DUBLIN

DUBLIN

A VIEW FROM THE GROUND

Neil Hegarty

PORTRAIT

PORTRAIT

First published in Great Britain in 2007 by Portrait Books

Copyright © 2007 by Neil Hegarty

The moral right of the author has been asserted

A CIP catalogue record for this book
is available from the British Library

ISBN 978-0-7499-5149 8

Edited by Carl Cutler
Text design by Paul Saunders

Typeset in Sabon by Phoenix Photosetting, Chatham, Kent
www.phoenixphotosetting.co.uk
Printed and bound in Great Britain by MPG Books, Bodmin, Cornwall

Portrait
An imprint of
Little, Brown Book Group
100 Victoria Embankment
London EC4Y 0DY

An Hachette Livre UK Company

www.portraitbooks.com

CONTENTS

CONTENTS

'You have a skeleton of actual reality to build about
with fulness & veins & beauty.'

Herman Melville, letter to Nathaniel Hawthorne,
13 August 1852

ACKNOWLEDGEMENTS

The extract from 'The Yellow Book: Axel's Castle', from *Collected Poems* by Derek Mahon (1999), is reprinted by kind permission of the author and of The Gallery Press, Loughcrew, Oldcastle, County Meath. 'Inscription for a Tombstone', from *Selected Poems* by Austin Clarke (Hugh Maxton ed., 1991), is reprinted by kind permission of Lilliput Press, Dublin. The extract from 'A Melancholy Love', from *Collected Poems, 1938–83* by Sheila Wingfield (1983), is reprinted by kind permission of Enitharmon Press, London. The extract from 'Sunday', from *The Nowhere Birds* by Caitríona O'Reilly (2001), is reprinted by kind permission of the author and of Bloodaxe Books, Tarset, Northumberland. The extract from 'The Closing Album I: Dublin', in *Selected Poems* (Michael Longley ed., 1988), is reprinted by kind permission of the Estate of Louis MacNeice and of Faber & Faber, London. The extracts from *Dublin 1742* (2002) by John Banville are reprinted by kind permission of the author and of Sheil Land Associates, London.

I am grateful to my editor, Albert DePetrillo, for floating the original proposal for this book, and for steering it so smoothly through to completion. My thanks and gratitude also to Denise

Dwyer and to all at Portrait; to Robin Wade and all at Wade & Doherty; and to the following: Laurence Browne, Gillian Cope, Paul Delaney, Aileen Douglas, Stephen Faloon, Vanessa Harriss, Marie Gethins, Seamus Gethins, Sean Hogan, Anne Mary Luttrell, Niamh McManus, John Murphy, Mairéad Ní Eithir, Jane O'Halloran, Caitríona O'Reilly, Bernard Seymour, Malcolm Shifrin and Catherine Toal. Thanks are also due to the staff of Pembroke Library, Dublin; of the National Library of Ireland; and of the Library of Trinity College Dublin – in particular to John McManus for much generosity. Warmest thanks to my family in Ireland, Britain and France, and in particular to Maureen and Charles Hegarty, and to John Lovett.

INTRODUCTION

⚗

Plum-blue hills for a background: Dublin, of course.

'A Melancholy Love' SHEILA WINGFIELD

Midsummer in Dublin and the weather is cool and bright. A summer storm passed through in the night; the waters of the Grand Canal, as I came over the lock this morning, were choked with leaves torn from the trees. The water itself was choppy; it felt like an autumn day. Now, at lunchtime, I make a cup of tea and carry it with me upstairs, onto the roof of my apartment building.

Up here are the rudiments of a garden. Onto this flat roof we have hauled heavy sacks of earth and compost, pots and containers in tasteful terracotta and tasteless plastic and set about creating a garden. Now, after two years, we are beginning to see the effects. Old-fashioned white roses are at their June best, laden with bloom and heavily scented. A buddleia bush, ravaged with greenfly earlier in the year, is now putting forth long spears of flower; feverfew and wild geraniums have self-seeded in our pots; and the passion flower which was doubtfully planted in March (could it survive the wind?) has responded well to the glow of the warm, red-brick walls. Our garden is beginning to be a success.

That we have an accessible roof at all, much less a garden to grow upon it, owes much to the provenance of this sturdy building. It is that rare thing in Dublin: a purpose-built apartment block dating from the 1950s, when urban living, apartment living, was a less than common lifestyle choice in this city. It is a classic building of its kind: utilitarian and unrelieved by much in the way of decoration, but with a plain grace and symmetry that has come to be appreciated with the years. The facing brick – or so I have been told, at any rate – was saved from a stately home in Northern Ireland when the wrecker's ball set to work. Warm and red and beautifully textured, and saved and brought to Dublin to augment this plain post-war building. I cannot say for certain whether this story is true or not, but I hope that it is. I am no traditionalist but there is something intrinsically pleasing in the idea of the bones of one building being retrieved and scavenged to form the bones of another. And the fitful Dublin sun, when it shines on these earth- and rust-coloured bricks, kindles them into life.

This building, close to the waters of the Grand Canal and embedded in the business heart of the city, is my home and so is symbolic enough for me. But it is a curious, a significant building in many ways. Solid, harmonious of scale and built to last, it represents the architectural values of another age. It contrasts starkly with the new apartment blocks thrown up in these last 15 years of Irish economic prosperity, ill-designed and showing their manifest defects all too clearly after a scant few years of existence. It contrasts just as starkly too with the buildings of Dublin's eighteenth-century Georgian heyday, just a stone's throw away. It is a pure modernist building, despised by many for this very reason, cherished by others, by me.

Although a mere 50-odd years old, the building has nonetheless managed to gather a few historic layers in the form of notable residents, coming and going and leaving their mark. The Irish writers Frank O'Connor and Liam O'Flaherty made their homes here, the former in the 1960s, the latter for years until his death in 1984. And Christine Keeler came here, they say, in the aftermath of the Profumo scandal of 1963, to keep her head down, to hide from the cameras, and to pick up the pieces of her life. And there were more – not bad for a relatively youthful building.

On the street outside, stories unfold. This area is busy with mainstream commerce by day, and at lunchtime the streets heave with suit-clad workers clutching sandwich bags and takeaway coffees. But by night, and on silent Sunday afternoons, a different breed of commerce takes over. Women are dropped off and take up their stations on the footpaths, by the railings of the little triangular park across the way, under the chestnut trees; cars appear, negotiations take place, are rapidly concluded and the cars take off again. Pimps, lurking in the shadows. Sometimes, a prostitute will simply take a client into the courtyard of an adjoining office building and emerge a few minutes later, task accomplished. Occasionally, the police take an interest; more often, though, they do not and the women and their clients are allowed to get on with it. In years gone by, there was more activity on the streets: on icy winter nights, indeed, the women would sometimes set fire to a litter bin as though it was a Girl Guide brazier aglow with charcoal and would gather round it to stay warm, gin bottles in hand. Today, apparently, mobile phones make the job easier and less chilly; there is less need to stand on windswept kerbs by night. But for all that, the oldest job is still visible on the streets; on Sunday morning, the ground is littered with mini-bottles of mouthwash – and with other evidence too. And so, there is much to look out at from this roof, if you have a mind – although it is the case too that some of the action down below can pall after a while.

A building, then, stitched into the fabric of the city; and up on this roof, the elaborate weave and texture of Dublin reveals itself. In the little park today, the beech and chestnut trees sway in full, delicate-green summer leaf, and, just beyond, the waters of the Grand Canal glint in the sunshine. Today, the office workers sun themselves on the canal bank, eat an al fresco lunch, sip their coffees. A floating café has recently opened on the barge moored on this stretch of the canal and up here on my perch, I can hear and glimpse pleased diners clinking and chattering on its deck.

The canal provides a measure of tranquillity to a neighbourhood in ferment. Two vast cranes hang in the sky directly above me: two buildings are under construction between here and the canal, and more are planned. One is an office development, slick and inoffensive enough, nearing completion now and being faced with green glass. The other is an apartment building, shoehorned into a small triangular site and still half built. I was at first inclined to be sniffy about it: probably the windows would be uPVC, I thought sourly, and the dimensions terrible. But no, the building is not half bad, boasting long terraces on the upper floors and balconies, generous of scale, down below; and not a plastic window in sight. These apartments will make good homes. I could do without the cranes hovering above my very head, but I can't complain too much about the fruits of their labour.

On the other side of our building, meanwhile, just next door, is a much larger vacant site. It was sold off by the government last year and is awaiting the green light for development. My neighbours are watching the site and awaiting the plans with a fair degree of trepidation. Already, we have headed off the first planning application, which proposed great towers of apartments rising into the air, dwarfing and shadowing every building within a mile radius and giving us all screaming nightmares. Too much, the planners eventually said, way too much. Now, the application is in abeyance and we have stood down our troops

– but we haven't paid them off, because the enemy will certainly be back.

To the north and west lies the city centre of Dublin. A stone's throw away marches the rear elevation of a long and imposing terrace: a classic Georgian line fencing in the east side of Fitzwilliam Square, small and exquisite. Beyond rises the pompous Edwardian dome of Government Buildings, which was taken over by the state in the 1980s, refurbished at vast expense and renamed in such a dull manner. Beyond it again ranges an arc of familiar sights: in the background, the lonely high-rise of Liberty Hall stands on the quays of the city; in the foreground, the modernist, bronze-clad mass of the Bank of Ireland rears spectacularly out of the Georgian streetscape; to the east, the skyline is thick with more cranes, testament to the intensive development of Dublin's docklands now under way; to the west, the steeple of St Patrick's Cathedral, crowned by its newly gilded cross, peeps over chimney stacks and slate roofs.

And if context is your thing, then this roof also affords views of Dublin's superb hinterland too. To the south are clear and matchless views of the Wicklow Mountains. Although in other countries and other cities, this range would be hills only, to Dublin they are mountains. And fair enough too, because they are undeniably dramatic, their very proximity to the city's southern suburbs a thrill in itself. Now flecked and veined with snow, now vanishing into a heat haze on a summer day, now green, looming and immediate as rain threatens the city itself, now plum-blue under cloudy skies – the mountains are a bellwether, an ubiquitous and ever-changing floor show.

Best of all, though only if I stand on the tips of my toes, I can see the Irish Sea from this roof, two little triangles of deep blue glimpsed through the rooftops on this sunny afternoon. Occasionally, the white sail of a yacht skims through, a ferry ploughs up the blue on its way across the water to Wales. For the most part, though, this small glimpse remains inviolate: a reminder of why this city exists in the first place. These views of the sea and of blue hazy hills and of the rooftops of the city in between – they enable one to transcend the small vexations of mundane life, whether these be the drills and hammers of the construction work next door or the greenfly on our roses or the sweeping shadow of the silent crane as it swings by overhead again, and again and again. All life is here, all set out for free public viewing: the various triumphs of Dublin and its various failures, the mistakes of planning and architecture, the colonial history of this city, its present prosperity, its beautiful and miraculous hinterland of hills and water. All this, all set out below a rooftop perch on a cool and blustery summer day, as the shadows of cranes hang and slide silently across the blue and white zenith of the sky.

— ◄o► —

I first came to Dublin as a student, at the beginning of the 1990s and I scarcely knew the city when I first arrived. My family never visited Dublin when I was growing up; there was no reason to do so. We had no family living here and my parents had never lived in Dublin or forged any particular connection with it. So that, when I got off the inter-city coach and onto a city bus and eventually dragged my suitcase into my new and very disagreeable student basement flat, I hardly knew where I was going; and I didn't know a soul.

I remember that my first winter in Dublin, the winter of 1990–91, as being amazingly dry and chilly. In those days – not too long ago, though long enough – coal could still be burned within the city limits. I remember the smoke hanging above the streets, and, more evocative and penetrating still, the potent scent of roasting barley coming down from the Guinness Brewery and suffusing the still winter air. Dublin felt like an altogether different city in those days, and a poorer one. I walked down through Rathmines each morning on my way into town, past grand family homes long since converted to bedsits and looking ramshackle now, with neglected gardens and stained net curtains hanging at the windows. Between the canal and the city centre was an area of public housing that looked even worse: underinvestment and poverty writ large.

But the economy was stirring in those days and a burst of prosperity was just around the corner; and in the 16-odd years since I got off the bus in central Dublin, this city has changed radically. I was fortunate, I think now, to arrive in a city on the cusp of such a change: I can remember the last breaths taken by another city, one that was more in tune with the past than the present; I can better appreciate the pleasures available to the citizens of this new and modern Dublin too; and I feel able to compare the two, to get a better understanding of the history and identity of Dublin in the process.

Dublin commands attention, as one of only a handful of cities in the world able to rely on its name and its fame. This is not by reason of vast economic pulling power, nor as a result of a powerful and prosperous past – but on cultural terms alone. Ask anyone to come up with images of Dublin and watch the results flood. Often, these images will be clichéd – think of Molly Malone, think of a cold pint of Guinness in a crowded pub, think of the graceful span of the Ha'penny Bridge reflected perfectly in the waters of the river Liffey on a cool, still evening. But the fact remains: that this city has never been short of images, of symbols – of a potent and seemingly inexhaustible supply of cultural capital.

As a nation, of course, Ireland has long relied on this considerable cultural clout: the country's history, its enormous diaspora, its experience of colonialism all explain the influence of the country today – and as the Irish capital, Dublin pulls in the lion's share of attention. The city's character and energy, though, is also self-generated and always has been. The list of cultural landmarks for which Dublin has been responsible is – clichés notwithstanding – considerable and impressive in its breadth and depth, ranging from the work of the glittering playwrights of the eighteenth century to that of music icons of today. It is this cultural capital that has given Dublin the power it presently enjoys.

This is a strength, to be sure – but it is a weakness too, tending as it does to push into the foreground aspects of this city's life and history, while excluding others. There is more to history, after all, than a chain of events and a series of recognisable images – of rulers anointed and dethroned and battles lost and won. It is true that this city, this Dublin, has been the prey of outside events through the course of a long and tempestuous history. Often, Dublin's story has been thrust violently upon it by forces outside its city walls and from abroad; it has been obliged to respond to events instead of shaping them. Dublin has lacked a sense of control over its own affairs – this, of course, being part of a pattern characteristic of colonised societies. Not that this is the whole story. View history from the side or from below and a different world emerges, one that can be viewed in the round, one in which the stories are different or subtly coloured and nuanced. View history in this way – view the history of Dublin in this way – and it becomes easier to catch at the heart of the matter.

Does Dublin possess a character, a personality of its own? Yes, in the sense that a multitude of lives lived here, layered in this one place over hundreds of years, will inevitably leave their mark. Yes, in the sense that the construction of great civic buildings and of private houses, the compositions of scores and plays and novels, the brewing of beer and the laying of water pipes and train tracks and tram lines and the whole cycle of human birth and death – all this involves energy. And this energy, which has gone into building this city and living in it, will be distilled into the place and will leave its trace. Does it possess an essence? Emphatically not, to my mind, for the world is various and Dublin is too; and essences are disagreeably pure.

Forget the essence, then, and look for the character. This book is written to catch at the personality of this city, this Dublin. This is one history, among many.

PART ONE

Bitter is the wind tonight.
It tosses the ocean's white hair.
Tonight I fear not the fierce warriors of Norway
Coursing on the Irish Sea.

ANONYMOUS (ninth-century Ireland)

Chapter 1

FOUNDATIONS

I magine, if you will, a ship nearing the Irish coast on a spring day in the ninth century AD. This eastern shore of the island gently shelves into the sea for the most part, with an island here and there and the occasional rocky horror to be avoided at all costs. It is a coastline that has been long known: the Romans were familiar with the Irish Sea, although they never crossed it in force to conquer damp and unwelcoming Hibernia. The mariners on this ship have also long known about and contemplated the Irish coast, from their bases in Scotland, on the Isle of Man and elsewhere. For many years, they have surveyed and criss-crossed these waters, getting to know their moods, dangers and opportunities. Their ships indeed, being shallow-draughted and agile, are uniquely suited to scouting unknown seas and, in the process, to keeping danger to a minimum.

At a point some 100 miles south and east of the Isle of Man, the ship noses past a high and rocky headland, on the tip of which a famous lighthouse will shine in later days, and enters a wide, semi-circular bay. The rocky headland is part of a peninsula, it seems, that bounds the bay to the north. Another cape – taller and equally rocky, equally treacherous – can be seen across the water, bounding the bay to the south.

This wide bay appears to be a safe anchorage and so the ship enters slowly. But it runs into problems at once: the waters are in fact shallow, tangled with shoals and not altogether promising, and the ship is forced to nudge and nose its way, seeking a channel that will lead towards the coast. And happily, such a channel is to be found, although to the north and south the shoals and sandbars continue to collect; a little island slips by to the right of the ship. The channel persists, a sure and certain sign that a river is pouring into the bay – perhaps coming down from the high range of hills that are outlined some miles away on the southern skyline.

Slowly, the coast – flat, for the most part, and gently rising inland – closes in, and before long the ship finds the mouth of the river: wide, with long gravelled beaches on both banks. The river is not especially easy to navigate either: it too is shallow and shoals of sand and gravel break the surface here and there, but the tide is high and this shallow-draughted boat can manage to ride it without too much difficulty.

On this clear spring afternoon, much of the landscape is clearly visible. It is partially wooded, but the great old-growth forests that once held sway over much of this land are long gone and the trees do not come down to the water's edge, as they might have done in ages past. Instead, great swathes of land have been substantially cleared and turned to pasturage. A small river flows into the main stream from the south; on the northern shore are bluffs and slightly higher ground.

Gradually now, the river narrows; any further navigation would be unwise and the ship begins to cast around for a suitable beaching spot. In the distance, the southern bank rises into a low escarpment; another, slightly larger, tributary stream curves around its foot and feeds into the main river. And signs of habitation? There are small houses dotted here and there, both on the escarpment and at its base and on the banks of the small stream.

And occasional larger buildings too, built of stone. Now, the longboat puts gently onto the southern shore, its hull crunching on gravel, and the mariners jump out, making landfall for the first time.

This river is the Liffey. And this landscape, this escarpment, this valley threaded with streams and pastures: this is Dublin, at the dawn of the Viking age.

Fanciful? Without a doubt, for the sources are sketchy when it comes to descriptions of the first Viking landfalls in Dublin. It is hardly likely, for a start, that a single ship would have nosed its way up the Liffey: this was not the Viking style at all. Rather more likely, as the *Annals of Ulster* later had it, a great fleet of 65 ships came up the Liffey in 837 and, as was usually the way with the arrival of fearsome Viking fleets, consternation and fear spread among the population. What did the Vikings have in mind for this new land? A great deal, if their past track record was anything to go by, and none of it particularly pleasant.

But the description of the Liffey – all shallows and shoals and gravelled banks – is realistic enough. And so too is the description of the landscapes that the Vikings would have silently contemplated as they sailed west, slowly against the stream. Ireland was already a populated island – long populated, with a system of governance and religious observance that had already stood the test of time. Dublin may have celebrated its millennium in 1988, but that date was notional, for the fact is that the Liffey valley, the escarpment and the banks of the stream that wound at its foot, had by AD 988 been long settled and ordered.

Humans had, in fact, inhabited the valley of the Liffey for thousands of years before the arrival of the Vikings. Ample evidence of their early presence, in the form of a dolmen here and a tumulus

there, can still be found today sprinkled throughout the city's hinterland. Those long-ago first settlers clung to the banks of a river
that was at best treacherous, unstable and not to be trusted. The
Liffey was then a broad, shallow expanse of water at its mouth, still
tidal perhaps ten miles upstream from the sea, bounded by gravelled
banks and shoals, and its estuary a tangle of sandbars. The land
upon which today's city centre is built was then either water or shifting sand; certainly a large part of what is today central Dublin, a
great many of its most important buildings and nearly all of its commercial heart was only a thousand years ago under water.

In earliest prehistoric times, the Liffey would have flowed
between banks that were heavily wooded. The ice retreated from
the northern half of Ireland a mere 12,000 years ago – a blink of
an eye in geological time – after which dense broad-leaf forests
grew to take its place. Most of the island was covered by these
thick woods inhabited by wolf, bear, elk and boar – and it was
only with the passage of thousands of years that these woods
began to be felled and a permanent human presence established.
The Mesolithic dwellers on the shore of Dublin Bay some 7,000
years ago left only scant reminders of their presence, but their later
Neolithic descendants have bequeathed enough in the way of
stone blades and tools for us to build up a picture of what was
becoming an increasingly complex society. Farming and more
thorough exploitation of the land now replaced a nomadic culture
of hunting and wandering. Ritual began to dominate, as shown in
the passage tombs – elaborate and of remarkable antiquity – of
Newgrange, Knowth and Dowth in the valley of the river Boyne
north-west of Dublin. The hill of Tara, nearby, assumed a long-
lasting political, symbolic and strategic importance in the affairs
of the island. And so it can be seen that the hinterland of Dublin
was already a centre of power and authority in the country.

And it was natural that the settlement at Dublin should have
developed where it did. The Irish climate, though seldom beguiling,

was kinder on the island's east coast, and the presence of the sea and of lands beyond it – Roman and later, Anglo-Saxon Britain and the great expanse of Europe to the east – brought early traders to the area. The roads of ancient Ireland – the Slighe Midluachra coming down from Ulster in the north, the Slighe Mór across the flat inland plain from Connacht in the west, the Slighe Dála coming up from Munster in the south-west and the Slighe Chualann running up from Leinster in the south – all met in the Liffey valley. This convergence, too, was a result of economics as well as a fact of geography: the Liffey estuary providing something of a natural point of contact between Ireland and its European neighbours. Moreover, the Liffey could be forded at this point. And so the river crossing and the settlement that grew up beside it came to be known as Áth Cliath – the hurdle ford.

It was not a good ford, not by any means. The tides of the river – rising and falling by 3 metres (10 feet), then as now – meant that the ford could be used for only 12 hours in every 24. Even then it was a wet crossing, involving much in the way of wading and splashing through deep water. The local inhabitants did their best to render it a little more usable, understanding well that the local economy would be better served if its infrastructure was improved a little. They created a makeshift passageway across the shallow river by dint of binding saplings together, stretching them into a rough path laid underwater – the 'hurdle' – and fastening a sketchy rail of branches to them at right angles. Such a contraption could have made little enough difference to the difficult business of crossing the river, of course – but a disagreeable and impractical ford was a good deal better than no ford at all. And so the crossing in the river gradually assumed an importance in Irish affairs.

Pushing upriver from the sea, the river began to narrow towards the hurdle ford. It was at this point that the southern shore took on the fortuitous arrangement glimpsed by the Vikings

7

on their arrival in 837: an escarpment rising above the water and a little tributary river curving around the foot of this rise to join the main flow of the Liffey. These very particular topographical arrangements dictated the formation of the first permanent settlements at Dublin, and this topography can still be seen today, over a thousand years later. Walk west, with the sea behind you and the city before you and you will see that the river still narrows and the ground still rises above the southern shore, to be crowned today by the sturdy square tower of Christ Church Cathedral.

This Gaelic settlement of Áth Cliath, then, grew up on this slope above the hurdle ford. The Liffey, running through stones and shoals in its narrow valley, was always liable to flood and so the escarpment provided shelter and protection from flood waters, as well as from all manner of raids. And this settlement, it is generally agreed, was the original centre of population at Dublin. It is an interesting twist to the story, however, that for several hundred years Dublin consisted of twin communities, side by side in the Liffey valley; and that it is the overshadowed second settlement that gives its name to the modern city of Dublin.

At the foot of the great stone embankments of the Liffey, as it flows below Wellington Quay in the heart of the modern city, can be seen what looks like a little outflow pipe. It is a hole just at the high-tide level, closed by a portcullis-like iron grating that is itself partially covered by green seaweed. It is through this dispiriting hole on Wellington Quay – rather than as 'a tongue of liquid sewage' hanging out of Wood Quay, as pungently imagined in *Ulysses* – that the little river Poddle, the tributary river that once curved around the feet of the hill of Christ Church, today flows out into the Liffey. Buried and dispirited though it may be now, however, the Poddle is a significant river in the history of the city. In those early days, when the Liffey was broader than it is at present, the Poddle ran in its own bed under the sky and widened into a dark tidal pool as it flowed at the foot of the hill. That pool, the *dubh linn* or dark pool, gave its name to the city of Dublin.

The history of the pre-Viking period is incomplete at best, but a good deal of archaeological work has been undertaken in the last 30 years, and today a rather more coherent picture begins to emerge of the settlement in the years before the Vikings arrived in force. That Christianity had arrived in the fifth century with the shadowy figure of Patrick is manifest: archaeology and oral history show the swift bedding down of the new religion in the valley of the Liffey, the building of numerous churches and, later, the establishment of monasteries and priories in the hinterland of the settlements. Oral tradition also speaks of Patrick himself baptising Dublin's first Christians on an island in the Poddle. At some point in the fifth century a chapel was raised to commemorate this crucial moment, and St Patrick's Cathedral now stands on the spot, making it the oldest consecrated ground in the city.

The settlement by the Liffey fords, Áth Cliath, was predominantly secular and commercial in focus. This was natural enough, dominated as it was by the crossings of the Liffey and by the meeting of the roads coming in from all over Ireland. Dubh Linn, the settlement by the dark pool of the Poddle, was monastic and ecclesiastical in focus and was dominated by a series of small churches strung out along the shore of the stream and by the principal church of St Patrick itself. But of course, the two settlements were in close proximity to each other and it is clear that a great deal of commerce passed between the two, and from them into the wider hinterland of Dublin. As was always the case, the monasteries and priories in the area became sources of trade and prosperity, stimulating both the local and wider economy and establishing, once and for all, the fords of the Liffey as a crucial centre of population and commerce.

Chapter 2

⚙

THE HEATHEN MEN

It was this hum of commerce, of course, that drew the Vikings, who had been busily raiding the coasts of Britain and Ireland for fifty or so years before their first appearance in Dublin Bay. The most infamous of these attacks was visited on the Irish-founded monastery at the holy island of Lindisfarne, off the coast of north-east England, in the year 793. 'This year came dreadful forewarnings over the land of the Northumbrians,' squeals the *Anglo-Saxon Chronicle*:

> terrifying the people most woefully: these were immense sheets of light rushing through the air, and whirlwinds, and fiery dragons flying across the firmament. These tremendous tokens were soon followed by a great famine: and not long after, on the sixth day before the ides of January in the same year, the harrowing inroads of heathen men made lamentable havoc in the church of God in Holy-island, by rapine and slaughter.[1]

St Columba's monastery on Iona and the settlements on the Irish island of Rathlin and on Lambey Island just north of Dublin Bay were attacked for the first time two years later and raids on the Irish coast began in earnest in the early years of the ninth century.

Nor did these Northmen focus exclusively on these islands' network of monasteries. Saxon London was attacked in 842 and although this first assault was beaten back, the Norse returned nine years later and sacked the city. It is within this wider context that the first Viking raids on Dublin should be viewed.

The twin settlements at Dublin, if not quite an urban centre as we would properly understand the term, nevertheless possessed many of the ingredients of a town: ecclesiastical foundations and a degree of wealth, commercial activity within the settlement and in its hinterland and economic activity reaching across Ireland. It is also worth emphasising that the political situation in Dublin and in pre-Viking Ireland in general was unstable at best. The country was, in general terms, divided into two kingdoms, centred at Cashel in the south and at Tara, and these suzerainties were subdivided into a multitude of smaller territories. There was, therefore, little in the way of central authority, and politics in general was a game of continually shifting allegiances. Given this generally favourable economic and political context, perhaps the only oddity about the Viking attacks on Dublin is that they did not happen a great deal sooner.

Viking, or Norse, fleets appeared in Dublin Bay, then, a full 44 years after the sacking of the monastery on Lindisfarne. Norse communities were already well established in Scotland, England and on the Isle of Man and were already beginning the transition from mere raiding marauders into traders and landowners. All the same, their reputation must have preceded them: if that anonymous ninth-century Irish poet feared not the fierce warriors of Norway coursing on the Irish Sea – well, he was probably the only one who wasn't afraid. Even as the longboats pushed up the Liffey, the inhabitants of the settlements at Dublin must have thought with horror that their way of life was at an end. Because the Viking propensity to violence and gore was well known and had lost nothing in the telling along the coasts of Ireland and Britain, those first Dubliners may have thought that they would all, down to babes in arms, be put to the sword. But not a bit of it.

So little evidence remains of these earliest times in Dublin and of the presence of the first Vikings in the settlement that it has been left, once again, to archaeology to come up with clues and evidence as to what occurred in these first years of the Norse era. And archaeology has proved that the pagan Vikings did not wipe out the early Christian presence in Dublin, as was once imagined, and that life continued in the area. Not quite as normal, perhaps, because dark layers in the various digs do indeed point, silently, to burning and destruction by fire; and it seems safe enough to pin some of the responsibility for this destruction on the Vikings. But not all of it: fires were after all a fact of life amid the wood and thatch of these early settlements and the Vikings cannot be held to blame for every spark that flew upwards from a cottage fire. And besides, we have only shreds and threads of evidence to show what constituted normality in those times, and so the Vikings cannot confidently be held accountable for disrupting normal life.

It is of course the truth that the Vikings were set loose on Europe by a desire for wealth and easy pickings from the famous monasteries of Ireland and Britain. But this is not the whole truth. They were also driven by a swelling population, a lack of fertile land at home and a talent for trade and commerce – not to mention the Christian political and military movements initiated by Charlemagne in continental Europe, which had the effect of piling pressure onto the pagan Vikings in their Scandinavian homelands and which had an inevitably defensive knock-on effect. And finally there is the presence, in this complicated geo-political equation, of the Great Climactic Optimum: the inexplicable warming of the climate of parts of the northern hemisphere around the turn of the first millennium. This warmed the seas, dampened winter storms and spurred the development of Europe in general, in particular its trading routes and commerce. The existence of the Great Climactic Optimum eased along the development of all of Europe's urban centres, greased the wheels of the Viking maritime adventure from Russia and Turkey in the east to Greenland and Newfoundland in the west, and led – in part at least – to the beginning of the next phase of Dublin's history. These larger facts and phenomena are crucial in any discussion of Dublin, so that the Vikings cannot merely be seen – as has happened so often in the past – as simply raiders hell-bent on bloodshed. Rather it is the case that many events and facts, great and small, pinpointed and inexplicable, led to the beginning of the Viking age in Dublin and to the drawing of the nascent town into a truly pan-European trading network.

The archaeological digs that have taken place in Dublin in the last 30 years have uncovered a great deal of information about the Viking age in Dublin. The Christian churches that pre-dated the Norse arrival largely continued to function – this we know. We also know that the Vikings, when they arrived, gradually came to be a good deal more concerned with trading and the acquisition of land than with destruction and pillage. In short, the process of acculturation, whereby layers of experience and familiarity are laid upon the incomers until they become citizens themselves, began more or less at once. Violence, although it certainly took place, was not the principal order of the day. The Vikings, after all, were just like everyone else: they had to eat. When you imagine, then, those first mariners surveying the gravelled shores of the Liffey and the bogs and fields beyond, imagine men with a speculative eye and a keen interest in trading and economics.

The location of the first Norse settlement and anchorage at Dublin has been the subject of a good deal of academic dispute over the last 30 or so years. The unearthing of a Viking burial ground some miles upriver at Islandbridge – close to where the Liffey weir and the superb Lutyens-designed War Memorial

Gardens now stand – led to a good deal of speculation that the newcomers established their principal base there. But the increasing shallowness and narrowness of the river at this point make this location unlikely; and the most recent scholarship suggests instead the obvious setting: the fords of Áth Cliath and the dark tidal pool of Dubh Linn nearby.

Indeed, it is now supposed that the black pool on the Poddle was the very place of the Viking *longphort* – or longboat anchorage and harbour. This pool, after all, was a natural settlement spot. It was easily defended and a safe anchorage and, at any rate, until it began to silt up around the fourteenth century, it formed a centre of economic activity. Pottery, bones, metals and more have been unearthed over the last three decades, and painstakingly documented and classified – and this evidence has gradually built up a picture of probability. Each excavated section, each layer of history, each discovered shard and shred has shed a little more light on the lives lived by those men and women, those first Dubliners who settled by the Liffey fords, by the dark pool on the Poddle and on the hill above.

Although the Vikings were ferocious warriors, they did not always have the upper hand in Dublin – far from it. The *Annals of Ulster* refer to a year-round Viking settlement at Dublin from 841 on – but in fact this settlement lasted only until 902, when the local Irish chieftains combined to drive the Norse leaders from Dublin. They lived in exile in Scotland and the Isle of Man before returning in 917 – this time for good. The process of acculturation had most likely already begun by this point though, and so the expulsion of the Vikings from Dublin as recorded in the history books hardly refers to a wholesale eviction of the Norse population. Such a massive act of ethnic cleansing would of course have been impossible in any case: the Norse and Irish did not live in hermetically sealed worlds; 60 years of settlement and of human relationships, of deals struck, children born and potent family connections forged, would have meant that a connection between the existing inhabitants and the newcomers was inevitable. Much more likely that it was only the leaders of the Norse community in Dublin who were evicted and that a large section of the population, including craftsmen and artisans, stayed exactly where it was.

But in 917, the Viking leaders returned in force to Dublin. Throughout the century, their settlement on the fortified hill above the Liffey and in the anchorages at its foot came under periodic attack and even temporary conquest from the native Irish, but this time the Norse were there to stay. A site just east of the town was established as the Thing, or local parliament, which was a phenomenon characteristic of all Norse settlements. It was at the Thing, whether the Norse settlement was in Ireland or in Greenland or on the Norwegian coast, that the Norsemen came to hear the law read aloud, to settle quarrels and to do deals. A tall standing stone was set up on the shores of the Liffey to mark their first landfall in Dublin and, perhaps more to the point, to fill the role of a lighthouse, warning sailors against the shoals and shallow waters along this stretch of anchorage. Some 3 metres (10 feet) in height, this Long Stone stood on the same spot for some 800 years before it was toppled and carried away in the eighteenth century.

The sites of the Thing and of the Long Stone now lie in the very heart of the modern city centre, and time and change – artificial and natural – have combined to alter the landscape beyond all recognition. Take the Long Stone: a replica of the original monument now stands on a large traffic island at the junction of Pearse Street and D'Olier Street. To one side is a cinema, to the other the grey hulking monstrosity that is Hawkins House, home today to the Department of Health, while the Long Stone public house sits nearby and the Liffey flows between its massive stone embankments 100 metres (330 feet) to the north. Difficult and strange to imagine that, in the middle of the ninth century, Viking longboats pulled up on the shore at this point where the small river Steine flowed out into the Liffey.

Or take the site of the Thing: modern Andrew Street, where Dublin Tourism is headquartered in the now-deconsecrated St Andrew's Church. The streets nearby, because of their proximity to the enormous tourist magnet that is Trinity College, are a jangle of T-shirt shops, cafés and sandwich joints; tourist buses roll by every few minutes. The great mound of the Thing was levelled in 1685 and the soil used to raise the height of nearby Nassau Street, which was prone to repeated flooding; even today, the street still runs several metres higher than the adjacent grounds of Trinity. And again, in keeping with an Irish way of doing things, there was until recently another public house, the Thing Mote, within shouting distance of the site of the original Thing.

It is because we know the precise location of these significant and ancient places, however, that their sites become peculiarly evocative, in spite of, or perhaps because of, the prosaic nature of their modern surroundings. As we pass under the shadow of Hawkins House, looming over the replica Long Stone, and as we push through the tourists crowding the railings of Trinity College, we may feel a frisson to think that the ancient past still leaves a ghostly trace in the lines of the modern city; and that the medieval shoreline and the lines of the old rivers are everywhere to be found in the modern city centre. That here, on this very spot, the Liffey once flowed shallow between its gravelled banks, that here the Steine, which now flows silently underground, gurgled past the foot of the Thing on its way down to join the Liffey, that here, tidewaters rose and fell twice a day where now sandwich shops offer their chicken tikka wraps; and that here, on this very spot and more than one thousand years ago, the keel of a Viking longboat crunched on gravel as warriors stepped ashore at Dublin for the very first time. Such reminders of the past are evocative and also something of a relief, summoning an era when the surroundings were wilder but also less prosaic, when the waters might have run unchecked and menacing, and when there was not a sandwich shop in sight.

As the Norse gradually established themselves in Dublin, so their settlement became more specifically urban in character. Although much of the detail of this period must be inferred, it seems clear enough that Norse activity went through a number of different phases. The earliest phase, which was characterised by so-called 'smash and grab' tactics aimed at maximising plunder and minimising contact with the native Irish, gradually gave way to rather more nuanced dealings and, by the time of the return of the Viking elite from exile, trade and economics were the order of the day. This second Viking occupation has been much mulled over by historians, keen to establish the facts of a period much muddied by the tides of history. But it seems clear that when the Viking elite returned early in the tenth century, they came back to a settlement that had never really ceased to grow, and in which progress had continued to take place. It is certainly the case, however, that the return of the Norse leaders in 917 significantly upped the pace of Dublin's growth.

In this second period of settlement – the so-called *dún* or fortress phase – the Vikings fortified their *longphort* on the banks of the Poddle's black pool, and began to build houses and create streets in the vicinity of their new stockade, the better to defend their assets and investments. New urban fortifications were constructed, consisting of earthen embankments crowned by a dry stone wall. The area encircled by this new wall was of course small by modern standards: no more than 10 or so hectares (approximately 25 acres) and consisting largely of the crown of the hill and its steep slopes, taking in most of the precincts of modern Dublin

Castle and Christ Church. The fortified town itself contained a stockade or stronghold, and recent archaeological work has unearthed remains of these first fortifications in and around the Castle itself. It was at this time, in the first half of the tenth century, that the name Áth Cliath fell out of common usage, to be replaced in the records by Dún Dublinn, the fortress of the black pool – the Dyflinn of the Icelandic sagas.

It was a busy place in those days and culturally complex too. Irish and Norse lived increasingly cheek by jowl within the walls of the new *dún* and the spreading suburbs beyond. The atmosphere would have been riven by tensions between the different ethnic groups who lived alongside each other and by the frequent attacks on the town walls from without. But this same heady mixture enriched the settlement, as talents were shared and improved upon and as foreign trade brought in ideas as well as people and goods. New houses, for example, used Irish materials and processes – all wattle and thatch – but were built to traditional Norse designs; and Viking design in general began to impact on the Irish way of doing things. Until this point, native Irish design, in jewellery and in all manner of craft, shows evidence of a strong Anglo-Saxon influence. Now, though, we begin to see Viking influence creeping in, with its emphasis upon symmetry, on tightly clustered and interlacing detailing of metalwork; gradually it becomes impossible to distinguish separate Norse and Irish styles. This, more than anything else, demonstrates that acculturation was the inevitable result of different peoples living side by side, driven by need, instinct and inclination to rub along together and eventually and inevitably to begin to fuse.

And so, although Dublin, as an organised settlement, long predates the arrival of the Vikings, it was these newcomers who provided a catalyst to its development. Far from being the mere marauders and monsters of popular lore, they brought with them principles of urbanisation which had been long honed in their other towns and harbours all over northern Europe, and economic and trading skills and principles that would serve their new base well.

Dublin was never at peace in these years, but its commercial life continued nothing daunted, for the town was now plugged into a Europe-wide trading network, which reached from Iceland to Russia and south to what is now Turkey. Goods created and ships built in Dublin have been traced all over the continent. Shoes stitched from animal hide were exported across Europe. Jewellery, skins and pelts, amber and slaves were traded in the markets of the city, wines and pottery were imported from France and beer was introduced to an enthusiastic population. Dublin's craftsmen began to work with glass and jet, and the city began to mint its own coins by the end of the tenth century. It became necessary to augment the traditional diet of oats, barley, wheat, rye and dairy products, and so corn was imported and traded in the new streets on the ridge west of the city walls, where Cornmarket now runs from Christ Church towards the Guinness Brewery. And so, chronic political instability notwithstanding, Dublin prospered – the lesson being that chieftains may come and chieftains may go but people will, given half a chance, buy and sell and work together regardless.

Dublin's Norse population converted to Christianity – eventually, slowly but in the end comprehensively and by the end of the tenth century the process was essentially complete. The principal result of this, as far as architects and archaeologists are concerned, is that Christ Church was constructed on the highest point of the hill of Dublin in or around 1036. Earlier churches had stood on this spot, but this was the first dedicated cathedral church for the walled town of Dublin. The Norse also constructed the church of St Olav, locating it a little further down the hill in the direction of the Liffey. This building, of which no trace survives, continued in use until the sixteenth century. It seems from all this religious activity that the Vikings were like other converts before and since: that is, zealous in their new faith. And they were instrumental in drawing the English gaze hither – not for the first time, perhaps, and certainly not for the last. It is a fascinating fact that the Viking bishops of Dublin were tied to the English see of Canterbury rather than to that of Armagh – then as now the ecclesiastical capital of Ireland. This fact, maybe more than any other, ties this early phase in Dublin's history into a larger and wider foreign picture and prefigures a great deal of Irish history to come.

The foundation of Christ Church also illustrates the persistence of the Norse presence in Dublin, even when the political and military tide was no longer running in their favour. Some twenty or so years before Christ Church was established, the Battle of Clontarf had taken place just north of Dublin. This battle, the details of which are familiar to every Irish schoolchild, has often been regarded as pivotal in Irish affairs, marking the demise of Viking power in Dublin and Ireland and the onset of a new age. The facts are rather subtler, however, and it is more the case that the battle was the latest point in a long and complicated ebbing and flowing of the tide of Irish history in this era.

The context of the battle is characterised by a shift in Irish politics towards a notion of a centralised authority. Brian Boruma (Brian Boru), who was the chieftain of the Dalcassians of northern Munster, had declared himself High King of Ireland in 1002. Such a declaration, as well as being substantially untrue, was as a red rag to a bull to other players in the Irish political scene and made conflict almost inevitable. And it is a measure of the strategic and political importance of Dublin and its environs that the battle, when it at last came, took place in the suburbs of the town in 1014.

The splendidly named Sitric Silkbeard was the Norse king of Dublin at this time and he allied the city with Maelmordha of Leinster in resisting Brian Boru's pretensions to national power.

Sitric also promised the support, insofar as it could be delivered, of his Viking brothers from overseas. Some of the annalists have dismissed these warriors, rather laconically, as 'foreigners'; others, happily, are a little more informative and so we know that among the 'choicest brave men and heroes' fighting that day were representatives of Norse societies from across north-western Europe.

Viking fleets moored in Dublin Bay on Palm Sunday 1014 and battle itself was joined five days later, on Good Friday. The site of the battle was north of the Viking city, on a very wide range of open and more or less flat ground stretching north of today's O'Connell Street to the river Tolka, east to the sea and south towards the Liffey. The battle was mythologised, as battles will always be, but it is clear that towards sunset, the 'foreign' Norse were decisively defeated. They were pursued towards their ships, many drowning on the way, while their Dublin brethren withdrew inside the walls of the city. But Brian Boru himself was killed – inside his own tent, as it turned out, because he had been too old to fight in the battle itself – and so were many of his captains. It was a rather weaker victorious side, therefore, that surveyed the battlefield at sunset that Good Friday.

These same myths would have it that the events of the day broke Norse power in Ireland, but this is not the case. Certainly they remained in control, more or less, of Dublin, as the foundation of Christ Church by Sitric some 20 years later demonstrates. It seems rather that their domination, which was never unquestioned or complete, was gradually diminished, partly by military defeat but principally through the inexorable processes of acculturation. This slow evolution of a new and distinctive society – what historians call Hiberno-Norse Dublin – continued through the eleventh century and into the twelfth. It would take another rupture in the fabric of history to end this period of economic prosperity and slow social change, and, once more, this rupture would be administered by newcomers.

Chapter 3

A TASTE OF DUBLIN

Today, time has done its work and the earliest Norse stockade, the dark pool and the Poddle itself have vanished from sight. The buildings and lawns of the modern Dublin Castle now cover the place where the waters of the pool once lapped. The Poddle flows on below the grounds of the castle and down into the Liffey through its seaweed-stained portcullis; and if you cross the threshold of the castle's lower gates, it is there – gurgling right below your feet. It is consistent and pleasing that this site of trade and contact should remain, a millennium later, one of the principal focuses of administrative and political power in the modern city.

The pool itself is commemorated in the site of the Dubh Linn Gardens, one of the most charming and sensitive areas of the Castle. Lying behind the main complex and in front of the old Coach House, this circular lawn is inlaid with brick set in a Celtic design. It is a peaceful, restful spot in any weather and even on warm summer days is never busy, as visitors pause a moment on their way into and out of the nearby Chester Beatty Library, and Dubliners take a shortcut through the castle grounds on their way elsewhere and glance at the careful planting, at the brick tracery set into the grass and at the usual sprinkling, so characteristic of Dublin, of memorials and statuary. Most relevant to modern eyes is the small memorial to Veronica Guerin, the investigative journalist who dug deep into the violent underworld of Dublin's drugs scene and who was, in retaliation, shot and killed in her own car in 1996. A quiet spot then, although perhaps not quite so serene as one might initially imagine.

The castle itself has been at the centre of power in Dublin and in Ireland for a thousand years. It has been built and rebuilt over the centuries and has changed as the society around it has changed, with the result that today it is unrecognisable from the earliest stockades raised on the site. Yet it retains some of the lines and forms of its earliest incarnations, in particular its arrangement around a pair of quadrangles. The nomenclature of course is deceptive: tourists expecting a castle in the Disney style will be disappointed, for this complex of government buildings, museums and grassy lawns ambles and rambles but seldom reaches into towering picturesque turrets. And Dubliners themselves also tend to disregard the castle and its precincts, as other seemingly fixed and unchanging landmarks in other cities are similarly disregarded. This disregard is surprising, all the same, for Dublin Castle has a good deal going for it. Its tranquillity, for one thing: step off Dame Street and into the Lower Yard and the dirt and roar of the city's traffic instantly recedes. And the hum of authority and power that emanates from its buildings, for another: as this remains very much a working government complex and civil servants come and go, wielding authority quietly and effectively.

The long, sloping and cobbled Upper and Lower Yards are fenced in by largely eighteenth- and nineteenth-century façades, painstakingly restored but modest rather than in any sense striking. The 1970s Stamping Office building anchors the Lower Yard, festooned in falling creepers and greenery. In true Dublin style, sadly, these otherwise harmonious public spaces are given over largely to car parks, so that the initial impression tends to be of clutter and offence: no possibility of admiring the surroundings in

23

serenity for fear of taking a black government limo in the small of one's back. Given the amount of money that has been ploughed into creating the gleaming infrastructure of the castle in recent years, this car-friendly policy is, to say the least, surprising; small wonder if visitors turn on their heel and get the hell out of there.

This quibble aside, though, the castle remains an agreeable enough place and the antiquity of the area adds another level of interest. It is possible to glimpse a little of the beating heart of medieval Dublin, though you would have to dig quite a bit to discover the facts for oneself. Happily, then, this digging has already been done for us: archaeological work has turned up evocative results throughout the castle precincts, and some of these digs have been retained as attractions in their own right. But it is not to mull on violence and drugs or on Celtic motifs or on car-friendly policies that a great throng of the Dublin populace is gathered here, on a hot morning late in June. No indeed, they are drawn to the Dubh Linn Gardens by pure greed. And I cannot wrinkle up my nose in disgust at the sight, for I am among them and the same motives have drawn me hither.

The specific occasion is a jamboree named A Taste of Dublin, designed as an opportunity for Dublin's restaurateurs and food producers to showcase their wares. The event is to take place in the Dubh Linn Gardens and already, as I have taken a short cut through the grounds of the castle a few days previously, I have seen the marquees and gazebos under construction. My curiosity has been whetted and, even though this is A Taste of Dublin's first outing and I have no clear idea what to expect, I am determined to go along in any case. Admission to the exhibition is something of a deterrent: either €25, €45 or an amazing €75, depending on the level of privileges one expects for one's cash. I expect full privileges, naturally, but I also expect not to have to pay for them and so I ring up and request a press pass. Amazingly, A Taste of Dublin agrees, and my stomach rumbles in agreeable expectation.

In truth, the alarm bells are already clanging in my head as I make my way through a Sunday-quiet town and up to the castle. I have read the advance publicity and €25, €45 or €75 seems like an awful lot of money to spend simply for admission to the event, with a handful of vouchers thrown in for good measure. You have to pay extra, it seems, once you're inside in order to sample the wares on offer. Still, I will keep a moderately open mind. I queue up, grab my ticket and plunge through the portals.

My open mind, alas, begins to creak shut the instant I enter. I can put it down to the marketing, which is embarrassing in the extreme: I have apparently stepped out of the eurozone and into quite another zone in which the 'florin' is the only acceptable currency. I can exchange my euro for their florins, it seems, at a conversion rate of one euro to one florin. No way, I think, and I begin to make my way through the throng. I want free stuff.

Near the entrance, foxgloves and giant purple alliums are arranged in mock Roman vases, and celebrity chefs are taking the crowds through the preparation of key dishes. On a stage nearby, one of these is showing the masses how to make Irish soda bread with the aid of a booming and whistling microphone. Free Sunday newspapers are being handed out; since they cost not a florin I stow a copy away in my backpack. People as greedy as I queue at a seafood stall to spear free langoustines onto cocktail sticks, and further in, other people queue up for free mini-samples of Spanish and French wines. I pass on the wine – it being altogether too early in the day – and instead accept a complimentary Greek tartlet consisting of a morsel of feta cheese and a wrinkled petal of roasted red pepper; accompanying this tartlet is a very large paper bag containing nothing except a complimentary disc of Irish shortbread.

As I move around, pushing through the masses of people, I feel my anxiety levels spiral ever upwards. Determined as I am not to spend a florin, I feel obliged to queue up with other cheapskates for free mini-samples of Toulouse sausage, sea salt-sprinkled bread sticks and Starbucks coffee (Kenyan blend). I find myself trying to poke a cocktail stick into a marinated and therefore slippery clove of garlic – fruitlessly, of course. But then again, those of my companions who have dug deep in their pockets for florins seem no better off, for the expensive restaurants are doling out portions (equally minuscule in dimension, to my eyes) of their food onto little paper plates. Surely proper plates could have been provided? Metal cutlery instead of plastic? I'm better off, I understand, with my cocktail sticks and free sausages – although this realisation does not improve my mood.

All around me are folk plying their wares. There is even a well-known credit card company amid the throng, although I notice that nearly everyone seems to be giving it a wide berth. As I pass the Starbucks stand for a second time, its representative homes in on me – drawn, perhaps, by the sight of my pen and notebook. Am I a food journalist? Ought he to butter me up? Amazingly, Starbucks has only recently embarked on its conquest of Dublin and Ireland, and so perhaps this emissary feels the need to go the extra PR mile. Not that I care about Starbucks, or indeed about anything at all by this point, but I know I ought to do my duty and so I ask, limply, a few questions about coffee ethics, about Starbuck fairtrade policies. He presses a mini-cup of Kenyan blend into my hand; he answers enthusiastically, if not quite relevantly, and I nod, I nod and nod; he keeps looking expectantly at the virgin-white pages of my notebook, at my pen. But I don't write anything down, I feel too exhausted and my pen stays firmly capped.

'Coffees are like fine wines,' he tells me earnestly. I sip my Kenyan blend and he says, 'Do you get the bitterness?'

I do indeed.

'On the back of the tongue?' he asks me. 'Or the sides?'

I think about the bitterness. 'On the back.' Thankfully, it's the right answer.

'Right!' he carols. 'On the back! That's where you should get it! – right on the back! That's where you get the hit!' He looks and sounds genuinely evangelical and I step away in alarm.

'I have to go now,' I mumble and set my Kenyan blend aside, and I feel my backpack bash people in the face.

'Right, right!' he says again. 'But take a leaflet!' He crams one into my closed fist. He doesn't instruct me to have a nice day, I notice; one glance into my face has doubtless convinced him that I'm a lost cause.

I push back through the melee towards the exit. Marinated garlic cloves are still being fruitlessly prodded, langoustines sucked from their shells and consumed with abandon and chefs still booming and whistling into their mikes about Irish soda bread. I squeeze through the exit and into the tranquillity of the outside world and stumble home, feeling judgemental. As I go, I busily theorise. Perhaps A Taste of Dublin epitomises the greed, vapidity and lack of style of the modern city? I resolve to make some notes to this effect as soon as I get home. So eloquently do I theorise, in fact, that an alternative thought does not strike me until rather later.

The grass and Celtic tracery of the Dubh Linn Gardens were hidden underneath A Taste of Dublin: underneath the tramping feet, discarded cocktail sticks and prawn shells and billowing gazebo canvases, but they were present nevertheless. And below all, the Poddle silently runs, recalling the time when a tidal pool rose and fell on this site, when deeds were done and goods and services exchanged. Maybe A Taste of Dublin, for all of its expense, paper plates and mock Roman urns, was following in a long and honourable Dublin tradition. After all, it was in its own way a marketplace; and so too was that early settlement at Dublin a marketplace. The connection was maybe unknown to the organisers of A Taste of Dublin, but it is a connection all the same. In the dim past, Norse and Irish exchanged iron from Sweden, silver from Russia, cloth and jewellery from Asia. Today's citizens exchange Portuguese wine, Italian olives and Starbucks Kenyan blend coffee – but maybe the same principle applies.

And so, instead, I make a different set of notes; it is better, after all, not to be jaundiced. And it is easier, in any case, to wax lyrical. Perhaps, a thousand years hence, an archaeologist will turn up a ground or two of Kenyan coffee in the soil of what was once Dublin Castle and marvel at Dublin's consistent place in a great trading network, this time spanning the globe.

Well, perhaps – but I doubt it.

Chapter 4

❦

THE COLONY

Eight hundred years of oppression. This particular phrase, whether passionately cried or murmured and sighed, has become a trademark slogan of Irish history. The story of the city of Dublin and of Ireland as a whole is threaded with foreign interventions. These have been large and small, seismic and less so – and all very much picked over. The most significant of all these interventions, however, and the one that truly mattered to the future of Dublin and of Ireland, did indeed take place just over eight hundred years ago.

Diarmuid MacMurrough, King of Leinster, had been banished from Ireland in 1166 and, in order to have vengeance and his lands restored to him, took ship to Bristol and later France in order to seek the assistance of Henry II, the Anglo-Norman King of England. MacMurrough, therefore, holds a special place in Irish history, as the agent who precipitated the first English intervention in Irish affairs. A glance at the context of the time, however, shows that the truth is rather more nuanced and complex. Henry was at this moment, some one hundred years after the Battle of Hastings and the Norman invasion of England, much engaged in pulling Wales and Scotland more firmly within the English sphere of influence. It was a natural progression to include

Ireland in these plans, and so MacMurrough's plea to the English crown must have been eagerly seized upon, providing as it did a pretext to invade Ireland and begin its occupation.

But a philosophical and legal framework had already been set in place that would provide a series of other pretexts. English meddling in Scottish and Welsh affairs might be excused by appealing to a potent combination of mythology and doubtful historical records which sought to establish a prior English claim to Scotland and Wales. With Ireland, no such claim could be established, but the Crown could, happily, point to the words and actions of the Pope himself as providing a reason for an invasion. The Laudabiliter of 1155, penned by Adrian IV, who was the first and only English Pope, had conferred on the King of England the right to occupy Ireland 'in order to enlarge the boundaries of the Church'.

This is an early example, perhaps the first, of a persistent motif in the relationship between England and Ireland. English actions would always be undertaken in the name of God and later of civilisation: by bringing the light of culture into the lives of the barbarian and feckless Irish, they were in fact doing those same Irish a favour. It is merely one of the ironies of history that it was the Pope himself who provided the first opportunity for this argument to be used. That the bloodshed and massacre accompanying the invasion was being actually visited upon a Christian and not a pagan people was glossed over by the apologists of the time, although these facts do not lose their impact in the telling.

The invasion, then, was inevitable. It had already been ordained by force of politics and strategy, and MacMurrough's appeal to the Crown merely provided the opportunity. It also, however, furnished another pretext, albeit a powerful one: that of free will. MacMurrough, himself Irish, was appealing to the Crown to establish itself in Ireland; he was acting, therefore, as spokesman for all of Ireland and therefore it might be claimed that the English intervention in Ireland had been invited by Ireland itself. This, at any rate, was the claim made at the time.

So much for the tanglings of history and propaganda. The impact of the Anglo-Norman invasion of Ireland is of course abundantly clear with the benefit of hindsight. This was the first significant English invasion of the island of Ireland; it changed the course of Irish history and it fixed the destiny of Dublin as the chief city of the island. So much is clear. What is also evident, however, is that the Anglo-Norman landings must also have been viewed at the time as truly epoch-making. For the people of Dublin and of south-eastern Ireland, it would have been painfully evident that these soldiers – heavily armed, well resourced, organised, purposeful and highly effective as they were – were heralds of a new age.

This powerful force – consisting principally of French-speaking, Welsh-based Anglo-Norman landowners and barons, all acting in the name of a French-speaking king – landed in County Wexford, 80 or so miles south of Dublin, in the spring of 1169. There they wintered and, in August of the following year, another, stronger force sailed across from Wales to join them. This force was led by Strongbow – Richard de Clare, Earl of Pembroke, who remains one of the pivotal figures in Irish history.

Strongbow had agreed to lead the invasion only in return for a number of guarantees. MacMurrough must promise to give Strongbow his daughter, Aoife, as part of a dynastic marriage and – more potently – must agree that the kingship of Leinster would be his upon MacMurrough's own death. In this way, Strongbow reasoned, his claim upon his new Irish lands would be copper-fastened both legally and morally. These promises duly given, Strongbow's Anglo-Norman force landed in Waterford harbour, occupied the old Viking port of Waterford and massacred its inhabitants, at which point the marriage of Strongbow and Aoife took place, 'while the streets ran red with blood'. The vast canvas of Daniel Maclise's *The Marriage of Strongbow and Aoife* (1854), which today hangs in the National Gallery of Ireland on Dublin's Merrion Square, vividly portrays this massacre even as it romanticises it: the lovers – Aoife sharply lit, Strongbow shadowed – are wed amid a throng of quasi-Greek and Roman divinities, while corpses lie piled all around.

The combined Anglo-Norman army immediately made its way to Dublin, recognising the town as the cockpit of authority for the whole island. The Hiberno-Norse population of Dublin set out to defend the town as best it could. Indeed, Dublin was theoretically easily defended by any attack from the south: the narrow coastal strip could be secured by a modest force of soldiers, while inland the Wicklow Mountains presented a formidable barrier to any invading army. Unfortunately for the people of Dublin, they reckoned without the local knowledge of MacMurrough: by-passing the coastal defences, he simply led the Anglo-Normans onto secure tracks over the moors and wilderness of the mountains and down into the valley of the Liffey. The Anglo-Norman army was numerically far smaller than the number of men available for the defence of Dublin but they were a very great deal better equipped, with chain mail, helmets, padded tunics, great long bows of yew and deadly steel-tipped arrows. Descending in this way from the mountains, the Anglo-Norman army was at the gates of the city before its defenders could mobilise. A small contingent of troops forced their way through the gates and commenced slaughtering the population. King Asculph fled on a ship that had been made ready on the Liffey and Dublin surrendered on 21 September 1170.

Efforts were made by the Irish to recapture the city in the following year: at a battle on Hoggen Green (now College Green) just east of the city, an Irish attack was defeated comprehensively; and in the same year, a long siege of Dublin was ultimately ended by an Anglo-Norman counter-attack which broke the besieging army and scattered its forces. But September 1170 remains the date on which a new era began for Dublin and for the island as a whole. When MacMurrough died in the following year, Strongbow declared himself King of Leinster, and the new order seemed assured.

It is at this point that one sees the quickening in the pace of history and the immediacy of events and consequences. King Henry II, watching these unfolding events in Ireland, was alarmed at the rapid progress his – the nominal his – forces were making in Ireland. Soon, it seemed, the whole island might be overrun and with it a new power might arise that would challenge the authority of the English Crown. Strongbow, the King feared, might rapidly graduate from being a mere King of Leinster into being quite another king – that of Ireland itself.

With this in mind, Henry hastened to Dublin himself, arriving in October 1171, and he was the first English monarch to land in person in Ireland. He came in some haste, indeed, clutching the papal bull which asserted his lordship over Ireland, and at the head of a vast army. Strongbow's uppity behaviour, however, was not the only reason behind Henry's decision to cross the Irish Sea. The Pope's legate was on his way from Rome to England at the same time, to accuse the King of being the brains behind the 'murder in the cathedral': the killing of Thomas à Becket at Canterbury Cathedral. Better for all concerned, therefore, that the papal representative should find Henry from home.

During his stay in Dublin, the King was put up in an elaborate wickerwork tent on the site of the Thing. There he spent a busy winter of 1171 to 1172, wining and dining selected Irish chieftains, planning the future governance of Dublin and asserting his authority over the town. Henry, in fact, showed a good deal of cunning in his dealings with the new order in Ireland and with the people of Dublin. Having reminded Strongbow by show of arms that he was boss, Henry confirmed him in his title as King of

Leinster. At the same time, however, he deprived Strongbow of an economic power base in Ireland by removing Dublin from his control. Authority over the city and its economic activities was instead granted by royal charter to the merchants of Bristol. The King bestowed on the new colony a liberty: a tangible liberty of some six square miles, within which economic regulations were eased and financial autonomy granted. Henceforth, Dublin would operate as an independent entity – a colony or city-state – within Ireland. As for Strongbow himself, he lived only a few more years before succumbing (somewhat ingloriously) to a foot infection in April 1176.

In granting the city to the merchants of Bristol, Henry would change the face of Dublin beyond all recognition. The final ending of Viking influence in the city severed the potent ties that bound it to a network of Norse-founded trading settlements across Europe. Now, Dublin would look principally to England for its trade and its cultural and economic influences. It was dependent on England, in other words, for its laws and its wealth and its economic well-being, for its very security and for much else besides.

The Anglo-Normans lost no time in imposing their values and culture on the city. It could be said that the new regime brought to Dublin a proto-modern economic culture and sensibility. The institutions that were forming across Europe for the purposes of supporting civic life were now introduced to Dublin too and, for the first time, we can trace the evolution of town councils and mayors and fairs, of trading guilds in the form that we understand them and of all the paraphernalia of urban life. The city's markets and trades, as in the English fashion, became focused on specific districts of the town, so that the fish markets were located on today's Fishamble Street, taverns on Winetavern Street, bakeries on Cook Street and so on. The wealthy section of the population sustained the importation of such luxuries as saffron, ginger and other spices. We can glimpse in all of this activity the beginnings of capitalism in Dublin, as the economic liberties given to the city spurred its citizens towards greater autonomy and more fervent wealth creation.

The Anglo-Normans also immediately began to imprint their culture on the architecture and planning of the city. In or around 1186, work began on rebuilding and enlarging Christ Church in the late Romanesque style; similarly rebuilding work began on creating a suitably sized St Patrick's Cathedral in 1192. New fortifications were undertaken from 1209 and engineering works began on the Liffey and Poddle, so that the new city of Dublin might be surrounded by deep water on three sides. King John had ascended to the English throne in 1199 and, having decided that the city required an updated fortress, he gave orders five years later to build a new stone Dublin Castle, 'making it as strong as you can with good dykes and strong walls. But you are first to build a tower, to which a castle and bailey and other requirements may be conveniently added: for all of these you have our authority.' This more than anything indicates the bedding down of Anglo-Norman influence in this, their new colony. But they also had rather more bracing gifts to bestow.

Dublin had always thrived on the fusing of cultures, and the arrival of the Anglo-Normans meant that additional ethnic groups and influences were now flung into the pot. Not, of course, that everything continued as heretofore – far from it. The new rulers of Dublin had very specific ideas on the subject of cultural fusion, and they lost no time putting these ideas into action. In the first place, the authorities busied themselves with the enactment of a series of laws, statutes and ordinances that set out to bolster their position in this new land. In common with other Irish colonial towns, they banned the native Hiberno-Norse population of Dublin from membership of the new city guilds that were then being created and from taking up apprenticeships in the trades.

Across Europe, indeed, similar phenomena could be witnessed at this time, as colonial authorities strove to assert their authority over local populations.

At the same time, and even more radically, the city authorities ordered the expulsion of the city's native population, which was obliged to remove north across the Liffey to what became the new suburb of Oxmantown (deriving from Ostmen, which was another term used for the Vikings of Dublin). This, more than anything, indicates the new nature of life and politics in Dublin. The city's population would henceforth speak forms of old English and French. Norse and Irish would continue to be spoken in the lanes and marketplaces of Dublin, but principally now by visitors to the city.

But the expulsion of the Hiberno-Norse population of Dublin was, as with the earlier Viking removals, of necessity incomplete. Indeed, it is certainly the case that the new Anglo-Norman government had no intention of expelling every man, woman and child from Dublin, even if this was possible. As in the past, craftsmen, artisans and other representatives of the old order remained where they were and continued to work as they had done before, maintaining Dublin's economic buoyancy in the process. Presumably the Anglo-Normans realised, as we generally realise today, that it's the economy, stupid: that trade, rather than ideological purity, will always comes first.

However patchy and flawed the practice was, however, the paperwork was always in order. The statutes and laws enacted in these years betray an obsession with blood, purity and power on the part of the Anglo-Norman authorities. It is the case, perhaps, that the exhaustive nature of these statutes – detailed and all-enveloping as they were – were substitutive and compensatory in nature; they betray the dawning understanding that the purity these laws sought to impose could never in truth be realised. The very fact, for example, that Dublin was subject to repeated cleansings of its population over the centuries indicates this basic truth.

The agitation and anxiety revealed in the laws, however, is striking and is part of a pattern that was repeated across Europe. Among German-speaking urban populations planted in the east of the continent, among the Anglo-Norman settlers clustered in the new colonial keeps and castles of Wales, and here in Ireland, the same echoes of fear may be heard. The colonists were isolated and, as they saw it, marooned on an alien sea and remote from their mother culture. Their power was tenuous and dependent on support from overseas, their supply lines were weak and all the ties that bound them to their original homes were stretched almost to breaking point.

And if this syndrome was everywhere the same, so too was the response, and it rested on notions of systematic discrimination. Accompanying the plethora of statutes concerning guild member-ships, the hiring of apprentices, and so on, were other broader, cul-tural, measures. The native Irish were excluded, insofar as this was possible, from ecclesiastical office; later this was altered to bar anyone from office who could not speak English with reason-able fluency. The law was obsessively meddlesome, in fact, con-cerning itself with everything from the manner in which the colonists might dress to the way in which they could ride their horses to the sports that might legally be played. In all cases, these measures were drawn to evoke a distinct separateness and gap between the Anglo-Normans and the native Irish. And in all cases, it is an easy matter to glimpse the creeping realisation that coloni-sation, no matter how systematically it may be applied and no matter how overwhelming may be the military might that accom-panies it, can never be complete and never wholly victorious. Colonisers the world over have always discovered this fact for themselves, and the Anglo-Norman colonial authorities in Dublin discovered it too.

Chapter 5

※

A MAP OF THE WORLD

On a Saturday morning in July, I make my way to the bus stop on Baggot Street. The road is almost deserted; filled, that is to say, with the particular kind of silence that has always been disconcerting to me, for the streets of this part of the city – broad streets, and old and grey, the edge of the Georgian quarter – can never seem to fill themselves adequately with activity and human life. Nor is it even a special weekend phenomenon, for I feel it too at the height of the working week, even in this presently frenetic Dublin of head offices and cafés dispensing bad coffee, froth, cream cheese-smeared bagels galore.

I used to think it was just me – something about the spaces of the city that pressed and prodded restlessly in my head – until I read Elizabeth Bowen and saw that she, as a child in the Edwardian city, had felt the same Dublin atmosphere. 'There never was much movement,' she writes, 'though I took this for granted (as being the rule of cities) I saw too few people in view of the height and space. The tyrannical grandeur of this quarter seemed to exist for itself alone.'[1] Bowen put it down to the fading and failing of the colonial city and the decay of her Anglo-Irish class, but it seems to me that she would feel and smell the same miasma even today, a hundred years later.

It is still quite early, no more than ten o'clock, but already warm and humid, and the number 10 bus, when it finally arrives, comes in the form of a corrective to the enveloping quiet: it is stuffed to the gills with Spanish exchange students on their raucous way to somewhere or other. Spanish language students are something of a dominant motif of the summer in the city, for such are the cultural affinities between Spain and Ireland that Dublin is a natural destination for hundreds of these young Spaniards who are eager to brush up on their English and who are infinitely more exuberant, expressive and stylish – not to mention better of complexion – than their pallid Irish peers.

The heat is uncomfortable, the city has been festering unpleasantly in the middle of a heatwave for several weeks, and the bus is stuffy and deafening – and I wish that the Spanish students would keep it down. I am already pink and damp; I do not, and Dublin does not, suffer heat graciously. The proximity of the sea always tempers matters, of course, but summer heat brings out on show skin that is winter-pale, that ought to be veiled and cosseted in at least several layers of fabric. Not on this hot morning. And take into account also the early twenty-first-century penchant for immodesty in matters of dress and fashion, so that navels, tattoos and sagging stomachs are on display, proudly, for the world to see. Such is the scene aboard the number 10, and so, when it eventually draws up at the Suffolk Street stop – heaving and immodest and bellowing as if it was a many-tongued Pandaemonium – I am eager to make a relieved escape.

I have decided to visit Dublinia, the permanent exhibition on Viking and medieval Dublin housed in the neo-Gothic Synod Hall neighbouring Christ Church. I have never been to the exhibition before, in spite of the fact that it has been installed for some 12 years. This failure is largely due, of course, to a sense of cultural superiority on my part. After all, such exhibitions tend to exist largely for the benefit of tourists, rather than for the permanent residents of the city. Or so I have always thought, insofar as I have thought about it at all, and so I feel rather pleased with myself on this morning, flushed with a new and quite unexpected sense of broadmindedness.

Today, Christ Church still sits on the hill of Dublin and the old streets continue to run as they ever did in the days of the medieval city: Winetavern Street falling steeply north and down to the line of the Liffey; Cornmarket running along the crest of the ridge towards St James's Gate, the Guinness Brewery and the western suburbs; Clanbrassil Street sloping away south towards the mountains. The cathedral itself, however, sits today no longer on the crest of its hill, but in a concavity several metres below the level of the surrounding streets. The reason for this sag is both perfectly prosaic and yet evocative too. Houses have burned or been crushed or have fallen and new houses and structures have been raised in their place; detritus and filth and mud of various sorts has settled, little by little, and over the course of a thousand tempestuous years the height of the hill has increased by a metre or two. Only the environs of the cathedral itself have been immune to this settling and sedimentation. Today, therefore, the building rests in its saucer, as the city has grown and been destroyed and layered itself all around.

The Synod Hall was built on the site of St Michael's, a long-vanished medieval church and is joined to the main bulk of the cathedral by a stone bridge of Victorian provenance, which crosses Winetavern Street. The hall is a work of the nineteenth century, as is the Christ Church of today: its Gothic detail and flying buttresses cannot disguise the fact that the Victorians undertook more of a thorough rebuilding of the cathedral rather than an actual restoration. Only the crypt and some masonry remain to point to the antiquity of this, the most distinguished of Dublin's landmarks.

I am first in the queue to plunge into Dublinia on this hot summer morning. Only a few earnest German and English tourists are with me as I pay the rather hefty entrance charge and begin my tour. I begrudge this entrance charge. Naturally I begrudge it, as each of Ireland's publicly owned national collections and cultural institutions is free to all comers, so I naturally believe that all museums and galleries the world over should be similarly free.

As it turns out, Dublinia – in spite of my grumbling stinginess – is worth the money. The exhibition manages to cut through the sometimes clogging and confusing eddies of Ireland's medieval past, with its plethora of strong characters, political weddings, blood-red massacres and foreign interventions, to present a portrait of a city where actual lives were lived, where profits were won and lost and where the ferocious difficulties of life were offset by a degree of pleasure and leisure that the history books often forget to mention. Nor does the exhibition veil some of the more recent events that have caused much of this past to be lost to us for ever.

Take the Wood Quay controversy of the 1970s. Today, the looming headquarters of Dublin City Council occupies the ground sloping from the north front of Christ Church down to the Liffey embankments on Wood Quay. The planning and construction of this complex of buildings was accompanied by a great deal of controversy. Initial excavations of the site revealed to the public what historians already guessed: that the ground in this area was thick with buried treasure. Viking and medieval Dublin had grown up in this area and, although the tides of time had swept away the evidence of the lives that were lived on the slopes of the hill above the Liffey, these first excavations had shown what might be brought to light. Bones of people and of animals, necklaces and pottery and a million other things besides – this was an opportunity to illuminate the past, if only the political will was there to allow the excavations to continue, and if only the resources were made available to the archaeologists.

It transpired that the political will was not there, the resources were not made available and it was only with the greatest difficulty that even a limited dig at Wood Quay was permitted to proceed. Dublin Corporation was determined to have its new civic headquarters built, come hell or high water, and it persevered with this determination, even as public interest in the Wood Quay site mounted. Much of the site was bulldozed and the archaeological evidence it contained destroyed for good, but a dig was permitted for a limited period of time on the remainder of the site. The result of this determination was that a vast number of artefacts were brought to the surface, remarkable and evocative in themselves but also serving as a painful reminder of what might have been, and of what was lost. And this, in the face of a public campaign which saw a petition signed by some 200,000 people, in the face of a Council of Europe appeal that the site be preserved, in the face of very considerable international protest.

There was never any question that the Wood Quay site should be preserved as a sort of open-air archaeological park. The site – exposed as it was, north-facing and steeply sloping – was not suitable for a park of any kind. Besides, this area had been profoundly urban since the beginnings of the city, and it was correct and proper that it continue to function in this way, rather than essentially fossilise as a sort of open-air museum. The tragedy of the Wood Quay site, rather, was that its importance was not officially recognised by the city authorities, that the excavations were not permitted to run for as long as necessary, and that the vast buildings which eventually came to be erected here were less than sympathetic to their surroundings. Although later additions to the complex have softened their impact from the Liffey, they still look monstrously large when viewed from the south. But a measure of good came out of the affair too, in the shape of a renewed interest in the city's medieval and Norse past.

The exhibition at Dublinia is as bracing in its assessment of the Wood Quay episode as diplomacy permits. But it seems to me, on this hot Saturday morning, that the potency of this section of the exhibition lies not so much in its overt commentary as in the silent power of the objects on display, demonstrating what has been preserved from the developers and what has not. The lower level of the museum consists of largely interactive exhibits: rooms to peer into in order to witness the fashion of the time and a good many invitingly large red buttons to press. For me, though, the real treasures of the museum are to be found on the upper floors, where a large relief model of Dublin is laid out on the floor, and where the treasures salvaged from the Wood Quay site are on display.

The skeleton of a female is stretched in a glass case; it looks complete, to my untutored mind, with not a bone missing. Nearby, the woman's features have been restored with the aid of computer graphics. It is evident that she lived a tough life: her bones reveal the arthritis she suffered, her mouth was swollen with abscesses that could not be treated. She used her teeth as tools and so they are cracked and broken; many are missing and I am told that she suffered considerable pain before her death. And of course she is short of stature, a good deal shorter than the average height today, and this more than anything seems to reveal the gulf of time that separates this medieval Dubliner from the modern population. Nearby are other bones: of dogs and cats and of a whale too, imported, maybe, from Scandinavia – and a wolf skin, evidence of a time before the species was hunted to extinction in Ireland.

Around this skeleton lie an abundance of pins and brooches and the medieval taste for the grotesque and horrible is also vividly demonstrated, with pottery jugs and vessels galore, festooned with leering griffins and gargoyles. But the most arresting artefacts on display, to my mind, are the tiny dice and whistles and harp pegs wrought of ivory and bone. An oral culture, of course, leaves no trace and is notoriously susceptible to disaster. A break in transmission of a tradition, a story or a song as a result of disease or war or social upheaval can be fatal. That song, story or tradition may, as a result, vanish for good. But a largely oral culture has implements and potency at its disposal too; and tools, touching and affecting indeed, are on display in Dublinia for the world to see and the imagination to take and carry away. We know a good deal about the harshness of life at this time, from the skeleton I see and from many other sources. But it is through the scanty evidence of pleasure and leisure that I feel past Dubliners reaching out and becoming tangible and human, as they plucked the harp or played games with dice as we do today.

Nearby are other objects that help to kindle the medieval city to life. Dublin was known in those days for the strong currents of religious energy that ran through civic life. This was epitomised not only in the two very large rival cathedrals within spitting distance of each other, but also in the plethora of other churches crammed within the city walls and in the roaring trade in religious pilgrimages in which the city engaged. These pilgrims have left enough evidence behind them to demonstrate that while much has changed in intervening years, more than enough has stayed the same.

I had passed through the Marian shrine village of Knock in the west of Ireland only a few weeks before, on my way to a wedding on the west coast, and memories of this experience were still vivid in my mind on that hot Saturday morning. Knock is the very oddest of places: lost on a windswept bog and a long distance from any substantial centre of population yet with an international airport a stone's throw away. Short on charm and beauty, and yet for over a hundred years – ever since the Virgin Mary took it upon herself to appear in the middle of this bog in 1879 – a centre of Irish pilgrimage and spirituality and dominated by a vast and ugly basilica.

In my mind, Knock will always stand for the horrid string of kitschy shops strung out the length of its main street. These shops sell what such shops the world over sell: Virgin Mary ashtrays and mugs and plates, rosary beads in every hue and in all materials, screw-top plastic bottles wrought in the image of the Virgin (her head comes off and her body may be filled with holy water), Virgin Mary snow globes and statues of her that glow in the dark and the Lord knows what else. Pope John Paul visited here during his famous trip to Ireland in 1979, and so this clatter of junk presumably retains the blessing of God Himself.

I am reminded vividly of my visit to Knock this morning in Dublinia, as I gaze at the knick-knacks left behind by pilgrims 700 years ago and subsequently excavated from beneath the streets of the city. In the absence of screw-top Marys, these unknown men and women adorned themselves with copper alloy badges and brooches, which identified them as members of the devout and as pilgrims. They came from across Europe to view and pray over the relics gathered together under the roofs of the vast array of churches within the walls of Dublin and in the city's hinterland, and to stop and rest on their laborious way to St Patrick's Purgatory on Lough Derg in far-away Ulster, and to Croagh Patrick, the sacred mountain of Ireland in Connacht. They would have taken part in the myriad religious processions through the streets of the city, many of which – in the manner of the English mystery play pageants at Coventry, Wakefield and other cities, all centred around universal feast days such as Corpus Christi — were sponsored and performed by the members of the city guilds.

Christ Church in particular was a magnet for pilgrims, containing as it did enough precious relics to satisfy the most fervent believer. As well as claiming to possess the bones of Peter and Andrew, the cathedral held in its keeping the precious Bachall Íosa, the Crozier of St Patrick, which was said to have originally been the staff of Christ. An English colony Dublin may have been then, but in those days of a universal Catholic Church Ireland's past and its religious present provided as much of a tie as commerce in binding the city into the mainstream of European life.

So much we know and, as with the harp pegs, the dice and the whistles next door, so too do the little copper pilgrimage badges carry a power, an immediacy, a strength disproportionate to their size.

After a while, I go next door to study the large relief model of Dublin. The new Anglo-Norman walled city is shown on the higher southern bank of the Liffey, and the Poddle, now widened and dredged, curls around the eastern fortifications. Already, a thousand years ago, the Liffey is being tamed, deepened and narrowed. Wooden palisades have been pushed into the riverbed from north and south, the land behind filled with earth and rubble, and houses and harbourage constructed on the new ground. Christ Church rises on the crest of the hill, as it has ever done, and St Patrick's, surrounded by its jumble of outbuildings and estate houses, lies just south of the city walls. Other churches and monasteries are scattered across the landscape, testament to the power of the Church in this society: St Mary de Hogges lying on the site of what is now Trinity College, to the east of the city, St Mary's Abbey sitting north of the Liffey, and many others. Oxmantown spreads out on the flat landscape on the river's northern bank, demonstrating the physical consequences of the expulsion of the native population by the colonial authorities.

These priories and monasteries scattered around the city's hinterland acted as potent engines of economic growth, and now new suburbs like Oxmantown – albeit created with other purposes in mind – spurred this growth yet onwards. Indeed, Oxmantown's position, adjacent as it was to St Mary's, was no accident. The Abbey, which was founded by the Cistercians in 1139, made no bones about its economic importance: it maintained its own harbour on the Liffey and owned another on Dublin Bay, and trade was carried on in its own marketplace. The economic clout of this religious foundation, and the many others like it laid out in the hinterland of the city, can be judged from the records. They possessed large swathes of land, covering on occasion hundreds of hectares; they were landlords to all manner of traders and artisans; and they were also the principal charitable foundations in the city. All this, and their spiritual activities too.

The new scale of this city, its suburbs and its impressive fortifications, are very evident in the relief map on display. But so too is its vulnerability, impressive defences or not. In the southern distance rise the Wicklow Mountains, a fastness for centuries for the native Irish opposed to the English toehold in Ireland in the valley below. West of the city sit the fortified posts – gates of a sort, though attached to no wall, as the relief map makes pitilessly clear – designed to protect the unwalled suburbs and which actually demonstrate the very vulnerability of these suburbs. These are situated all around the city, a vast hinterland on which the new city relies for food and supplies, yet which lies beyond any meaningful control. Much has been made of the fact that the people of the city dined as standard on salmon, oysters and an abundance of seafood – but famine was a grinding commonplace in Dublin in these years for all that. Here are all of these unmistakable facts, evident in this map of Dublin's world, and they display most effectively the fact that this new colony's hold on prosperity and viability was tenuous at best.

Not that all visitors to Dublinia find the exhibition a clarifying experience. As I leave, I pass a small family group gathered in querulous debate.

'Naw,' says a plump teenager crossly and in carrying North American tones, 'that was the other Henry, Dad. The eighth one. He was the one that did that.'

'Yeh, the eighth,' his sister murmurs in agreement. 'It was the eighth.'

'Wait,' says Dad. 'The eighth – he was the one with all the wives, right?'

'The Six Wives, yeh.'

'Yeh. Right, well, he's the Henry I was talkin' about. He's the one who killed the guy.'

'Naw, Dad – no way.'

I hang around in a blatant fashion for another minute or so, until they begin to look at me suspiciously and to edge away. I never discover, though, which Henry they mean, or the identity of the guy he was supposed to have killed.

Chapter 6

⚛

HISTORY HANDED DOWN
FROM ABOVE

Here is a first point. On Easter Monday 1209 – some 40-odd years after Dublin surrendered to Strongbow – a large party of citizens sallied forth from the city. Their destination was what is now Ranelagh, a kilometre or two south of the city centre. Today, this is a highly agreeable district of town, being green and über-fashionable, with restaurants, cafés, farmers' markets and gleaming new tram stops, and, as a result, property prices that are high enough to bring on an attack of screaming vertigo. As is the case in many south-Dublin neighbourhoods, the Wicklow Mountains appear surprisingly close: lift your eyes on a clear day and you might reach out, it seems, and grasp the fields and coniferous plantations of the lower slopes.

Even back in 1209, it would have been a pleasant spot. The district was lightly wooded in those days and the ground firm and rising towards the swelling mountains in the distance – in all, a change from the marshy land close to the city walls, from the ditches and gravel and tides along the Liffey and Poddle rivers. It was distant enough too from the congestion, din and odours of Dublin, yet close enough to feel secure. All important matters to the good burghers of the newly Anglo-Norman Dublin and all good reasons why this district had been chosen by the townsfolk

49

for a game of hurling – fast, skilful and physical, a contact sport as celebrated today in Ireland as it was then. It was Easter Monday, and the game, together with a fair and general merry-making, had been arranged as part of the holiday celebrations. As an occasion, it must have been anticipated with pleasure, marking as it did the coming of spring and the end of the long and unpleasant Irish winter, and acting as a welcome diversion from the difficulties of life at that time. Hundreds of townsfolk, then, congregated in Cullens Wood in Ranelagh, anticipating an agreeable day out.

As it turned out, however, the new colonists in the city had little to celebrate at the end of that day. They had taken scant account of their own safety, as it seems, presuming that the hinterland of the city had been secured from attack. But local Irish chieftains of the O'Toole and O'Byrne clans, who had been dispossessed of their lands, came down out of the looming mountains and, approaching in secret through the woods, attacked the crowd. In the ensuing massacre, some 500 citizens of the city were killed.

Inevitably, the event became known as 'Black Monday'. Such an enormous loss of life would have been shattering for this small city – economically, socially and psychologically. It was certainly the case that the ranks of citizens were so decimated that new colonists had to be drafted in hastily from England. And moreover, the fact the episode was commemorated in Dublin for over 600 years is illustrative of its impact on the psychology of the city.

Here is a second point. In 1314, the Scottish army of Robert the Bruce recorded a famous victory over the English at Bannockburn. The victory, it was hoped among enemies of England in Wales, Scotland and Ireland, marked a turning point in the tide of fortune: the advance of the English Crown and of English influence might now at last be stemmed. In the aftermath of the battle, messages were sent from the Irish chieftains of Ulster to Robert, requesting that his brother Edward sail for Ireland with an army. Perhaps, the native Irish reasoned, a similar victory could be scored over the English on this side of the Irish Sea and the English expelled from Ireland into the bargain.

Edward duly arrived in the port of Larne on the Ulster coast in the spring of 1315. A full two years later Edward was joined by Robert himself and together they marched on Dublin, destroying everything in their path. There was every reason to think that the city would fall: its fortifications had been neglected and the population of the city and its hinterland had been much reduced by disease. Presumably the authorities in Dublin had no great faith in their defences either, for drastic measures were taken to ensure the city's protection. The stone bridge over the Liffey to Oxmantown was torn down, and church belfries – and on occasion whole churches and church property – demolished too in order to rebuild the city walls. Most drastically of all, the north-western suburbs – beyond which the Bruce army was encamped – were set alight as a means of deterring an attack.

And the measures worked. The Scots army possessed none of the paraphernalia needed to besiege the city and in the face of this fact and of the fire raging before them they departed, handing the victory to the people of the city. But the victory, such as it was, exacted a price, for the fire got entirely out of hand and burned a large section of the walled city, including part of Christ Church itself. The colony had been saved, but at the cost of its own partial destruction and of another year of general famine to come. It would have been small consolation to the defenders of the city that the Scots army under Edward was first starved by the same famine it had helped to create, and eventually defeated; and that Edward himself met a gruesome end, for he was quartered in the following year.

Here is a third point. In late July or early August 1348, some 30 years after the Scots campaign had ended, the Black Death was first reported in Ireland. It appeared first at Drogheda, on the

51

coast north of Dublin, and in the harbours at Dalkey and Howth on Dublin Bay, a little south and north of the city itself. The plague had already swept through southern Europe in the early part of the year, passing from city to city with frightful speed, and using well-worked trading paths and shipping lanes to cut a swathe of death across the continent. The disease may have arrived in Dublin via Bristol or Chester, or it may have come on ships plying the well-worn shipping lanes between France and Dublin, carrying their precious cargoes of wine for the Irish market; it is impossible today to pinpoint its origins, nor does it, in any case, matter very much.

The social, economic and demographic impact of the Black Death on European society is already well recorded. In Dublin, its impact was equally devastating: in the second half of that dreadful year, 14,000 people were said to have died – a large proportion of the city's population. As is generally the way the poor probably suffered the most. The stone houses of Dublin's wealthy elite served a little better than the mean, filthy and crowded houses of the poor to keep the plague-carrying rats at bay. But nobody in the city and surrounding area would be immune – far from it; the Black Death was notably indiscriminate, after all, and no respecter of class difference, and it has been calculated than some two-thirds of the English colonists in Ireland were carried off by plague.

The Black Death was famously a potent agent of social change in this feudal medieval Europe. It weakened the aristocratic hold over the general population: fewer people were left to work the land, and as a result those who had survived were better able to call the shots – or leave the land for the growing towns. In England, shrill and hasty laws forbade demands for higher wages, forbade peasants from abandoning their land for the cities, forbade all manner of revolutionary actions and deeds – but these laws had little effect. The plague had changed the fabric of life, permanently.

In Ireland and in Dublin, this change appeared in ways that responded to the specific conditions of the country. It is estimated, for example, that the impact of the disease lessened in more rural areas of Ireland. While the population of Dublin's low-lying hinterland was decimated, for example, the clans of the Wicklow Mountains were hardly affected at all, and this was hardly good news for the authorities in Dublin. Moreover, the greater tendency of the population to migrate in search of better wages, better conditions and a better life led to changes in the character of Dublin's population. The endless ordinances and proclamations designed to maintain the purity of the city's population continued unabated, but migration would have its effect, and Dublin, as the medieval period wore on, became increasingly a mixed city.

So much analysis of demographics and economic change is all very well but the plague's visitations had effects more urgent and pressing on a city with Dublin's specific position and conditions. Put simply, the colony could not afford death on such a grand scale. The Black Death would carry away a large portion of the European population, but it would not carry away everyone. Once this became clear, once it became evident that the end of the world had not come, once the disease had come and gone, other towns and cities of Europe could set about slowly rebuilding their strength and wealth. Dublin, though, had no such philosophical luxuries to fall back on: it was a city on the edge even at the best of times, and the effects of the Black Death were therefore truly specific to it and potentially cataclysmic. The significance of such mass death on an already hard-pressed colony – on its morale, its economy, its spirit and character – should not be underestimated.

Three glimpses, then, of life in the medieval city, and horrendous and livid glimpses, to be sure. But also highly representative: attacks on the city from surrounding populations were common and sustained; and plague was a common feature of life at the time, so common in fact that after the first attack in 1348 it was only mentioned by the annalists in passing – though dreadful and traumatic all the same. Fires in the medieval city were even more common than plague or assault from outside. Dublin, in common with every other medieval European city, was regularly swept by deadly conflagrations. The average life expectancy, across all classes, was a mere 26 years. Together, these episodes and facts reveal how marginal and grinding life would have been for ordinary people even in a continental European city and how much more difficult it was for a population of a colony such as Dublin.

The difficulty and distress of these years lays bare the extent to which the fate of medieval Dublin lay outside its control. The attitude of the Irish beyond the Pale – the area around Dublin where the Crown's writ still more or less ran – was understood: they would never be reconciled to the presence of this colony on the east coast of the island. Of equal significance, however, was the attitude of the English authorities in London and for much of the medieval period, they had much bigger fish to fry. Indeed, when Richard II came to Ireland in 1394 and 1399, his aim was not so much to reconquer the territories which were slipping from his control as to assert his authority over the diminished realm he still maintained in Ireland, and during his second expedition the throne was usurped in his absence. There followed the lengthy and tumultuous Wars of the Roses, during which the Crown had little energy to invest in its beleaguered outpost at Dublin.

The political instability and upheaval that mark the medieval period – the jockeying for possession of the English Crown and the wars with France in particular – meant that the colonists in Ireland were left largely to their own devices. Colonists, both English-born and those who had been born and raised in the city, began to abandon Dublin to return to England, so much so that yet further ordinances were proclaimed, this time banning Irish immigration into England. And, in a stroke of delightful irony, the ban on native Irish immigration into Dublin itself meant that the city's population could legally not be replenished even by this means. Taken all in all, then, it is no wonder that by the late medieval period the city was falling into ruin. Abandoned and derelict buildings were a standard feature of the cityscape, the tax base was shrinking, and the city's fortifications and two great cathedrals were falling into decay. The Pale, which had never in any case been much larger than 48 kilometres (30 miles) long by 32 kilometres (20 miles) broad, began to shrink, its bounds contracting gradually in the direction of Dublin and the sea.

The results of this extreme isolation were inevitable. The colony at Dublin was forced to turn to the land around it for sustenance and intercourse; immigration from the countryside into Dublin became part of a necessary pattern of life, regardless of the blizzard of laws that forbade its existence; intermarriage as a result became more usual; Irish was heard as a matter of course once more on the streets of Dublin, and the differences between the native-born Irish and the Anglo-Irish began to break down. It was a situation being repeated on a much greater scale, across Ireland, as a thoroughgoing Gaelicisation of the country took root. And it was a situation that was intolerable to the Crown. When, at length, the Tudors were established on the English throne in 1485, with time and resources to spare for Ireland, they set about reconquering a city and an island that had largely slipped from English control.

The following 200-odd years, from 1485 to the restoration of the monarchy in 1666, were strikingly tempestuous, even by Irish standards. As the Tudor reconquest of Ireland wanes and waxes, the history of the country is punctuated with plantations of new settlers, with Spanish landings on the south coast, with rebellions across the island, with endless change and destruction imposed from above and from without. Throughout the period, Dublin remains the cockpit of English authority and power in Ireland. It might be imagined that the city would therefore naturally have witnessed considerable investment, as the English strove to reassert their authority in Ireland. In fact, the opposite was the case: the dwindling of Dublin's population may have been finally arrested by this burst of new activity and by steadily increasing interaction with the rest of Ireland, but the fabric of the city continued its decline even as English arms and power were landed on the docks and flowed into the rest of Ireland. In essence, Dublin remained in the medieval age even as that age was itself drawing to a close.

This process of decay can be observed as late as the seventeenth century and is best symbolised by the collapse of the roof of the nave of St Patrick's in 1542, and by the collapse of the roof and south wall of Christ Church in 1562. The city's merchants signalled their priorities by clustering their stone warehouses around the deep-water port at Dalkey on the southern edge of Dublin Bay, even as the silting of the Liffey continued unabated until navigation into and out of the city itself became hazardous. In 1573, the Lord Deputy, Sir Henry Sidney, reported that the neglected Dublin Castle was 'ruinous, foul, filthy and greatly decayed' and set about reconstructing a building that was falling down around his ears. And human actions too played their part in the decline of the city: in 1597 over 200 citizens were killed and a vast amount of damage done to Dublin's decaying buildings when a store of gunpowder exploded while being unloaded on Merchant's Quay.

Even the Reformation in Dublin principally serves to emphasise a sense of decline in the city and neglect on the part of the Crown. Picture the scene in 1538, for example, when a bonfire was piled up in front of Christ Church and set ablaze. As the kindling lit and the fire spread, many of the ancient religious relics housed in the cathedral were brought out and dumped unceremoniously into the flames, including the Bachall Íosa, the precious Crozier of St Patrick. The archbishop of the day was George Browne: he had been appointed by Henry VIII, he had previously officiated at the King's marriage to Anne Boleyn and now he ordered the destruction of the relics, viewing them as symbols of idolatry. The religious and political fervour displayed by such an action does not, maybe, accord well with the idea of a crumbling and neglected city – until we set this bonfire in a wider context.

The Reformation led to the dissolution of the monasteries in Dublin, as in England itself, and, as a result, institutions that had been a part of city life for centuries vanished in the space of a few years from 1537 to 1544. Nearly all of the venerable priories and monasteries that dotted the city's hinterland disappeared in this way; and today, these ancient buildings and institutions have, for the most part, utterly vanished from the city's landscape. Only the scant but evocative remains of the chapter house of St Mary's Abbey can be explored, nestled on a lane close to Mary Street in the north inner city, and hinting at the economic and spiritual power of the foundation that once stood here. The importance, influence and longevity of these religious houses, however, can still be glimpsed by any walker in Dublin, wandering the streets of the city with map in hand. Mary Street, Kevin Street, Bride Street, Stephen's Street, Dame Street, and many others – these are all named after abbeys and priories that have disappeared, leaving only their names behind.

Even before the Reformation, these institutions had for the most part been in steady decline for many years and had no longer been fulfilling the crucial roles – as centres of education, medicine and charity – that they once had. As a result, it is clear that their dissolution did not in fact have the disastrous social consequences that were once imagined. It is significant, however, that the buildings, once abandoned by the religious orders, more often than not fell rapidly into ruin or were demolished. Trinity College, for example, was founded in 1592 on the site of one of these monasteries, that of All Saints which was suppressed in 1538; and it is recorded that the former priory buildings were found to be in ruins by the time of the college's establishment. In short, the city and its inhabitants simply did not have the wealth or economic vigour needed to maintain all of these foundations, and this in itself tells us all we need to know of the parlous state of Dublin at the time.

Actions such as the dissolution of the monasteries and the bonfire of the vanities before Christ Church – these are in themselves dramatic, stirring episodes and lend themselves to a lurid and highly coloured conception of Irish history in these years. We only have to look a little more carefully, however, to glimpse that creeping neglect behind these high colours, this drama. The bonfire may have been lit; behind it, however, the roof of Christ Church was crumbling and ready to collapse, which it duly did, not 25 years later. The authorities demanded that the monasteries surrender themselves, but these same monasteries were already in a state of spiritual and physical ruin, and most of them would be simply demolished and their stones carted off to repair other crumbling buildings around Dublin. Most striking of all is the sense that in spite of this city's massive strategic importance and its position as a seat of government in Ireland, the destiny of Dublin lay always in the hands of other authorities. History handed down from above – and always more marked when this destiny leads to decay and collapse.

Given this fact, it is unsurprising that this sorry period in the history of the city would end only when English society entered into a new and radical phase. The period of the Commonwealth and Protectorate in England from 1649 to 1660 – when the monarchy was overthrown, when Parliament asserted its will and when ultimately Oliver Cromwell ruled in England, Scotland and Ireland as Lord Protector – is rightly seen as a crucial phase in Britain's transition to a modern state. And, as Dublin was by this time so decisively connected to the tides of British political power, the period proved to be crucial to the destiny of this city also.

Cromwell landed at Dublin at the head of a large army on

15 August 1649. The city had previously witnessed the Battle of Rathmines, fought in the southern suburbs between forces loyal to Cromwell and those loyal to the Irish Confederate Catholics, who at this time ruled most of Ireland and who were in alliance with English Royalists. Only Dublin and Derry were in parliamentary hands at that time, and both cities were under continual threat. The clash at Rathmines on 2 August had been won by the Cromwellites, who therefore succeeded in their objective of securing the city's harbour for the passage of their master and his army. If this battle had been lost, the Cromwellian invasion of Ireland might well not have achieved its objectives, and Cromwell might never have had the opportunity to express his disdain for all things Anglican by using the patched-up nave of St Patrick's as stabling for his horses.

Cromwell, however, certainly did achieve his objectives, and at the cost of massive loss of life in Ireland. The settlement imposed on the country was punitive in the extreme, resulting in mass confiscations of Catholic land, the effective destruction of the Irish Catholic landowning class and the unrolling of the Penal Laws across the country. As for Dublin itself, the city was spared much in the way of massacre, but its economy suffered greatly from the impact of spiralling taxes levied to pay for the war, as well as from continuing attacks of famine and plague. It must have been difficult for the citizens of Dublin to believe that dramatic changes were on the way, and that the ceaseless cycle of disease, famine, hardship, neglect and economic deprivation was about to end. And yet it was, for the imposition of a political settlement – punitive and harsh though it was to the Catholic population of Ireland – combined with the later restoration of Charles II to the throne in London, inaugurated a new and altogether dramatic period in the history of the city.

PART TWO

I keep much in the Country because it is more unlike
Dublin than anything I can find this side the Channel.[1]

JONATHAN SWIFT

Chapter 7

LENDERS AND BORROWERS

On a warm afternoon late in September, I make my way through the south city centre. The broad roads surrounding St Stephen's Green are littered with fallen leaf-covered branches, the gutters and pavements are choked by more leaves, torn from the trees, and the scene, in general, looks as though someone has really gone for it with a chainsaw. The truth is a little more prosaic, though dramatic enough: the remnants of Tropical Storm Gordon passed through in the night and wreaked havoc as he went. Ireland lies in the path of Atlantic weather systems, of course, but dying hurricanes and disintegrating tropical storms are nevertheless rare events – blessedly rare, I think, as I pick my way through the sodden debris.

Out the other side of St Stephen's Green and onto Kevin Street, heading west towards the Liberties, and the style and tone of the streetscape abruptly changes. The Georgian terraces that still – up to a point – edge the Green now disappear and twentieth-century buildings, some good and some very bad, take their place. This kind of rapid transition is characteristic of Dublin's city centre, where grandly substantial public edifices and terraces can often appear to be little more than skins or membranes, behind which are tucked neighbourhoods of quite different provenance.

A few minutes west of the Green lies St Patrick's: the larger of the city's twin Church of Ireland cathedrals and, although not the older, the more historically resonant. Like Christ Church, it has been radically altered down the centuries; the Victorians took St Patrick's firmly in hand too, essentially reconstructing its medieval fabric. Its location is a good deal less favourable than that of Christ Church, which sits perched atop its hill a few hundred metres away. St Patrick's lies on the gentle southern slope of this same hill, and, today, road widening and a clatter of poorly designed and unsympathetic apartment developments on the opposite side of Patrick Street combine to impact grievously on the environment of the cathedral. But it is an impressive building in spite of this: the largest medieval church in Ireland, still striking today and with enough fine buildings and public spaces in its immediate environment to neutralise the bad.

Adjoining the cathedral to the north is the square of St Patrick's Park, which does a good deal to throw the building's ornate design into relief; nearby too lie the Victorian buildings of the Iveagh Trust, confident, muscular and handsome, and helping to lessen the sins of those rearing and cheap buildings of the early 1990s that ought never to be been allowed in the first place.

'A person shall not consume intoxicating liquor or inhale, inject or absorb controlled drugs or solvents.' So warns the notice at the entrance to the park. One can hardly blame Dublin City Council for dispensing this advice; this is a tough neighbourhood, the proximity of the cathedral notwithstanding, and maybe, I think, it is as well to keep people on their guard. It reminds the unwary back-packed visitor, distracted perhaps by the promise of park and cathedral and a sunny day, of additional realities of life in a modern city.

There are plenty of folk about: the high season may be just over but the park is full of strolling visitors and tour buses are neatly lined up across the road. And it is a fine spot on this bright day:

the lawns are neat and, although the dahlias have clearly taken a battering from Tropical Storm Gordon, they are blooming valiantly just the same. I pass a graceful little grove of silver birches to my left, beyond which loom the mighty walls of the cathedral itself. A well-known actor, whom the gossip columns tell me is in town shooting a film, struts along; he pushes out his pecs boastfully as he passes me. I want to kick myself; most people in this country pride themselves in coolly ignoring passing celebs, but I was just an instant too late to look away nonchalantly, to gaze studiously over his shoulder at the Gothic detail – so absorbing – on the cathedral walls.

I have been to St Patrick's many times, of course, but the church is not my destination today. Instead, I skirt its western wall, noticing the steps that lead down into the principal entrance – for St Patrick's, like Christ Church, lies in a saucer that has gradually become deeper and deeper as the city has filled up all around – and turn down St Patrick's Close. Beyond the cathedral churchyard stands a most exquisite Queen Anne building. This is Marsh's Library, unexpected and venerable – the oldest public library in the country.

Marsh's was founded in 1701 by the eponymous Narcissus Marsh, Church of Ireland Archbishop of Dublin, close to the site of the ancient and now largely vanished priory of St Sepulchre's. The library began functioning two years later, and today it is one of those few buildings in the city that is still used for its original purpose. Indeed, the place gives every appearance of not having changed in the slightest since it first opened. Fine granite steps climb up from the road, rosemary and geraniums peep over the stone sills of the steps, and, once inside, a broad wooden staircase ascends to the library doors; a vast portrait of Marsh gazes down from red-painted walls. I ring the bell and a moment later the panelled door creaks open and admits me.

I have been told, many times, about Marsh's Library and its many virtues – and indeed, the beauty and elegance of the place strike me forcibly. The sober walls are panelled in oak and a carpeted path leads down a long gallery between rows of high oak bookcases. Lighting is subdued and subtle; the sashed windows are blinded. This is a real library, as all libraries are meant to be (the sentimental side of me murmurs, with a sigh), what with the broad oaken floors and walls and these high bookcases, their shelves buckling gracefully under the accumulated weight of years.

Earlier in the day, I had told a friend I was off to Marsh's and she said to me excitedly, 'Will you ask about library loading?'

'Library loading?'

She is having some work done to her house, this friend, and her builder has already told her that steel wall reinforcements – horrendously expensive, naturally – must be fitted in order to take the weight of her bookshelves. Can this be true? If so, then how, she has asked hopelessly, did institutions such as Marsh's manage in the days before magic steel reinforcement rods? I promised I would ask.

I cannot, of course, imagine ever handling any of the leather-bound books on these heavy bookcases. Indeed, the whole building and its contents are distinctly museum-like. And so it is well that I already know that appearances can be deceptive: Marsh's is a working library, research institute and conservation centre, complete with a keeper. The leather-bound books are there to be touched, like any books in any library – so long as you have a reason to touch them. Best of all, and lest we forget who founded this library and why, each bookcase is topped off by a mitre.

Marsh's, in fact, feels distinctly welcoming to the idle and the curious – as I soon notice. The staff ask questions of each newcomer, the tourist literature arrives – befitting such a scholarly institution – in a wide variety of languages and alphabets, and the exhibitions change frequently. At the moment, the library is displaying its treasures on the theme of the discovery and exploration of the New World, and an array of books and maps and sketches are set out in glassed mahogany display cabinets that remind me of those in old-fashioned department stores; I half expect leather gloves and ties to be on sale, *Are You Being Served?*-style, tucked in drawers below.

The bell rings again and again as I nose around the first gallery, taking in the mitres and the maps.

'Where are you from?' the library representative asks each new visitor.

'Oh! Germany!' carols one caller, a little coquettishly.

'Sweden, is it?' the attendant asks a flaxen-haired goddess, his hand hovering over a little tower of Swedish-language booklets. She shakes her blonde hair out impatiently and frowns. In Ireland, we still have a tendency to assume that every blonde in the world is Swedish. It must be the influence of ABBA; it occasionally jars with people who are blonde and not Swedish.

'I am from Poland.'

'Oh, Poland. Well, we have Polish too!'

They do too. And Japanese. And Portuguese. There are information booklets in each language, handed out with some pride.

The library is roughly L-shaped, with a reading room in the angle, and the exhibition continues through the length of the two galleries. Trees wave against the uncovered windows of the reading room, and I peer out at the little garden set in the angle of the building itself and at the lower storeys boasting their original Queen Anne windows. At the distant end of the second gallery lie the features that attract most visitors: a white death mask of Jonathan Swift, housed in yet another glass mahogany display cabinet and part of the collection of death masks held in St Patrick's, where Swift served as Dean; and the three readers' cages that line the wall nearby. Readers, I was told, were formerly locked into these cages – each of which is also adorned with a decorative mitre – in order to consult the library's most precious books, thus illustrating most effectively the universal truth that library users, in whatever era or jurisdiction, can never ever be trusted not to steal books.

When, a little later, I finally get around to some desultory reading about Marsh's and its history, it becomes clear that this library was positively tormented by thieves for many long years. The cages in fact were originally intended to guard only the most precious volumes in the collection – not necessarily to lock scholars in with these volumes. In 1738, however, we read that the then Keeper of the Library, John Wynne, reported to the governors that 'a great number of books … were very lately stolen out of the Library and that many other books were abused and rendered imperfect by having whole tracts, Maps, Pictures, etc., tore out of them'. Greater vigilance was called for, and doubtless applied, but the thefts continued and in the end the library's manuscripts – the most easily pilfered items in the collection – were locked away in the cages for safe keeping. Ninety years later, however, it is clear that the thievery has continued, for the governors order that all books must be taken from the bookshelves only in the presence of the library staff and furthermore, that all volumes must be read 'at the publick Table, in the Librarian's room'. Under the librarian's nose, in other words. Comical or shocking, depending on one's point of view, but it is oddly pleasing that the much-repeated stories regarding the cages are not merely a myth of history, and pleasing too that this old institution has always been a living and breathing organism with very specific issues of its own to handle.

When I go back to the main doors, I say to the attendant, 'Um, I was wondering about the question of library loading.' I am right to sound unsure of myself, since I hardly know what I'm talking about.

'Library loading?' says the attendant and I explain to him, clumsy and long-winded. He listens and then laughs and gestures down to the boards on the floor. The old, broad boards, stained a deep brown – and clearly not going anywhere in a hurry. 'The keeper's apartments are directly underneath,' the attendant says, 'and I can't see the floor caving in just yet, can you?'

I can't. I don't have an answer to my friend's library-loading issues. Maybe there are load-bearing arches in the keeper's quarters? I can hardly knock and ask to see for myself.

— ◄○► —

As for Narcissus Marsh himself: he was an Englishman, born in Wiltshire in 1638, educated at Oxford and sent to Ireland as Provost of Trinity College in 1679. It was not, it seems, an appointment he particularly welcomed: being a scholarly man, he disliked the 'impertinent [useless, trivial, irrelevant] Visits', the public duties and administrative chores that accompanied his position. He disliked the 'rude & ignorant' Trinity students; and as for 'this lewd debauch'd town', suffice to say that he did not appear to like Dublin all that much either. And so, if he had to push his way through the equally lewd and debauched streets of Dublin on a Saturday night early in the twenty-first century, it is comforting to know that he would doubtless recognise the city instantly and dislike it all over again.

Marsh is an odd character: to a modern eye, he is something of a curate's egg, appearing by turns both expansive and narrowly conservative, a holder of a host of positions and opinions that seem mutually exclusive. As Provost of Trinity, for example, Marsh was instrumental in preparing for print the first translation of the Old Testament into the Irish language; the edition appeared in 1685. Moreover, he had noted that, whereas Irish-born students in Trinity could speak the language, they invariably could neither read nor write it. In order to remedy this situation, he employed a former Catholic priest to teach Irish to the student body and to preach a monthly Irish sermon, and he insisted that all future

Irish-born students who entered Trinity must be able to speak, read and write the Irish language.

To modern eyes, this is radical stuff – and to be sure, contemporary critics were fierce in their condemnation of Marsh for his actions. The propagation of Irish in the city could be seen to be an incendiary activity; this was, after all, the Dublin of the 1680s, when recent history was too recent, when the throne in London was still disputed between Catholics and Protestants, when the new, post-Cromwellian dispensation in Ireland was still taking root and when the new Protestant ruling class were by no means bedded down in their power and authority. Who wanted a provost racing around inside Trinity encouraging its students to speak, to study, and be preached to, in the Irish language? Not the ruling elite of the established Church in Ireland, for sure.

So much for this context. There are other contexts too, and these give the lie to any notion of Marsh as a radical. He might have been keen to foster a use of the Irish language – but his keenness sprang from an evangelical will to spread the true and reformed word of God around a country that was still predominantly Irish-speaking. It is clear that his philosophy had clarity: Trinity was the only university in the city and in the country, and its graduates – or some of them at any rate – might be relied upon to go out and evangelise among the Catholic multitudes. Marsh can hardly be blamed for failing to be acquainted with the lessons of history – that such evangelising never, or hardly ever, works. And there are other details that also help to locate Marsh more properly in the political and religious culture of the day, notably his action in propagating the Penal Laws.

Marsh himself was notably mild in his attitude to some religious dissenters and notably less mild to others. Following the revocation of the Edict of Nantes by Louis XIV of France, for example, some 10,000 Protestant Huguenots left France and settled in Ireland, and a high proportion of these came to Dublin.

Marsh embraced this swelling immigrant community in the city, permitting the Huguenots to worship in the Lady Chapel of St Patrick's in the absence of a place of worship of their own, and in spite of the substantial doctrinal differences between them and the Church of Ireland. The ultimate result of this general tolerance was that the Huguenots were assimilated into the mainstream of the Church of Ireland much more rapidly than might otherwise have been the case.

He was, on the other hand, no great ally of Ireland's Presbyterian population, and still less of Ireland's Catholics. As Archbishop of Cashel, he is to be glimpsed mourning the still-rebellious state of the country, of 'these sad, calamitous times wherein I am forced to live from home; & do hear almost every day of the murther of some or other Protestant'. Hardly surprising then, that as Archbishop of Dublin and therefore an active member of the Irish House of Lords in the city, he seems to have played a not inconsiderable part in the drafting of key aspects of penal legislation, including the Banishment Act (1697) ordering the expulsion of papist clergy and religious from Ireland and the Inter-marriage Act (1697), which forbade Protestants from marrying Catholics.

He also (for he was an Englishman after all) drafted a key piece of economic legislation – the so-called Woollen Act (1699) – designed to prohibit the export of Irish woollen materials. This Act, which was expressly created to protect the woollen industry in England, had the effect of promoting the creation of the famous linen industry in Ulster as a substitute for the banned woollen trade, but also of causing considerable economic distress in Ireland itself. It also, of course, highlighted the utterly subordinate position of the Irish Parliament in Dublin to that of Westminster.

This was a state of affairs that had been sealed by the so-called Poyning's Law of 1494. At a meeting of the Irish Parliament at Drogheda in that year, Sir Edward Poyning, Lord Deputy to

Henry VII, had declared that Ireland's Parliament would hence-forth be under the authority of the Parliament in London. In practice, this meant that all legislation passed in Ireland must be rubber-stamped in England before it became law, copper-fastening Ireland's status as an English, and later British, colony. This situation would be consistently seized upon and utilised by pro-ponents of Irish independence in the eighteenth century. As far as Marsh was concerned, however, this was an inevitable way of conducting affairs; after all, Ireland had no business claiming any form of autonomy and the Irish Parliament in Dublin naturally was subservient to the mother Parliament. Champion of the Irish language or no champion of the Irish language, there was no gain-saying the dominant facts of Marsh's life.

And yet, on the other hand, there is the existence of his library, founded as a public library and prepared to admit anyone (women included) provided they could read what was put in front of them. Here's the rub, of course, since such a public library could not be so very public if a large section of the population was unable to read its contents. But even with this knowledge, there is a sense of generosity and expansiveness here. It is difficult to possess wholly jaundiced feelings for someone who goes to the trouble of estab-lishing a public library.

Jonathan Swift, though, did his best. He disliked Marsh very much, blaming him in part for his own lack of advancement in the Church; and he was busily damning Marsh even before his death:

Marsh has the reputation of most profound and universal learn-ing; this is the general opinion, neither can it be easily disproved. An old rusty iron-chest in a banker's shop, strongly lockt, and wonderful heavy, is full of gold; this is the general opinion, neither can it be disproved, provided the key be lost, and what is in it be wedged so close that it will not by any motion discover the metal by the chinking ...[1]

What, then, are we to make of Marsh and of this mass of contra-dictions? Simply this, perhaps: that Marsh encapsulates the con-tradictory nature of Irish culture and society at this rapidly moving phase in Dublin's history. And Marsh's Library is an important feature in terms of the city itself and of its development. It helps to epitomise Dublin's belated shift from the medieval world into an age of modernity. For the first time in the city's his-tory, after all, the authorities were free to build and develop with-out fear of attack and possible destruction from without. The mournful litany of Penal Laws, repression and economic distress provides ample evidence, to be sure, of other doubts and fears floating on the surface of Dublin life. But this was the beginning of a new economic and architectural age just the same.

Chapter 8

LIFE AND LIBERTY

After I leave Marsh's, I turn west, skirt the great walls of the cathedral once more and cross roaring Patrick Street. Not by the pedestrian crossing, not by any means, but in the time-honoured Irish way that involves stepping out into the road and hoping to dodge the traffic successfully en route to the other side of the road. It is not at all a system that would go down well in Switzerland, say, where I would doubtless be subject to a citizen's arrest in a trice. Or in the United States, where as a summering student, on a sunny street in downtown San Diego, I was once threatened with a fine for jaywalking. I could hardly blame the cop, given that I had run across the road right in front of him; it must have been a matter of pride for him. At that time, I managed to steer clear of the law's punitive arm only by pleading (entirely shamefully) the excuse of my nationality, by playing the hoary old Irish card. This, I squeaked, was the way things were done in Ireland, I didn't know any better. This is a way of doing things that is universally familiar to members of the Irish diaspora, accustomed as they are to using their nationality like a magic wand. It worked, sort of, in San Diego too.

'Yeh? Well, you better go back to Ireland, sir, before you get yourself killed.'

But in Dublin, in Ireland, everyone jaywalks. Lots of people speed too, even more unforgivable, although my family played the Irish card even here, in order to get away with a speeding crime while on a trip to Florida. Having hired a fabulous Cadillac, we headed north from Miami, glorying in the environmentally unfriendly vastness and air conditioning of the car. This was back in the 1980s, you understand, when Cadillacs were few and far between in Ireland and we coolly overtook the Highway Patrol while doing an effortless million miles an hour.

The poor Highway Patrol, they really had no option but to flag us down. When they heard our collective accents, however, and the usual old excuse, 'this is the way things are done in Ireland; we didn't know any better!', their knees seemed to turn to jelly. Their collective ancestors came from the Old Sod, it appeared, and so we ended up having a good old laugh right there, on the hard shoulder of the freeway, with the traffic screaming past under the Florida sun.

'But sir,' they told my father when they eventually departed, 'try not to do this again. Please. Because, y'know, it makes things very difficult for us.'

It is an interesting syndrome, this benevolence that arises at the sight of an Irish passport. I hardly know how to account for it. As for the speeding and jaywalking (and a good many other crimes too), these are, presumably, an illustration of that perennial colonial mindset which holds that laws exist to be broken, or at the very least utterly scorned and ignored, a mindset that persists long after the coloniser has given up in despair and gone home.

A dense system of streets stretches east of Patrick Street, rising up onto the long historic escarpment above the Liffey. This area is the Liberties, one of the oldest districts in the city and its first true suburb. The city walls lay just east of this area, on the highest point of the long hill; and as the centuries went by, so this part of Dublin acquired a character and vibrancy all of its own. The street names – Fumbally Lane, Pimlico, Carman's Hall, Mill Street, Weavers Street – point to the district's antiquity and character and centuries of associations accumulated like so many layers of cob-webbed dust.

The *liberties*, which gave their name to this district of Dublin, like the original liberty granted to the city of Dublin by Henry II, were economic rights and privileges given to the ecclesiastical foundations which grew up as Dublin itself grew up, and which have now, for the most part, long vanished. They were free of the charters and rules that bound trade in the city, were at as much liberty as was practicable to order their own destiny, were largely self-sufficient. And, as the medieval period came to its reluctant and belated end in Dublin and the old monasteries and priories were dissolved and broken up, so the Liberties too began to alter economically and socially. As we trace their history and the history of the city around them, in fact, we can see the extent to which the Liberties act as a bellwether of the health of the city as a whole.

Take the Huguenots, for example, who settled and concentrated around the Earl of Meath's Liberty – where Meath Street runs from north to south today – and who rapidly re-established the district as a centre of the Irish weaving industry. While the playing field was level, weaving in the city brought prosperity and wealth to this part of town: mansions were built amid the yards and manufacturing houses; and at length the Huguenot community was even in a position to build its own church of St Nicholas Without and St Luke's, a few hundred metres from the Lady Chapel at St Patrick's. The area throve but the swift and threatening success of the Irish woollen trade frightened the British authorities and led to the economic measures mentioned above, in which Archbishop Marsh had a hand; and with the passing of such protectionist statutes, weaving in Ireland collapsed. In 1974, the area around it still poor and the Huguenots long vanished as a distinct social group in Dublin, the church was at last closed and deconsecrated. The building was destroyed by fire in 1983.

The collapse of the weaving and other industrial trades caused changes, as persistent as they were profound, to the character of the Liberties. The area began to decline steadily, so that by the end of the eighteenth century it had a reputation as one of the most poverty-stricken areas in the city, its housing a byword for deprivation and despair. In 1798, James Whitelaw's census illustrated graphically the poverty and terrible want that had developed in the Liberties and in many other parts of Dublin too. In the outer suburbs, peasants lived packed in mud huts with small plots of land attached; in the more urban Liberties themselves, the accommodation was even more severely crowded, the lives even more characterised by poverty and 'a degree of filth and stench inconceivable, except by such as have visited these scenes of wretchedness'.[1]

Today, the area of the city around Meath Street is of course a good deal changed. Property prices have been on the up across the city for a decade, and they are up here too, and the economic advances of the last 15 years have left their mark on this cityscape. New private apartment buildings and excellent public housing – and today there are many that are impressively designed, slick and energy-efficient and thrown into relief by the jerry-built and the shabby nearby – have been slotted into the dense streets. New shops have opened and the city's new immigrant communities are catered to in the form of Nigerian and Bosnian grocery stores. Francis Street, traditionally the centre of Dublin's antique trade, now features expensive galleries and upmarket cafés, while the antique shops themselves have been updated to respond to changing economic circumstances.

More striking, however, is the consistency of atmosphere in this part of town; while other areas of Dublin have been profoundly altered by gentrification and the processes of change, the Liberties seems in a way to be curiously unchanged. German discount stores may have moved on to the main thoroughfare of Thomas Street, but you can still saunter into one of any number of shops and buy your weight in Tupperware for less than a fiver; and the market stalls, butchers and bakers on Meath Street itself still ply their wares as they ever did. The texture of street life is still vivid and loud, as dense with people and traders as the streetscape itself is dense with buildings.

Not that the authorities have always been exactly happy with this state of affairs. The Corporation of Dublin had the Liberties in its sights, in fact, as long ago as the end of the seventeenth century, when the workaday, anarchic character of the area and of the old city in general began to distress the planners and policymakers. The whole area was messy: hackney cabs and street traders and hawkers and sellers of various kinds were doing nothing for the image of Dublin, the streets themselves were 'nasty' as well as 'abominably dirty' and nobody was very happy about it at all. The authorities therefore tried a variety of methods of tidying the place up a little: the market regulations of 1683, for example, demonstrate a remarkable ability to legislate both sensibly and obsessively:

First That noe person be permitted to incumber the streets with any stalls, formes, stooles or otherwise to stop the passages of the streets; but all the streets shall be free for common passage for all people and for horses, coaches, carts etc., to pass to and fro without interruption.

Second That noe pease or beans be suffered to be shelled in Fishamble street, Warburg street or Skinners row, nor any annoyance suffered there or in any other streets of the cittie, to indanger by their stench the health of the citizens ...[2]

Whether any pease or beans ever were shelled subsequently on Fishamble Street has not been recorded.

Sections of these regulations are of course reasonable and laudable, concerned as they were with the elimination of disease from the city. They also demonstrate, at this significant moment in the history of Dublin, an increasing interest in modern principles of urban regulation and planning, in a clean and regular and sweet-smelling city. Of particular interest to us today, of course, is the extent to which these ambitions became manifest in the century that followed and the limited nature of these ambitions, as far as areas such as the Liberties were concerned. Because in the eighteenth century, and afterwards, the life of the area went on in its specific way, as the city was rebuilt around it.

Today, then, while property prices may be on the up across Dublin, they are generally less so in the Liberties, and gentrification has brought about fewer of the stark changes that can be witnessed elsewhere in the city. But perhaps part of this consistence can also be put down to the very continuity of life, of history, in this working-class neighbourhood of Dublin. The deep roots of a thousand years, maybe, that are not readily severed by a proliferation of new coffee machines.

Traces of the Liberties' ancient past has – for the most part and as is usually the way in this city – been swept away long ago, to be replaced by fresh layers of history that have settled over the years. In the nineteenth century, for example, ecclesiastical architects really went for it up here. As I climb up Francis Street, evidence of this awaits in the shape of a dome of granite, gleaming white Portland stone and green copper that rises above me: the dome of St Nicholas of Myra (1833). The church was built on the ancient, and now vanished, Franciscan friary that gave its name to the street itself. It sets the tone both architecturally and in terms of the consistency of history up here.

A few minutes later, as I reach – a little breathless and red of face – Thomas Street on the crest of the hill, the sharply chiselled spire and magnificent Gothic exterior of Pugin's Church of St

Augustine and St John (1874) appear before me. This church – 'John's Lane' to every true Dubliner – overlooks the Liffey and is visible for many miles around, providing a signature for the city. I push the door open and go in, and the traffic and incessant noise of Thomas Street fade away rapidly in the face of a soaring vaulted interior, rich decoration and glowing stained glass. John's Lane, in fact, resembles a cathedral very much more than it does the parish church of a poor, predominantly working-class district of the city. Which, presumably, was the point: such a building demonstrates, better and more eloquently than any essay or sermon ever could, the renewed power and authority of the Catholic Church in Dublin by the middle of the nineteenth century. Certainly, as I sit down in a pew and take in the remarkable fabric and air and confidence of the building, it seems difficult to believe that since John's Lane was opened, the heyday of the Catholic Church in Dublin has come and gone and left crisis in its wake.

There is much in the way of continuing neglect up here too, though, to be seen the moment I leave the church and come back out onto Thomas Street; painfully visible in the fabric of the streets and buildings. The ugly, badly built and unsympathetic apartments that face St Patrick's are copied repeatedly throughout the Liberties; and the road widening of the twentieth century has done the district no favours, slicing the area away from the city centre and leading to a sense of isolation.

Lately, the city has announced plans to address the damage of the past and draw the area once more within the orbit of the city centre. The plan envisages a stitching together of the Liberties, the district around the two cathedrals and the scant remains of the city walls into a sort of 'Cathedral Quarter' by means of carefully engineered pedestrian zones, lanes and other spaces. It might then become a pleasure to walk up the hill from Trinity College, say, via the Castle and so into the Liberties, avoiding the roar of main roads nearly the whole way – a pleasure and not the ordeal by automobile as it is today.

A part of this plan also calls for a new civic museum to be built close to the north front of Christ Church, on the steep slope between the cathedral and the river. After all, as the architects of this plan have noted, medieval cathedrals were not meant to stand in isolation, but instead to rise up amid a throng of other buildings. And so this new museum would respond to the Dublin of old, as opposed to the Dublin of dual carriageways that has been cut through this area. It is a good plan in theory – optimistic and civic-minded – even if the inevitable marketing-inspired 'Cathedral Quarter' moniker is a pity. Still, it is a truth universally acknowledged that every European city in possession of a good fortune must be in want of a Cathedral Quarter, and so I suppose Dublin had better have one too.

Not least among the merits of this plan is its emphasis upon a degree of conservation, where appropriate. They are values that are on the up in Dublin, albeit tentatively, and that have lately lent a new lease of life to some of the city's ancient buildings. Take the Tailors' Hall on the prosaically named Back Lane, where Cornmarket runs up to Christ Church. This building, the last remaining guildhall in the city, was built by the Tailors' Guild of Dublin on the site of a former Jesuit chapel. It is this popish association, in fact, that probably explains its secret and discreet entrance: the building is set well back from the street, to be approached through an archway and courtyard paved in stone.

The Tailors' Hall exemplifies the layers of silent history that can accumulate in Dublin's buildings. It was used variously by the tailors, the Freemasons and the judiciary and briefly by the British Army in the famous year of 1798. Its hall was the largest public space in the Dublin of the 1720s and, as a result, the great and the good were entertained there. Most fascinatingly, the Catholic Committee – founded in 1760 by the surviving Catholic gentry – organised a series of meetings in the hall in 1792. The function of this so-called Back Lane Parliament was to roll back the remains of the Penal Laws; its secretary was one Wolfe Tone, who went on to become one of the most prominent leaders of the United Irishmen and of the rebellion of 1798.

In spite of this historical significance, however, the Tailors' Hall gradually fell into ruin and was declared derelict and unsafe in the 1950s. Its gradual restoration began in the 1960s, and today the building is the national headquarters of An Taisce, the National Trust for Ireland. It was beautiful inside on the afternoon I visited, a few days previously, besuited as I was, scrubbed, self-satisfied and ready for a wedding reception.

I had made it my business to find out in advance a little about the Tailors' Hall and so I was curious to peep into the principal hall itself, to discover the shades of Tone and others. It was a beautifully impressive space, lit dazzlingly with autumn sunshine streaming through the tall and slender round-headed windows, supported by a ceiling featuring one simple oval rose, and centred by a white marble fireplace.

'Can I look around?' And, in the face of the catering person's reasonable reluctance – they were trying to get the place ready for a meal for 60, after all – 'I'm writing a book,' I said. I'm writing a book; of course I must have my way.

'It would be better if you came back a little later,' said the catering person, a little tartly. 'Dinner will be at six. Come back at six.'

I retired, vanquished, to the free bar downstairs. And later, as we sat down to dinner in the fading afternoon light, I got to see the hall for myself. The hearth was filled with candles and the double-height hall itself decorated with white fairy lights and wreaths of ivy; and later still, the basement, with its calp (limestone) walls and timber-beamed ceilings and doors opening onto the dark garden, was perfect for a party on a cool autumn night. It was altogether delightful, although truth to tell I was already altogether delighted with the stuffed loin of pork and the roasted vegetable salad, the lemon cheesecake and the platters of cheeses and membrillo. By that stage in the evening, indeed, I was so extremely delighted with myself that the ceiling, and its oval rose, might have come crashing down on top of our heads and I would-n't have noticed.

Chapter 9

LAWS AND ORDER

I have come out onto the streets of Dublin, in the branch-strewn aftermath of Tropical Storm Gordon, on something of a quest. Marsh's Library was my first port of call, but there is another building to visit on this same day, a building connected to Marsh's architecturally, and also in my imagination.

Down past Guinness, at the end of James's Street that runs along the long spine of the escarpment above the Liffey, the road forks. One branch runs on along the new tram lines towards St James's Hospital and so, at last, down into Inchicore and Kilmainham, while the other bends downhill and past St Patrick's psychiatric hospital. This foundation was endowed by Swift; his 'Verses on the Death of Dr Swift', composed some 15 years before his actual death in 1745, make his intentions bitingly clear:

> He gave the little wealth he had,
> To build a house for fools and mad;
> And showed by one satiric touch,
> No Nation wanted it so much.

The building was completed in 1757.

The road swings by a large new apartment complex and bridges the old Camac River flowing down to meet the Liffey, before curving and climbing uphill again. A set of fine granite gate posts and many old trees, still in full leaf in these early days of autumn, signal what might well be a private estate. Only the signs on the gates encourage one to enter, to walk along the deeply shaded path and up, suddenly, to a most magnificent building lying at the end of the drive. This is the Royal Hospital, home to the Irish Museum of Modern Art (IMMA), and one of the finest and most exquisite buildings in the country.

I ought, by rights, to have circled around the perimeter of the large demesne and entered the estate through its main gate, and so along the long and dramatic avenue that leads up to the west front of the building. But I was in no particular mood for a surfeit of drama. And besides, I like the east entrance to IMMA, in spite of the endless processions of tour buses which bellow up and down the hill, in spite of a forest of cranes at the bottom of the hill where new development is taking place; in spite of all this, of all the evidence to the contrary, this entrance feels almost secret, tucked away as it is underneath its trees. But the Royal Hospital, as an exercise in grace and beautiful symmetry, is a delight when approached from east, from west, from any direction at all.

First, the superlative setting. Although this district of Kilmainham is really no more than a stone's throw from the bustle of Dublin city centre, its setting is routinely described as 'villagey' or 'village-like' by the estate agents – and amazingly, this is no lie, for it does indeed lend itself to tranquillity. The Phoenix Park rises on the northern side of the Liffey, the rare formal beauty of the War Memorial Gardens lies along the bank of the Liffey weir and the great demesne of the Royal Hospital itself spreads through the centre of the district.

To the building's north and west, the grounds are extensive and look down and across the Liffey and up to the vast expanse of parkland on the far bank. The main motorway from Dublin to Galway and the west coast cuts along the edge of the estate, but it is just crucially far enough away to be out of sight, out of mind, and is further hidden by a screen of tall trees. Further along to the west the grounds are shaggier, spreading down to ancient cemetery grounds and the ruins of the foundations of the Knights Hospitaller priory that once occupied the site; and the long western avenue runs down to the imposing gate tower opposite Kilmainham Gaol.

Remote and elevated among these expansive grounds even today, this marvellous Renaissance building is never less than a surprising sight, with its four long and supremely elegant ranges set around an arcaded quadrangle, with a tower and spire topping the northern front. With its arcades and elaborate timber carving above the entrances, the building inevitably bears comparison with Les Invalides in Paris. No wonder, then, that it has drawn visitors since its completion in 1684. It was the first significant public building to be completed in Dublin in the aftermath of the Cromwellian settlement and its scale and ambition at this tentative moment in the city's history are commensurately startling; no beginning with small-scale construction for the new Dublin.

The building was created to provide accommodation for old soldiers, and was therefore very much in keeping with the militarised state of Irish society at that moment at the end of the seventeenth century. It was used and neglected and utilised again through its 300 years, most notably, maybe, during the 1916 Rising when 2,500 British soldiers took possession of the building – another good example of the layering effect of Irish history on the fabric of Dublin. Its future was finally secured in the 1980s when it was selected to be the home of the new Irish Museum of Modern Art. Remodelling of the building was begun anew and the museum opened to the public in 1991. These days, it also serves as the focus for the National Day of Commemoration, held annually to remember those Irish citizens who have died in the two world wars and in service with the United Nations.

I walk up the eastern drive and the building, as it comes into view beyond the rhododendron thickets, glows under perfectly blue skies. I walk into the courtyard to find the four long, arcaded walls hidden by a vast pink wall painting and a busy scene of spotlights, catering vans and long lengths of electrical cable.

'Michael Craig-Martin exhibition; it opens tonight,' says a museum person breathlessly, when I stop her in the midst of this hoo-ha; her cheeks are as pink as the painting.

I like the wall painting, I decide, although I hardly have the language to explain why. At the present moment, it seems enough to be delighted at the specificity of it: the long and elegant walls of the courtyard at IMMA, blanketed by painting that is pink and abstract; the juxtaposition manifestly works. I take a walk in the long galleries that line three of the four arms of the building, poke around the bookshop, drink a cup of filthy, tar-like coffee in the vaulted basement café, and then go outside again into the cool sunshine.

Below the main north front of the building lies the formal garden, the Master's Garden, which was a feature of the estate from its inception, 'laid out for the greater grace of the house'. Like all gardens, it has changed radically over the years, and today is in the midst of a process of reconstitution and restoration, although this is made a little difficult by the absence of reliable evidence regarding the original designs. No matter, though, nobody wants replication. Certainly I do not, as I walk along paths lined with espaliered fruit trees and beech hedging, with slowly growing box mazes tucked behind and a fountain gurgling in the very centre; fine and new and gravely beautiful on this bright day.

The Royal Hospital and Marsh's Library are separated by more than the Liberties. They are utterly different buildings, with utterly different purposes: the one monumental, designed as a residence, surrounded by spacious and airy grounds; the other profoundly internal in mood and content and purpose, profoundly urban in scale and setting. Yet they are both products of the same era of the city and both were up and running as institutions at the very beginning of Dublin's eighteenth-century growth spurt. In my mind, they seem to anchor this famous period of growth, both being assertions of confidence, both exercises in far-sightedness and future purpose. The two institutions, located just to the east and just to the west of the Liberties, combine in my mind with that deeply urban district of the city to create a natural, seamless and homogeneous whole. And no wonder, maybe, that they should be connected by threads, albeit often vanishingly discreet ones – for the two buildings share an architect: William Robinson, Surveyor-General of Ireland.

And maybe too they have more similarities than are immediately obvious. Both buildings are after all public, or at the least, only semi-private spaces – they favour anonymity; we move through them and work in them but we do not stay. They were both founded as symbols of an envisaged new Ireland, one in which the coloniser would at last have the firm upper hand. The established Church is an intrinsic force in the foundation of Marsh's, while it was surely no mistake that the benevolent creation of the Royal Hospital eclipses the existence of an earlier, pre-Reformation politico-religious foundation. In its evolution over the centuries, the Royal Hospital – always the more public of the two – has in effect moved up to meet Marsh's, so that today both buildings act as repositories of information and culture and classification. In this sense, both buildings are symbols of the Enlightenment in Dublin, being dedicated to order and symmetry. Both buildings appear at the beginning of the Enlightenment and have weathered the storms to emerge into the modern age, their stores of culture naturally altered or reconstituted – but still considerable.

As for the Enlightenment itself, the question of its impact upon Dublin is a vexed one. Certainly, many of the elements of modernity are present in Dublin at this moment in history: power and economic authority shifts decisively into the city, with a commensurate movement of people from the Irish countryside; the political power of religious organisations in Dublin is being supplanted by secular authority; the foundations of communal life, and the place of the individual within it, are becoming the subject of intensive investigation and evaluation. And specifically, many Irish figures played a crucial part in the development of Enlightenment thought in Europe: think of Robert Boyle (1627–91), the father of modern chemistry; and of Francis Hutcheson (1694–1746) whose writings on ethics, largely composed in Dublin, were crucial in the development of the Scottish Enlightenment; not to mention Swift; the philosopher and political theorist Edmund Burke; and others. It is also the case that the presence of buildings such as the Royal Hospital, dedicated to symmetry and to an ideal of perfection, and institutions such as Marsh's, dedicated to classification and to public knowledge, help to contextualise the history of the city in these years and to set it against a wider and more cosmopolitan backdrop, in which a variety of Irish philosophers and writers moved and worked.

But certainly it is also the case that the impact of the Penal Laws in the culture of the time subverts this evolving sense of secular rationalism in Irish law and philosophy, and it is the case too that the colonial presence in Dublin and Ireland in these years crucially removed the city and country from the mainstream of the various evolving Enlightenment movements in Europe. As for the reality of life in Dublin under the regime of the Penal Laws, this was more complex and nuanced than has been supposed.

— ◄o► —

So, at last, to these Penal Laws. They hold an inglorious position in Irish history and the first thing to say, perhaps, is that they were far from being a purely Irish phenomenon. Penal statutes designed to persecute various minorities had evolved across Europe over hundreds of years and a network of statutes targeting Catholics, Dissenters, Jews and others had of course existed in Ireland and England since the Reformation. The specific and infamous Irish Penal Laws, however, consisting of a dense web of statutes designed to regulate and marginalise Catholicism across Ireland, are generally taken to refer to those passed by the Irish Parliament, sitting in Dublin, between approximately 1691 and 1760.

Although too numerous and elaborate to list in full here, the Penal Laws included a ban on the right of any Catholic to vote and a ban on marriage between Catholics and Protestants. One infamous statute, the Banishment Act, ordered the transportation of all Catholic clergy from Ireland. Others were concerned with regulating the land seizures that had taken place in the aftermath of the Cromwellian invasion. And while education continued throughout Ireland, there were bars set on a Catholic education: 'no person of the Popish religion shall publicly or in public houses teach school, or instruct youth in learning within this realm', and, as a result, the network of so-called 'hedge schools' developed in secret throughout Ireland.

The Penal Laws make for fascinating reading. Their tone – even taking the jargon and wordy preambles of contemporary language into account – lurches between the deeply pragmatic on the one hand and the deeply paranoid on the other. On one side, they evoke fear of all manner of cunning Catholic stratagems, cooked up by papist prelates in Rome and designed to pull the wool over the eyes of God-fearing Protestants; on the other, they are founded upon a profoundly practical and matter-of-fact interest in land, landholdings and landowners. Take An Act to prevent Protestants intermarrying with Papists (Section One) (1697), which, in addition to legislating against Catholicism, betrays the usual horror of errant female sexuality:

Whereas many protestant women, heirs or heirs apparent to lands or other great substances in goods or chattels, or having considerable estates for life, or guardianship of children intitled [sic] to such estates, by flattery and other crafty insinuations of popish persons, have been seduced to contract matrimony with and take to husband, papists, to the great ruin of such estates, to the great loss of many protestant persons to whom the same might descend, and to the corrupting such protestant women that they forsake their religion and become papists, to the great dishonour of Almighty God, the great prejudice of the protestant interest, and the heavy sorrow of all their protestant friends, if any protestant woman having any estate or interest real or, if personal of a value of 500 pounds, shall take to husband any person without first having a certificate from the minister of the parish, bishop, and justice of the peace living near the place where such person shall be resident at the time of such marriage, that he is a known protestant, which certificate shall also be attested under the hands of 2 credible witnesses, that protestant woman, and the person she shall so marry, shall be incapable of holding or enjoying any of her aforesaid estates or interests.

And by such marriage all said estates and interests shall be vested in the next protestant of kin to whom such estate or interests would descend were such protestant woman dead. And such protestant person may sue for and recover such estates or interests at any time after such marriage.

The density and tone of these statutes appears overwhelming, pointing to an iron will to expunge the Catholic influence from Ireland. But the impact of the Penal Laws has in truth always been disputed keenly; they may have been ferocious on paper, but they were not consistently implemented with this fearsome iron will, and even when they were could still not be relied upon to have the desired effect. And the Penal Laws were as subject to the influence of context, of realpolitik, as any other laws. When the British government was obliged to set great store by its alliance with Catholic Austria in the eighteenth century, for example, its zeal in approving various penal statutes sent over from Dublin noticeably waned. It is the case, indeed, that the British authorities, for very good reasons of their own, not infrequently either blocked or thoroughly watered down the more zealous measures streaming from the Parliament in Dublin.

In Ireland itself, the network of penal legislation was subject to scathing criticism. To Edmund Burke – whose own family had Catholic antecedents – the code was 'a machine as well fitted for the oppression, impoverishment and degradation of a people, and the debasement in them of human nature itself, as ever proceeded from the perverted ingenuity of man'.[1] Later, Burke would criticise the Penal Laws for laying Ireland open to the temptations spawned by the French Revolution; by oppressing the great majority of the people of the island in such a way, he argued, the government of Ireland was barring these same people from tasting what he considered the sweet fruits of a British civilisation – thus laying them open to the false attractions of the anarchy and barbarism that ruled on the other side of the English Channel.

Furthermore, since the Penal Laws would always be rejected by a great proportion of the Irish public, they could never be assured of success in any case. As was the case with the earlier Anglo-Norman statutes on population and demographics, so it was with the Penal Laws in Dublin. As the Hiberno-Norse continued to drift into the 'pure' city from Oxmantown and as the native Irish continued to emigrate to Dublin from outside the Pale itself, so now, in the seventeenth and eighteenth century, the Penal Laws could simply not always and everywhere be successfully applied. To take one example, even supposing local state officials had the inclination and energy to drop everything in order to pursue fugitive

Catholic priests across the countryside, they would have to contend with an elaborate early warning system, polished and honed by the Catholic population (and not infrequently tacitly supported by the local Anglo-Irish population too) that generally ensured that the priests would slip through any nets set out to catch them.

And while it is certainly true that the temporal power of the Catholic Church was much diminished in these years, it is also the case that its spiritual authority was inevitably greatly enhanced, and that the Penal Laws set the stage for Catholic resurgence – typified in such glorious churches as John's Lane – in the years that followed. Such is a lesson of a colonised society, where the laws and authority of the colonising power are always and everywhere subject to seepage, to slippage.

This slippage is notably evident in Dublin. Even though the city's large population and distinct circumstances always renders its situation specific, the city provided opportunities for Catholics that were not always present in rural areas or smaller towns, and so immigration into the city was inevitable and ongoing throughout this period. Practical and economic factors would always come into play, in spite of what a variety of administrators and statutes might say.

One statistic illustrates this fact strikingly. Births in the city of Dublin did not exceed deaths until well into the nineteenth century, and therefore immigration into the city from the surrounding countryside was not simply inevitable, but was essential to the city's economic well-being. The eighteenth century, therefore, witnessed not only a swelling of the city's total population – from approximately 50,000 in 1695 to approximately 190,000 in 1798 – but also a rapid increase in the proportion of that population that was Catholic. In 1700 a mere 30 per cent of Dublin's population was Catholic, but a century later Catholics made up almost three-quarters of the population of the city, and Dublin was a Protestant stronghold no longer.

Needless to say, of course, the administration of the city remained in Protestant hands in spite of these facts – a system of gerrymandering that was of course repeated throughout Ireland, and that would remain an unlovely feature of life in Northern Ireland until well into the twentieth century. This system was explicitly embraced by the administration in Dublin even late in the eighteenth century, as the following extract of a shrill letter of 11 September 1792, from the Corporation of Dublin to the 'Protestants of Ireland', makes abundantly clear:

> [W]e consider the Protestant ascendancy to consist of a Protestant king in Ireland, a Protestant parliament, a Protestant hierarchy, Protestant electors and government, the benches of justice, the army and revenue, through all their branches and details, Protestant. And this system supported by a connection with the Protestant realm of Britain.[2]

At any rate, nobody could consider such a public position to be underhand.

As the composition of Dublin's population continued slowly to change through the course of the eighteenth century, then, so too did the reality on the ground. A slowly evolving Catholic middle class gained a foothold in a variety of professions – in the law and in medicine in particular – and the Catholic presence in various trades became increasingly marked as the century wore on. Indeed, it may be the case that several of the more breathtaking penal statutes put forward for approval by the Irish Parliament originated in a response to this evolving reality – a lashing out against a new and inevitable political and economic dispensation.

Chapter 10

⊗

THE TRUTH ACCORDING TO LAETITIA

The time is the early summer of 2002 and the location is The Ark – Dublin's cultural centre for children, located in a beautifully restored building in Temple Bar. A play entitled *Dublin 1742* is being staged, premised on the meeting and interaction between a group of notable and remarkable characters living in Dublin in the year 1742, the year that George Frideric Handel's *Messiah* was written and received its world premiere on Fishamble Street. It is an event obsessively referred to in most of Dublin's tourist literature, perhaps because such classical high-water marks are few and far between in the history of this city. An open-air production of the oratorio takes place at Easter each year close to the spot where the original *Messiah* was first aired; plaques commemorate the place and the time; and hotels and pubs are named – rather dubiously – after the composer.

I remember well walking slowly up the hill of Fishamble Street, on the western edge of Temple Bar, early on a Friday evening some years ago – and, as I passed the scene of the original, seeing a circle of German tourists being instructed in a rendition of the 'Hallelujah Chorus'. The parts were being handed out in a tidy and organised manner, and as I reached the top of the slope and turned the corner onto Cork Hill and escape, the group burst into fruity song. And such scenes are far from rare, Temple Bar being after all the tourist heart of the city, where visitors effortlessly out-number Dubliners by night and day, summer and winter alike, strolling its cobbled streets, drinking in its vast bars, and search-ing for some notional Dublin essence or authenticity.

This is an old part of the city, this thin slip of lanes and narrow streets wedged between the traffic of Dame Street and the waters of the Liffey. A thousand years ago, the river ran here through its shingle and sandbanks; and later, Temple Bar was one of the first districts of Dublin to be claimed by the people from the brackish river waters: slowly the piles were driven into the river bed and the land filled in behind with rubble and mud; slowly a tracery of lanes and houses appeared and were swept away and rebuilt in their turn; and slowly this web of lanes and alleys became fixed and established on the early maps. In the shadow of both the Castle and of Christ Church though it was, Temple Bar neverthe-less forged and maintained a reputation for a certain civic disor-der, a distinction made manifest not only in its taverns and theatres but also in its medieval street pattern that weathered Dublin's massive eighteenth-century re-engineering and that has survived up to the present day. And today, it is still possible to avoid the traffic and noise of Dame Street and walk all the way from Trinity up to Christ Church through this ancient network of narrow, cobbled and twisting lanes.

In the nineteenth and twentieth centuries, though, Temple Bar was a neighbourhood very much down on its luck, marginalised by these same new patterns and streetscapes of the city and increas-ingly bypassed by the business and profits that keep any district afloat. By the middle of the twentieth century, most of the property in the area had been acquired by CIE (the state transport author-ity) with the intention of razing the area and building a vast trans-port interchange in its place. This, famously, was the turning point in Temple Bar's fortunes: independent galleries, cafés and music shops took out temporary leases on buildings that were facing the axe; an alternative cultural scene took tentative root and then began gradually to thrive; the city authorities began to look askance at CIE's monolithic plans and to revisit the waxing charms of the district; and a good deal of well-judged lobbying was carried out in an effort to alter the course of the future. Eventually, in 1990, the ragged and disintegrating streets, cobbles and buildings of Temple Bar were duly given the chance to be not a gigantic bus station after all – but rather a state-sponsored cultural centre, a Latin Quarter, a *rive gauche* in which people might live, work and play. It was an optimistic civic vision and one to be praised too, even if the future has not exactly worked out as planned.

The atmospheric small bars that were once a prime feature of Temple Bar, for example, have largely vanished in these last years and monstrous superpubs have taken their place, cashing in on the area's popularity. Dublin's ongoing cultural currency combined with cheap airfares has brought throngs of tourists, hen parties and stag parties; the old streets and lanes of the area are, as a result, a sight to behold on Saturday nights, as long hours of cheap lager promotions take their toll. Temple Bar gets a fair amount of flack for the degree to which it has become a boozer's paradise, the extent to which its Latin Quarter credentials have failed to materialise. And to be sure, there is no gainsaying the fact that I would not be caught dead in Temple Bar on a weekend night in the summer season. But it's easy to carp, to fixate on drunken youths, on marauding hen parties, on the Irish predisposition to drink to excess and to hell with the consequences. For the fact remains that a good many people do indeed live, work and play in the area, and that a version of that founding cultural vision has managed to survive.

Through the 1990s, these old streets were tweaked a little, and new public squares and lanes dropped into the district's fabric. Some of the country's cultural institutions set up shop here too: The

Ark, with its child-sized theatre seats and its door handles positioned to suit children and not adults, so disorienting and so clever; the Irish Film Centre, settled under its glass roof in the old Quaker meeting house; the Gallery of Photography; the Photographic Archive and Project Arts Centre – and others like them. Commercial galleries were established and survive; and space – although not enough – was set aside for subsidised artists' studios. A handful of good, locally owned cafés and restaurants have thrived amid the pizza shops and Mexican restaurants. Markets take place each weekend, selling both food and fashion; open-air film screenings take place in the new enclosed Meeting House Square on summer Saturday nights, come wind or weather. The Temple Bar blueprint did not survive intact the commercial reality of the world, then – but a semblance of it did, and it is worth celebrating the fact.

But back to 2002 – or rather, to 1742. Handel is himself, in the child-scaled auditorium at The Ark, a character in this play based on the production of his oratorio; so too is Enlightenment idealist Bishop George Berkeley, gossip and memoirist Laetitia Pilkington, actress Peg Woffington, soprano Susanna Cibber and Cibber's composer brother, Thomas Arne. Not to mention Swift himself: that satirist, novelist, poet, wit and founder of a mental hospital for the psychological good of the city of Dublin. And at stake is the success or failure of *Messiah*, the destiny of which lies in the hands of the aged and fading Swift, who has not yet decided whether to release to Handel six young choristers from the cathedral choir of St Patrick's. In the opening scene, therefore, Handel appears in a state of controlled panic on the stage. To make matters worse, his chosen soprano, Susanna Cibber, is behaving like a diva; it is all he can do, it seems, not to slap her hard across the face. No – all is far from well:

> In one week, dear Susanna, just one week,
> My oratorio will be performed

Here in Fishamble Street, in this grand hall.
Already the performance is sold out.
Four hundred pounds our patrons have subscribed –
Four hundred pounds! And for their money, ma'am,
They will expect from you, from all of us,
The finest musical experience.
We must not disappoint them –[1]

As the play progresses, we encounter the embittered Swift, who has by now decided to leave to the city of Dublin a sum of money for the building of his mental hospital. Such an institution is in his opinion sorely needed, Dublin being a madhouse ('Was there e'er a place, that had more need of it?') and overbrimming with a despicable populace ('A nasty, mean, ungrateful, loathsome lot!'). As a result, he has insisted that the proceedings of the premiere go towards the relief of the ill of Dublin, and if he does not get his way, then he will pull the concert entirely. Swift, it is clear, is regarded as a madman by nearly everyone around him, and it is left to Laetitia Pilkington to try to arrange matters in order that the choristers are released, so that *Messiah* can go ahead, and that Swift himself is protected from his own increasing eccentricity. Pilkington is successful – naturally – in her endeavours, as she confides with some relief to her audience at the closing of the play:

The thirteenth day of April, in the year
Of seventeen and forty-two, the first
Performance of *Messiah* here took place,
In Dublin, at the Music Hall, before
A grand, polite and crowded audience.
And of the chorus, I have heard it said,
None sang so sweetly as the six young boys
That Doctor Swift so kindly had released.

The play's author is John Banville, winner a few years later of the Booker Prize for his novel *The Sea*. Banville has a name for austerity of style in his fiction, but *Dublin 1742* is an indicator, as it seems, of other fictional and dramatic interests. A year after the Booker, after all, he will pseudonymously publish a thriller set in 1950s Dublin, while *Dublin 1742* itself, in its agreeable exuberance, is very far from austere; just as well, since this is a drama for children. Instead, the costumes are truly sumptuous, the production values lavish, the direction and performances exuberant, the script itself sharp and ironic.

The form and structure of the play is unusual, involving much in the way of processing from space to space on the part of the audience, a good deal of direct involvement with the actors, and a private conversation with Pilkington, who delights in confiding in the children gathered around her. But there are a good many adults in the audience too, drawn to The Ark to see what Banville can do in the way of children's drama – a good deal, as it turns out, and *Dublin 1742* is a critical and commercial success. Its many virtues are heightened by the understanding that a fantasy is unfolding on stage: the audience can kick back and enjoy the acid, bitchy eighteenth-century meetings and minglings taking place in front of them.

Banville's script is of course based on a conceit: that such a collection of culturally and historically significant characters might indeed have congregated in the centre of Dublin in the days leading up to the first performance of *Messiah*. And yet – not so great a conceit. Not in that small city centre and not in the circles that Swift, Berkeley and Handel himself would have moved; one might easily believe that such a group of characters might be living and interacting within that small patch of city. After all, Dublin in those days may have been, as every modern guidebook so tediously points out, the second city of the British Empire – but it was still no more than a large town. And then, as now, its defining characteristic was intimacy. Banville's conceit, therefore, is far from being exaggerated. It is an easy matter to suspend one's disbelief and immerse oneself in the fiction unfolding from room to room at The Ark.

And besides, Banville's script is very much based on real life, as an entry in the *Dublin Journal* of March 1742 makes clear:

> For the relief of Prisoners in the several Gaols, and for the Support of Mercer's Hospital in Stephen's Street, and of the Charitable Infirmary on the Inns Quay, on Monday the 12th of April, will be performed at the Musick Hall on Fishamble Street, Mr Handel's new Grand Oratorio call'd the MESSIAH, in which the Gentlemen of the Choirs of both Cathedrals will assist, with some Concertos on the Organ by Mr Handel.

Nor is it mere accident that places Laetitia Pilkington (1712–50) at the heart of the play. Pilkington's *Memoirs* are a valuable source of insight into the world of eighteenth-century Dublin and it is fitting, therefore, that it was her narrative that provided *Dublin 1742* with symbolic structure and glue; that it was Pilkington herself who moved through the play supplying a voiceover here and a knowing aside there; that it was her confiding voiceover that fulfilled the function of supplying the spectator with a necessary cultural, political and religious context. In locating her at the centre of its dramatic narrative, *Dublin 1742* was responding to the available contemporary source material, to the force and energy of Pilkington as a historical character and to her literary legacy.

Pilkington's intimate associations with Swift and many other characters gave her rare and remarkable insights into the ticks and politics of fashionable Dublin. Her eyes and ears were open to the nuances of Dublin society, in all their complexity. Furthermore, her relationships and connections were with both Ireland and England – she lived in both countries, and her own highly coloured character and personal history give her journals a rare magnetism, as well as rich pickings for historians. Small wonder, then, that at the heart of *Dublin 1742* is that long, intimate and gossip-filled audience with Pilkington, during which she brings her journals, her insights, her inside information to life.

Pilkington would have vanished from history had she not set down an account of her life in her three volumes of *Memoirs*, the first two of which were published in 1748 and the third post-humously. In these volumes, she establishes a distinctive voice for herself, one marked by a good deal of cheerful good humour, an occasional dash of vituperation and a generally self-deprecating style that landed her in trouble with critics long after her death. In one short essay, Virginia Woolf, who tends in any case to be spar-ing in her compliments when it comes to Ireland and the Irish, is perplexed as to how Pilkington might be judged. She is 'shady, shifty' and as one reads on, it becomes apparent that Woolf hardly knows what to make of the *Memoirs*. Having put the boot in, however, Woolf eventually comforts herself through the discovery that Pilkington, after all, belongs to a noble line:

> Thus Laetitia is in the great tradition of English women of letters. It is her duty to entertain; it is her instinct to conceal. Still, though her room near the Royal Exchange is threadbare, and the table is spread with old play-bills instead of a cloth, and the butter is served in a shoe, and Mr. Worsdale has used the teapot to fetch small beer that very morning, still she presides, still she entertains. Her language is a trifle coarse, perhaps. But who taught her English? The great Doctor Swift.[2]

Here we have an excellent example of a most curious syndrome, and a consistent thread in the age-old and much-tormented rela-tionship between Ireland and England. Woolf has awarded to Pilkington the ultimate accolade, one that has been granted to unusually successful Irish sports stars, politicians, writers and soldiers down the years – she was in fact English all the time.

(Mind you, it seems that the boot can frequently be found on the other foot too, as I had discovered on my visit to the Royal Hospital. Michael Craig-Martin's connections to Ireland are tenuous at best – he was born in Dublin but never lived here. Instead, he lived in London and the United States and represented Britain at the 1998 Bienal de São Paulo. Not quite true-blue Irish then – not that that stops us from claiming him as one of our own.)

Still, Woolf does, albeit in her own extremely ungracious way, hit on at least one truth. Pilkington may indeed have been driven by poverty and want to bring her butter to the table in her shoe, but she was a successful memoirist nevertheless – precisely because she draws the reader in. Her writings are notably valuable documents, in fact, in that they illuminate the social and economic context of the Dublin of the day, and illuminate too the personal interactions that lift history out of the realm of the drily factual.

Pilkington was conscious from the outset of the difficult terrain she was traversing, and of the less than warm reception her *Memoirs* would meet – in certain circles at any rate, where memoirists and particularly female memoirists would be regarded with flint-eyed mistrust, as being highly biased, selective and full of spin. By the middle of the eighteenth century, Dublin had been brought so tightly, so unquestionably within the British sphere of influence that the cultural mores of London unquestionably applied to Dublin also. This was an age in which female legal and social freedoms were being gradually circumscribed. It is inevitable, therefore, that such memoirs as Pilkington's were viewed as transgressive in nature, emphasising as they did their author's independence of movement and thinking, their financial autonomy and their sexuality.

Most importantly of all, maybe, they circumvented conventional channels to appeal to an increasingly worldly, enlightened and liberal bourgeois audience, both in Dublin and outside it. They introduced a version of history and of lived behaviour that was never going to be received particularly well in the circles of power. Such notions are always especially potent in a colonial context, connecting as they do with other transgressive ways of behaving and thinking and of viewing society. Herein, maybe, lies Pilkington's particular value in eighteenth-century Dublin. She becomes a prime source of material on all manner of subjects related to this period. As a document of a woman's life, as a history of a Protestant woman in a predominantly Catholic country, and as the story of a consciously Irish woman in a colonised society, the *Memoirs* is a precious document, shedding a clear light on a much-picked-over era in Dublin life. And yet, Pilkington's manifest awareness of the critics is noticeable in the defensiveness of her opening ringing declaration:

> Altho' it has been the common Practice, with writers of memoirs, to fill their Volumes with their own Praises, which, whatever Pleasure thay may have afforded to the Authors, by indulging their Vanity, are seldom found to give any to their Readers; I am determined to quit this beaten Track; and by a strict Adherence to Truth, please even my greatest Enemies, by presenting them with a lively Picture of all my Faults, my Follies, and my Misfortunes, which have been consequential to them.[3]

Pilkington was born in Dublin in 1712. She was descended from aristocratic stock and was at pains to point out both these noble antecedents and the significance of her immediate, rather more middling, family; her father, the highly regarded physician and 'man midwife' Dr John van Lewen, can fairly claim to have been Ireland's first professional obstetrician. Born of a tentative bourgeoisie then asserting itself across western Europe, with access to education and new ideas and philosophies, Pilkington is already becoming an interesting object of study. And ironically, she had rather better claims to gentility than did Swift himself, in spite of the fact that the old man took a good deal of pleasure in looking down his social nose at her.

Notwithstanding this significant position in Dublin society, the young Laetitia had at first to fight in order to access privileges that ought, perhaps, to have been hers by right. 'From my earliest Infancy,' she tells us, 'I had a strong Disposition to Letters; but my Eyes being weak, after the Small-pox, I was not permitted to look at a Book; my Mother regarding more the Beauty of my Face, than the Improvement of my Mind; neither was I allow'd to learn to read.'[4] Pilkington's description of her situation – she taught herself to read, she tells us, by stealth and guile and risking many a slap and boxed ear in the process – illuminates very well the nature of gender relations in the Dublin of the day. It is difficult, after all, to imagine a boy of the middling classes being put in a similar position. That her parents were eventually won round to her way of thinking, she claims, owes much to the fact that her memory and artistic sensibilities were simply prodigious. They could hardly stand in the way of such swelling genius.

In 1725, Laetitia married the Reverend Matthew Pilkington in Dublin. The marriage lasted for 12 years, during which time the young couple lived in both London and Dublin. An unusual marriage at best, it would eventually decline into *Dallas*-like mud-slinging, adultery and hysteria, as both husband and wife took lovers, and went on to air their dirty linen in as public a fashion as they could manage. The *Memoirs*, in fact, are full of distracting references to sexual indiscretions, sexual advances, sexual paraphernalia of all kinds – and as a result it can be difficult enough to see beyond one's own delighted prurience and into the greater significance of Pilkington's writings.

Her marriage continued, for a few years at any rate, in spite of this air of ghastly dysfunction. Matthew Pilkington seems to have been the first to dabble in adultery but eventually Laetitia partook also. In the *Memoirs*, she raises her hackles to deny that any adultery took place at all, in spite of the fact that she was discovered with a gentleman in her bedchamber at an unreasonably late hour. No: the truth was that she was sitting up late, as she claims, to finish a new book.

> I own myself very indiscreet in permitting any Man to be in at an unseasonable Hour in my Bed-Chamber; but Lovers of Learning will, I am sure, pardon me, as I solemnly declare, it was the attractive charms of a new Book, which the Gentleman would not lend me, but consented to stay till I read it through, that was the sole Motive of my detaining him. But the Servants being bribed by their Master, let in twelve Watchmen at the Kitchen Window who, though they might have open'd the Chamber-Door, chose rather to break it to Pieces, and took the Gentleman and myself prisoners.[5]

As a result of these activities, her husband divorced Pilkington in the Dublin courts. She was barred from seeing her children – they later sought her out – and left Dublin for London. Her new status throws a pitiless light on the plight of an Irishwoman in such a specific situation. If Pilkington wished to remarry, for example, an Act of Parliament would be required under Irish law to enable her to do so. Furthermore, her husband was permitted to accuse her of all manner of wickednesses, without fear of being accused of libel, as a letter from Matthew Pilkington's solicitor makes clear:

> Sir, in the Absence of my Client, Mr Pilkington, I received your Letter, and he wou'd have you know, the Woman, you mention, is not his Wife, nor has he anything to say to the infamous Wretch; she fled to Ireland, where she ought to have been executed, for killing her Father, three of her Bastards, and Poisoning her Husband.[6]

There is no reason to believe that any of this torrent of invective is true, as Pilkington points out plaintively, 'Could one believe, that any thing less than Infernal Malice could have forg'd such an Accusation against an Innocent person? My very Blood thrilled with Horror, to think, there could be such a Monster of my Species.'[7] The court case and its aftermath highlights female inequality at this point in eighteenth-century Dublin: Pilkington could be exposed to public humiliation, libelled, barred from seeing her children and cast into outer social darkness without ever having any comeback through legal means. And given this situation, it is no surprise that she sought redress through the publication of her memoirs. The surprise, indeed, is that more women did not follow her example.

The remainder of Pilkington's life was spent shuttling between London and Dublin, ever poorer and ever more desperate in her search of a livelihood. She retained the affection of a few of her former well-connected friends, but for the most part she was cut out of polite society and reached her nadir with a spell in a debtors' prison. In writing her memoirs, therefore, she had nothing to lose and a good deal to gain. She died in Dublin on 29 July 1750.

— ◄o► —

There is a good deal more information to be gleaned from Pilkington's *Memoirs*, of course, than mere sexual tittle-tattle. In particular, Pilkington is an astute commentator on Dublin's cultural scene and remains a prime source of material on Swift's declining years. Swift was, of course, the pre-eminent cultural figure of these years, with such volumes as *Gulliver's Travels* (1726) and the brilliantly sustained satire of *A Modest Proposal* (1729) having helped to establish his reputation long before Pilkington came on the scene.

It is only comparatively recently, however, that Swift's Dublin experiences have received more than scant critical appraisal, in spite of the fact that he spent more than three-quarters of his life in Ireland and ended it as Dean of St Patrick's, and in spite of the fact that Ireland has left its trace on so much of his writing. He maintained, like Archbishop Marsh – and a good many other people, come to that, all Dubliners born and bred – a position of loud public dislike of the city, and had little or nothing to say of the world of Catholic Ireland beyond the city limits. But as prose writer and poet, as commentator on and participant in the fraught relationship between England and Ireland, and as a resident Dubliner himself, he was well able to see the city's squalid poverty and appalling need. Swift bequeathed a considerable literary and political legacy to Dublin.

The *Drapier Letters*, written under pseudonym between 1724 and 1725, attacking British economic and political policies in Ireland, are a good example of this engagement with Irish affairs. So too is *A Modest Proposal*, which suggests that the children of Irish peasants be killed and their flesh sold ('a young, healthy child is … a most delicious, nourishing and wholesome food, whether stewed, roasted, baked, or boiled') in order to bring in valuable income for Irish families reduced to desperation by such British economic policies as the Woollen Act. And this, before we even need mention the material bequest – written, if you recall, into *Dublin 1742* – to found a mental hospital in the city.

Critics have increasingly, and with some gusto, fought over this legacy: in recent years Swift has been labelled as misogynist and proto-feminist, conservative and radical, nationalist and colonialist; and there is a good deal in his corpus of work to support these arguments and many others like them. In many ways, indeed, Swift sums up rather neatly the Janus-faced position of Dublin itself in these years: as the undisputed principal city of Ireland and yet a British imperial city too; as a city run by and for its Protestant elite, yet with a burgeoning Catholic population that was inexorably becoming the majority community; and as a city both of remarkable and ostentatious wealth and of shocking deprivation.

In this context, it can be helpful to attend to Pilkington's *Memoirs*, which slice through this tangled mass of rhetoric to bring a version of the man himself to life. She very clearly understood the importance of trading on her association with Swift, who was the literary superstar of his time, for she introduces him as early as possible in her narrative. Swift, she confides at this point, was careful only to befriend and confide in those whom he knew were deserving of trust and affection:

> I had also the much envied Honour of being known to Doctor Swift, whose Genius excellent as it was, surpast not his Humanity in the most judicious and useful Charities, altho' often hid under a rough Appearance, till he was perfectly convinced both of the Honesty and Distress of those he bestowed it on: He was a perpetual friend to Merit and Learning; and utterly incapable of Envy, indeed why should he not? Who in true genuine Wit could fear no Rival.[8]

Such a person was Pilkington herself; we are left in no doubt of the fact.

In this first volume of her *Memoirs*, Pilkington takes time to gush over Swift – his genius, his taste, modesty and poetic sensibilities – and consistently attempts to connect his life and talent to her own, the better to stake a claim to literary authority. It was a tragedy, she claims, that he could never be prevailed upon to write a memoir of his own and therefore fortunate that she was available to step into the breach. And so on, for Pilkington is nothing if not a skilled propagandist in her own cause – although of course it is this very skill that makes her narrative so gripping. As Swift aged and became deaf, she writes, his circle contracted and he permitted into it only those with whom he was perfectly easy. Such as the Pilkingtons, of course, and it was this access to Swift that permitted her to build up an insight into the great man and to transmit this insight, in the fullness of time, out into the waiting world.

Yet she is also concerned to paint the man in his human colours, proffering vignette after vignette as she does so. And it is in these vignettes – describing Swift at his dinner, Swift the visitor, Swift socialising with the great and the good, and with lesser members of society – it is in these, more than in any number of essays on his literary and political leanings, that we catch a glimpse of the real Swift. This is even more clearly the case when Pilkington – as she frequently does – paints the man in a less than flattering light.

Swift, she tells us airily, 'whilst he was at the University of Dublin ... was so far from being distinguished for any superiority of Parts or Learning, that he was stopped of his Degree as a Dunce'.[9] He liked to make fun of the stature of both Pilkingtons – neither of whom were, we can gather, all that much taller than hobbits – and liked also to inspect carefully the lady's methods of housekeeping, and to criticise both the 'Lilliputian' dimensions of her home, and her hospitality if it fell short of his own exacting standards. He force-fed her gingerbread and rum, at first relying on persuasion to have his way but 'finding that would not avail, he threw me down, forced the Bottle into my Mouth, and pour'd some of the Liquor down my Throat, which I thought would set my very Stomach on Fire. He then gravely went to prayers'.[10]

And so it goes on, this copious description of Swift the man: charitable and generous, giving much out of his own less than generous church stipend for the relief of the poor of the city; a fearful misogynist, quite content to humiliate Pilkington at the drop of a hat. The cumulative effect of these descriptions, by turn generous, acid and cruel, is to make the reader giddy – but also to build up a touching figure of a man who could also be generous, acid and cruel, and frequently all at the same time.

As for Swift himself, his mentions of the Pilkingtons in his papers are rather less frequent, but they do occur from time to time. It is clear that he looked upon them as pet lambs, at least in the early days. They were, he notes:

> A middle kind both for understanding and fortune, who are perfectly easy, never impertinent, complying in everything, ready to do a hundred little offices that you and I may often want, who dine and sit with me five times for once that I ever go to them, and whom I can tell without offence, that I am otherwise engaged at present.[11]

This air of genial indulgence lifts entirely following the acrimonious dissolution of the Pilkington marriage, to be replaced by a cloud of condemnation. We know that the aged dean went through his correspondence and excised the very Pilkington name whenever he chanced across it; and it can be safely assumed that Pilkington's insights into Swift and his life ended at this point, and with similar abruptness. This situation must have been yet more painful for Pilkington when she came to write her *Memoirs* in later years, and its effect can be clearly seen in her third and final volume: it is a good deal more discursive and gossip-laden, less insightful and more generally prone to half-truth and unpleasant innuendo. Pilkington, it is clear, has run out of material.

Critics may have paid most attention to Pilkington's comments on Swift – but her more glancing thoughts and declarations are equally fascinating. She has much to say on the topic of the English, the Irish, her place in both countries, and these comments reveal much to do with the fractious nature of the relationship between the two countries at this significant moment of the eighteenth century. But they also reveal her inevitable isolation; her memoirs, like her life, were destined to end badly.

A memorial stone to Laetitia Pilkington was unveiled at St Ann's Church on Dawson Street in 1997. The memorial, set into the wall beside the west door of the church, pulls no punches in its judgement on her and on her life:

> In the Crypt of the Church, near the Body of her honoured Father John Van Lewen M.D., lies the mortal part of Mrs Lætitia Pilkington whose Spirit hopes for that Peace, in the Infinite Merit of Christ, which a cruel and merciless World never afforded her.

Chapter 11

RECONSTRUCTION

John Banville's play, Pilkington's memoirs, Marsh's Library, William Robinson's Royal Hospital, the records of the Irish Parliament's painstaking and paranoid Penal Laws, the street life and buildings of an always evolving Liberties and the regulations set in place to try to control its streets: all of these help reveal the nature, culture and various specific characteristics of eighteenth-century Dublin. Its politics were fraught, but in philosophy, in architecture, in economics and city planning and in letters, it was a city sparkling with vitality and energy. It was at last the undisputed capital of an island united politically and economically (if not ideologically or in terms of religion) under a single form of rule. And in human terms, it was a city of striking intimacy, with the members of its ruling elite – then as now – well acquainted both with one another and with the texture of life in Dublin as a whole. This intimacy in such a physically small urban setting also naturally meant that Dublin's grinding urban poverty was equally and unavoidably on display. In short, the lives of eighteenth-century Dubliners may have been leisurely and rich, or they may have been terribly poor – but they were lived out cheek by jowl, in sometimes grating proximity. Such intimacy, with its consequences and psychological ramifications, is brought home vividly in a series of small drawings in ink two centuries later. Harry Clarke (1889–1931) would of course become much better known as the creator, in the 1920s, of the famous glowing stained glass that today still shines in the interior of the former Bewley's coffee house on Grafton Street. Earlier in his career, however, Clarke drew a series of illustrations to accompany a new edition of Alexander Pope's *The Rape of the Lock*. Clarke's piece in this series, 'He Takes the Gift with Reverence and Extends', for example, is a malign little rococo-inspired scene that brilliantly suggests the continual surveillance and observation, combined with extreme ostrich-feathered formality, boredom and intrigue, that characterised eighteenth-century aristocratic society. Combine these attributes with a sense of the native claustrophobia of the Dublin of this period, and the little drawing comes to possess a power out of all proportion to its size.

The architectural legacy of these years has helped to record eighteenth-century Dublin for posterity. This city is rightly famous for its streetscape of Georgian squares, terraces and public spaces, a good deal of which have survived down to the present day unchanged – or at any rate more or less unscathed. Nearly all of this architectural stock is concentrated in the south-east and north-east quadrants of today's city centre, with other important districts and key public buildings scattered elsewhere throughout Dublin's core: the great set-piece open spaces of Merrion, Fitzwilliam and Mountjoy Squares; the long mounting elevations of Gardiner Street; the marching façades of Fitzwilliam Street vanishing towards the distant mountains; and the copper-green domes of the Four Courts and the Custom House reflected in the waters of the Liffey.

This architectural and social record has attracted visitors to Dublin from all over the world, although it is also the case that it has sometimes been more valued abroad than it has been at home. And by no means all of Georgian Dublin has survived, far from it.

Some of its remains have been grievously neglected, or otherwise mucked about with, and it is only comparatively recently that many of the city's finest buildings have received, once more, the attention they are due and have been painstakingly restored after decades of neglect. Take Gardiner Street, for example, which climbs up from the Liffey towards Mountjoy Square. Briefly the most fashionable area of the city, its enormous houses underwent a long, slow decline over two centuries, changing from brilliant aristocratic town houses into the worst and most shocking inner-city tenements. Today, many of the street's Georgian buildings have been demolished and apartment buildings raised in their place. These buildings, leggy on stilts to conceal underground car parking, were built in the first flush of 1990s prosperity and are a pastiche, of sorts, of the houses they replaced. With each proportion wrong, however, each window frame fashioned in indestructible uPVC, each railing wrought in cheap imitation of the original Georgian design and material and dimension, they are a kind of horrible mockery of the eighteenth-century buildings that once stood here. Maybe the original houses had deteriorated beyond repair, maybe they had reached the end of the road. If so, however, there seemed to be no conception of how an opportunity might have been taken to replace these terraces with high-quality buildings. No way – and instead the city is left with these horrors in pastiche, marching up the hill towards Mountjoy Square.

Or take the infamous Electricity Supply Board (ESB) building that was erected, in the teeth of public opposition, in place of a terrace of 17 late eighteenth-century houses on Fitzwilliam Street which were torn down in the 1960s. This terrace formed part of a longer avenue of Georgian houses that extended almost a kilometre north and east from Leeson Street towards the austere 1930s' front of the National Maternity Hospital on Holles Street: the longest Georgian streetscape, maybe, in the world. 'It has no special architectural coherence,' grumbled one architectural specialist, in the face of protests from conservationists. 'It is not a planned façade, nor an architectural entity. It is simply one damned house after another.'

The controversy at the time, which preceded by some years the Wood Quay debate, marked something of a watershed in Dublin's history: a moment when the politics of conservation connected with the public consciousness, and a moment when it became apparent that the remains of the Georgian city could not be simply picked off or demolished, piece by piece, when there existed a will to retain and maintain properly what was left. Until then, the Georgian buildings of the city centre had been viewed at best doubtfully or ambivalently or with dislike. The new Irish state had come into existence only in 1922; and in its haste to stamp its imprimatur and cultural authority on the country, maybe it was natural enough that it would look coldly on the architectural remains – the most obvious remains, as Dubliners moved daily through the city – of a too-recent colonial era. Maybe it was felt that money was better spent on symbols of the new Dublin, rather than on conserving the paraphernalia of the old.

Although in this case, the ESB got its way. The 17 houses duly vanished in 1965 and the replacement office block was opened in 1970. The new ESB headquarters is not a bad modern building – far from it, in fact, although it has become shabby with time. And other modern buildings in the area, such as the bronze-clad head-quarters of the Bank of Ireland around the corner, are contextu-alised well, even spectacularly, against their eighteenth-century surroundings, giving the lie in the process to the notion that such streetscapes must be preserved, forever unchanging, in aspic.

But these 'damned houses' on Fitzwilliam Street ought not to have been interrupted by the ESB in their march, one after another, south towards the line of the mountains. Their uneven lines and windows and absence of careful symmetry underscore their par-ticular grace. From my kitchen window, and from the roof of the apartment building, I can see the rear elevation of the houses, and it is their very haphazardness that lends them beauty and character. Today they are marked by fire escapes, satellite dishes, occasional extensions and the other grafted signs of modernity; their enormous landing windows are round-headed or thrust out into an occasional bow; their chimney stacks are elaborately decorated in brick; and the mews at the end of their long back gardens have been developed into desirable city-centre residences. One of the houses is skinny-thin in breadth – no wider than a room, in fact. But what a room! From my kitchen, I can see the vast window that illuminates this narrow room, and I can imagine the light that floods the house. Early in the morning, this crazy array of bow windows and square windows and long-arched many-paned windows catches the light of the rising sun and flashes back its radiance in pink and gold, and dazzling orange. And this is only the rear, seldom-seen elevation of these buildings.

From the front, they are more sombre, unrelieved except for their brightly painted front doors and ornate fanlights. They stretch into the distance, glowing red in Dublin's fitful sunshine or fading to a dark red-brown on a gloomy winter afternoon. They bear the unmistakable mark of houses that were built to be lived in, that were built one by one, without a grand and all-encompassing plan, maybe, but with a distinct and immediate sense of scale and of place. They are hardly 'one damned house after another', and they are worth looking at again, and worth treasuring.

— ◄o► —

The state authorities invested heavily in the new Dublin of the eighteenth century, seeking to build a city that would stand as a monument to their own endeavour, to their world and their empire. That a new Dublin came into existence in these years is of course all the more significant when we remember that this world was still far from secure: a Jacobite army swept south from Scotland into the English Midlands as late as 1746. Moreover, the first British Empire of the eighteenth century was, by 1770, in the process of disintegration: Canada had finally been secured from the French only in 1759, but the 13 American colonies peeled away a mere 17 years later; and Britain remained involved in bitter and debilitating conflict with France throughout much of the century. That Dublin assumed the form that it did must be partly, at least, the result of a reaction to this new world of insecurity and defeat for Britain. The result of a bitter resolution that imperial rivalries might be sustained for decade after exhausting decade, that colonies might be attained and colonies might be lost – but that one colony at least, the oldest, would never be relinquished.

Dublin's reconstruction in these years also owed much to rational philosophy – that of the Enlightenment, which ran as a current through the administrations of the time, the Penal Laws notwithstanding, and in which so many Irish figures played an important part. And the creation of some of Dublin's finest streetscapes and buildings makes this philosophy tangible. For, while the Liberties and other districts of Dublin festered in the most appalling deprivation, a new city arose in the east, planned and built rationally. The formation, for example, of the Wide Streets Commission in 1758 – probably the most powerful city planning organisation in European history – provided an opportunity for successive administrations to make the rational word flesh by enacting changes that created new streets and avenues, and permitted a cherished sense of order and modernity to assume control over a previously medieval and disordered landscape. Such thinking also acted as midwife to such symbols of Enlightenment perfection as the domes of the Royal Exchange (now City Hall), the Four Courts and the Custom House, all completed by century's end. And of course, all of these buildings and all of the new and monumental streets pushed through Dublin, connecting one locus of power with another and with another and another, all of these helped to accentuate the fact that while this new and remarkable city was a fitting capital of Ireland, it remained a colony nevertheless, and dependent upon another state for its economic and social well-being. The real power still lay elsewhere.

Dublin's growth was also driven by private investment; and it is to this speculation that we owe some of the city's finest buildings. Bartholomew Mosse was one such individual, famous for his opening in 1757 of the Lying-In Hospital that lies at the north end of what is today's O'Connell Street. The building, now the centre of the modern Rotunda hospital, is usually described as the world's first dedicated maternity hospital. This glosses over its original beginnings, 12 years before in 1745, in the seedy and unpleasant surrounding of George's Lane (now South Great George's Street), just beside the Castle in one of the oldest and most disagreeable parts of town. Mosse deployed his considerable energies in order to purchase a large piece of land on the other side of town, to raise money for the foundation of a new and altogether more glamorous institution and then – most impressively of all – to associate it with a quite remarkable degree of social cachet. The result was that the opening of the Lying-In Hospital in 1757 was accompanied by the sort of razzmatazz that social climbers dream of. The cream of society, including the Lord Lieutenant himself, attended the event – and it was an event distinctive in its own right.

Mosse arranged matters so that a phalanx of women, great with child and dressed in specially commissioned blue uniforms, were at hand to greet the great and the good as they arrived to inspect the new building. It was a form of spectacle, of theatre, although Mosse also understood that one can have too much of a good thing: for as soon as the initial impact had worn off, the aristocratic visitors were swept off to mingle and drink coffee, while the heavily pregnant women were made to vanish behind doors, up staircases and out of sight as quick as lightning.

In all this, perhaps Mosse's masterstroke was to form a financial association between his hospital – which might otherwise have been the sort of place from which the aristocracy would shrink in horror – and the adjoining money-making pleasure gardens that, combined with the nearby promenade of Sackville Mall, became one of the city's the most fashionable quarters. Virtuous charity, pleasure and spectacle are always a heady combination, and so it was here too. His gardens – all gravel sweeps, manicured lawns, clipped avenues of shrub and tree, musical entertainments, food and drink – combined to form an attractive evening package. And these were not closed spaces; they were, on the contrary, open to anyone who could afford the entry fee, which ruled out the poor but certainly not the city's upwardly mobile. And finally, as though to round off the attractions, the hospital added its domed Rotunda in 1767. It was by no means especially beautiful on the outside, but was nevertheless an impressive space within and provided yet another zone for public pleasure and spectacle. Given the Irish weather, the elite of Dublin must have been secretly relieved.

The manifold pleasures of these pleasure gardens would change, given time. Their day in the sun would be comparatively brief: by the 1780s, the aristocracy was giving up on their delights and the space was being filled by the less well off, the less cultured. Even before then, it had become necessary to lay down the law a little more sternly and to raise the walls that surrounded the gardens a little higher, for the place seemed to have a knack for bringing out the worst in its inmates. They allowed their children to run riot (later, children were banned altogether), but this wasn't the half of it: the gardens were, so the authorities felt, becoming a scene of general vice. The appearance of such uneasy sensations are not surprising, for the pleasure gardens were spaces in which the rules might be relaxed, at which women might appear unattended and unchaperoned, in which the inhabitants of an otherwise rigidly stratified city might mingle with those above and below them on the ladder, and inevitably let their hair down.

They were, in short, a place of unparalleled social freedom in eighteenth-century Dublin. No wonder, then, that they became so popular in the first place; and equally no wonder that eventually this popularity would tip over into ill-repute, since the phenomenon of the pleasure garden was persistently connected to ideas of female sexual freedom and emancipation. The very qualities that brought success, then, eventually brought failure too. The Gardens and Rotunda, together with the Assembly Rooms that are now home to the Gate Theatre – these institutions closed during the 1798 rising, reopened briefly just before the Act of Union, and then closed for good as the century ended.

We have private investors and entrepreneurs to thank too for the surviving squares and terraces of Georgian Dublin. In particular, the development of the Gardiner family estates in what is now the north-east inner city and the Pembroke estates south and east of the city centre provided a decisive fillip to the eastward growth of the city and in so doing marked indelibly the character of Dublin. The city moved decisively in these years away from the open spaces of the western suburbs and east towards the sea, and this was a development that was commented upon at the time. The prevailing wind in Ireland is of course from the west, bearing moist winds from the Atlantic, and the western reaches of Dublin were as a result sweeter-smelling and – in those anxious days – more healthy. To the east the landscape dropped, in marsh and sand and occasional flood, down into Dublin Bay. The area is agreeable today, because the landscape is controlled and regimented – but it was much less so in the eighteenth century.

But there were reasons why this ostensibly eastward thrust made a good deal of sense. The Liberties and Stoneybatter (the old Oxmantown of Anglo-Norman times), always the poorer and less salubrious working-class districts of Dublin, lay to the west of the old city. The fluctuating boundary of the Pale had run west of the medieval city too, and so perhaps there was a persistent and obscure sense, conscious or unconscious, that the east and the docks and the beaches of Dublin Bay were somehow safer for the city's aristocracy and new bourgeoisie than the open western suburbs, no matter how sweet-smelling they might be. Trinity College, now generously bankrolled by the Irish Parliament and beginning to unfold and expand in a series of monumental buildings and quadrangles, lay to the east too and provided an anchor to increased development in that direction. The new and exquisite Custom House opened its doors along the Liffey's eastern reaches in 1791. And last but not least, these two estates, Pembroke and Gardiner, happened to hold extensive lands in the east – lands now ripe for slow development.

The first significant developments north of the river were on Henrietta Street, where 15 vast town houses were built by the Gardiner estate from the 1720s until the 1750s. Until comparatively recently, Henrietta Street was something of a byword for the neglect of the eighteenth-century city. After a heyday as comparatively brief as the Lying-In Hospital's pleasure gardens, these enormous houses gradually but inexorably declined through the course of the nineteenth and twentieth centuries. They stood neglected, decaying and grim, and served as tenements at one time or another until conservation work began, falteringly, in the 1970s. Flora Mitchell, in the textual accompaniment to her evocative book of Dublin watercolours, describes the street as a dark 'canyon' climbing north and west up its hill. The crucial point, however – the amazing point, given the fate of some other Georgian streetscapes – is that Henrietta Street survived its long period of neglect virtually intact. Thirteen of the 15 houses still stand and it remains the best example of early Georgian architecture in the city.

I had wanted to get a good snoop around at least one of these enormous Henrietta Street houses for ages. I was glad therefore when, early in October, the *Irish Times* carried a piece on Open House Dublin, in which a host of the city's buildings 'open their doors for a unique experience of architecture. This is the first year that Dublin will join major cities around the world – including London, New York and Toronto – that host this exciting and immensely popular event annually.' Sounded good to me. But I was too late, of course, to reserve places on the best tours: no snoops for me, alas, around the double-height entrance hall and lavish interior of the Provost's House at Trinity College, which sits grandly behind its forecourt at the top of Grafton Street; or around the King's Inns at the top of Henrietta Street itself; or around half a dozen other of Dublin's most remarkable eighteenth-century buildings. I would have to be content sniffing around the less remarkable ones.

So I thought, at any rate. While I was sent packing from the Provost's House and King's Inns I reckoned, in my innocence, that some of the other buildings would be a piece of cake. Surely there would be no crowds assembling to look over the other buildings on the Open House list: apartment buildings in Temple Bar and, further afield, eco-buildings on Camden Street and other locations around the city centre, the tall trades-union tower at Liberty Hall on the banks of the Liffey, and so on. As it turned out, however, the Open House weekend was a victim of its own success.

I turn up, then, on the Saturday morning to get a tour of the Iveagh Buildings, Victorian and confident, bankrolled as social housing by the Guinnesses and overlooking St Patrick's Cathedral, only to find a queue of hundreds tumbling down Patrick Street. 'You won't get in,' says a harassed Open House person. 'You might as well go home; we're really sorry.' And later, I hear that most of the other sites on the list have had the same remarkable response. Liberty Hall, for example, is overwhelmed with citizens wanting to tour the building and catch the matchless views of Dublin from its roof. The problem seems to be that the buildings, for the most part, are open only for a couple of hours, nowhere near enough time to cope with the interest they have generated.

In spite of this disappointment – in spite of a general disappointment tangible in the crowd – there is a festive, pleasurable atmosphere running up and down Patrick Street on this sunny October Saturday. People are obviously delighted with themselves, having made the effort to come here at all; certainly I am. It has much to do with – or so it feels – the Open House idea: a sense of reclaiming the buildings and the streets, with an optimistic sense of asserting ownership of the fabric of Dublin itself, and of taking the opportunity to explore and to assess the detail that is often missed in the rush of an ordinary working day.

Since I can't get into the Iveagh Buildings, I take a look instead around the outside of this fascinating complex: at the kindergarten called, in the Dublin vernacular, the Beano, which the kids would be bribed to attend with buns and hot chocolate; at the elaborate brickwork decoration; and at the sheer height of the buildings – so unexpected and so rare in this low-slung city. It feels, in fact, like a European city in here; I might be in the midst of a complex of public housing in Vienna, for example, and not in Dublin at all. And all around, people are doing the same thing, poking and looking and becoming sightseers in their own city. This sense of civic curiosity and pride, it seems to me, might be latent or in abeyance most of the time – but it is potent in the extreme, if only it can be harnessed, and it is tangible on this autumnal weekend.

And so, to Henrietta Street the following day. These giant town houses are nothing if not austere – even in the clear, cool light of late October, with Open House crowds milling around. They have been beautifully restored, of course, with their woodwork and plasterwork and elaborate chimneypieces as fine as they must have been in their heyday. But they retain an air of cool external austerity. As E. M. Forster might have put it, 'Of course it must be a wonderful building. But how like a barn! And how very cold!' Devoid of much in the way of external decoration, they serve as reminders that these were buildings erected speculatively; there was no room for financial error.

Perhaps it is rather ungracious or cross-grained a reflection, but these houses seem to serve as potent reminders of how terribly difficult must have been the lives that were lived there, or some of the lives, at any rate. There was no piped water in the houses on Henrietta Street until at least 1740, and it boggles the mind to imagine the labour and exhausting effort it must have taken on the part of servants to keep these great houses habitable and their wealthy inhabitants fed and warm, clean and pleased. How great the armies of servants, how many the basins of water to be dragged upstairs throughout the day, how many the buckets of coal brought up, panting, to heat the huge rooms – and so it goes on.

And this, in a colonial city. No wonder that a fear of the servant class grew steadily throughout the eighteenth century, no wonder that Edmund Burke and many others warned against what might happen, no wonder these fears became hysterical as the Bastille was stormed and Louis XVI and Marie Antoinette lost their heads in 1793. These great houses on Henrietta Street acted as stages for all manner of power plays; and they would have witnessed all of human life.

— ◄o► —

Henrietta Street was the first significant development north of the Liffey, and it was soon followed by many others. Mountjoy

Square – originally the most perfect and harmonious of the city's Georgian squares – was established on high ground above the Liffey and seemed set to be the most desirable address in Dublin for many years to come. Its lofty setting, well placed to catch the air and with views across the city, was superb, and so too were the elevations, proportions and internal plasterwork of its town houses. But the square is a good example of the eventual fate of much of the development planned and executed north of the river in the eighteenth and early nineteenth centuries. While such areas in their heyday were at the very pinnacle of Dublin's fashionable world, their season – like that of Henrietta Street – was relatively short. By mid-century, the city's elite were beginning to follow the lead of the Earl of Kildare ('they will follow me wherever I go'), migrating south of the river, and setting up shop in the south-eastern quadrant of the city. Grave and austere Kildare House – now Leinster House, the seat of the Oireachtas or Irish legislature, upon which the Lying-In Hospital was modelled – was merely the most lavish manifestation of this new building boom; and by the end of the eighteenth century, the suddenly unfashionable north inner city was beginning its long, slow decline. At any rate, however, Mountjoy Square, Henrietta Street and many other areas escaped – by dint of luck, sluggishness and persistent economic weakness – the fate of the long terraces of houses on Gardiner Street. Much of Mountjoy Square was demolished in the 1970s, it is true, and the replacement buildings designed as pastiche, as replicas of what were lost. A heart-sinking idea, although possibly better than what might have happened instead.

South of the river, the Pembroke lands were intensively developed also, and here time has been kinder. The set-piece terraces and Merrion and Fitzwilliam Squares survive largely intact, and the squares in particular provide simply the best formal streetscapes that contemporary Dublin can offer. Fitzwilliam is small – almost tiny – and quiet and beautifully intimate, while

Merrion provides a public space on a grand scale. The terraces on three sides of the square are set off by the series of public buildings – the Natural History Museum, National Gallery of Ireland and Leinster House – that line the west side. Merrion Square is further enhanced too by later additions such as the Pepper Cannister Church (1824), star of many a Dublin film, set and framed at the climax of a long elegant perspective from the west end of the square. And the squares themselves provide green space in a city centre notably lacking in the stuff.

Or rather Merrion Square provides green space. The green park in the middle of Fitzwilliam Square, in an odd quirk of history, remains closed to the public and its central lawn can be barely glimpsed through the cunningly planted shrubberies on its perimeter. 'Disgraceful!' thunders an occasional letter in the *Irish Times*. A truly disgraceful state of affairs in this democratic day and age. Open it to the public, for God's sake. And disgraceful! I have often thought so too as I have walked past on a hot day, perspiring and thinking revolutionary, Bastille-esque thoughts.

That was until the day, not too long ago, that a friend – and keyholder – invited me to a picnic in the square on a warm summer day. We listened to the iron gates click satisfyingly shut behind us and laid out a white-and-red checked tablecloth on the manicured grass and dined on crusty bread, and cool butter and pâté, and blue cheese and apples. We drank champagne from real glass flutes (it might have been cheap sparkling wine in plastic glasses, but remains Möet et Chandon in my duplicitous memory) and ignored the passing and perspiring pedestrians peering murderously through the gates and realised that yes, Louis XVI and Marie Antoinette had been correct all along.

Still, Merrion Square is good enough for the hungry masses. Good enough for me too, most of the time and when I can't access champagne and privileged keys. The gardens at Merrion Square have come in for more than their fair share of flack, being derided as an essay in vulgarity, as gaudy, as ill-planned, as failing to attend to their context – and so on. But I like them. In the summer, various bands and orchestras pitch in summer concerts, and throughout the year there is plenty to see, in the form of colour and planting and busts and memorials innumerable. The Chilean government, for example, has contributed a memorial to Bernardo O'Higgins, one of the leaders of the nineteenth-century Chilean independence movement, in honour of his Irish ancestry; Independence hero Michael Collins is commemorated in a bronze bust; and Oscar Wilde – the 'fag on the crag', in charming Dublin vernacular – sits in glorious technicolor atop a rough quartz boulder opposite his former family home. Best of all is the remarkable streetscape that surrounds the park, and that can be glimpsed through the trees. The topmost windows of the great town houses seem to peep over the tree tops and into the square – a reminder of whose park this once, exclusively, was.

Dublin sometimes seems fated, at least in its Georgian manifestation, to be compared endlessly to London – socially, culturally, architecturally. Pick up any book about Dublin and these comparisons instantly jump off the page in a particularly tedious version of the second city syndrome. The city's Georgian squares are endlessly compared to their London equivalents and sometimes found wanting, sometimes not ('you have nothing in London so handsome as Merrion Square'); the width of their respective streets are subject to fretful comparison; the Liffey and its embankments contrasted with the Thames and its, in spite of the manifest fact that they are very different rivers; Dame Street compared (apparently) to Bond Street, the Royal Hospital to Chelsea and so on. Some of this, doubtless, can be put down to a form of eighteenth-century inferiority complex; and certainly there is little doubt too that such a habit of comparison between two such radically different cities is something of a curse.

But despite the flack, the park at Merrion Square is of course infinitely superior to any park in any setting in the whole of London, or indeed anywhere else in the world. It is owned by the Catholic Church, which has leased it to the city. And it would not have been a green space at all, if a plan formed by the Church in the 1930s to turn it into the site of an enormous Catholic cathedral had been realised. Such a building would have rectified that quirk of history that has given Dublin its two Protestant cathedrals – within a stone's throw of each other – but nary a Catholic one. It would also have provided the Catholic Church with a potent symbol of authority just across the road from the seat of secular power in the land. Maybe such a juxtaposition in mid-twentieth-century Ireland was too much to bear; maybe someone blinked first; maybe the Church, ultimately, didn't want to build its cathedral in the midst of colonial Dublin. Whatever the reason, the cathedral was never built, the city remains Catholic cathedral-less and we still have a park to loll around in on hot summer afternoons.

Chapter 12

REFORMATION

One more building from Dublin's eighteenth century, before we are done. At the eastern terminus of Dame Street lies College Green – the old Hoggen Green of Viking and Anglo-Norman Dublin, close to the site of the Norse Thing, and today bounded to the east by the monumental west front of Trinity College. College Green is in many ways a useful focus of a city that possesses no acknowledged centre – for Dublin is even today fractured by its division into northside and southside, split by the Liffey, with each half of the city centre possessing its own coherent structure and commercial heart. College Green, then, probably fits the bill as quasi-centre of the city better than anywhere else; it is no more than a stone's throw from the Liffey, with clear views up to O'Connell Street on the northern bank of the river, and even clearer views west along Dame Street and up the hill to Christ Church.

College Green epitomises the changes and the urban engineering that were driven through the eighteenth-century city. Dame Street is one of the Wide Street Commission's most important legacies. It was felt to be necessary, symbolically and practically, to provide an appropriately monumental connection between the Castle and Trinity, and then to drive further roads along the new

Westmoreland and D'Olier Streets and across the river to Sackville Street. Buildings were condemned, therefore, their residents removed and new elegant terraces created that fitted the aesthetic bill in this new city. Behind this membrane, Dublin continued as chaotic and squalid as ever – the narrow lanes of Temple Bar, for example, still led down to the river in a bawdy festoon of taverns and houses of ill repute, as they had ever done – but the main object was achieved just the same. And all of these networks and terraces and routes connected on College Green.

Traffic-clogged today, always noisy, always busy, its footpaths crowded day and night with pedestrians, its street frontage lined with a tangle of cafés and takeaways and bars, Dame Street is a far cry from Bond Street today, and far too from being the most attractive area of modern Dublin. But its essentials are largely unchanged. The area's dimensions remain impressive and the eye is still caught and carried west and up towards the Castle, or north along wide Westmoreland Street towards the river. A hundred little streets lead down into Temple Bar and the hulking front of Trinity College is no less vast than it ever was. College Green itself is today probably the busiest intersection in the city centre: traffic sweeps around its curves north and south and pedestrians crowd at the crossing points, waiting to dodge the traffic.

If this sounds unpromising, in many ways it is unpromising, especially in wet weather when the traffic snarls up, car horns sound incessantly and dripping golf umbrellas snag in raincoats and bags, and narrowly miss eyes. There is no room for senti-mentality, after all, in a modern city. But it is not all unpromising – the main gates of Trinity remain a favourite meeting point in the city centre, and a crowd of people wait and loiter here day and night, glancing up at the blue clock above the entrance arch. A branch of Habitat has moved in over the way, and tables and chairs have been set up (a little hopefully, maybe) outside its doors, screened from the traffic by lines of bay trees in pots. Next door is Books Upstairs, one of the best independent bookstores in the city. In the centre of College Green a bronze of the Irish patriot Thomas Davis presides over a restored fountain, and the presence of this water and of a throng of lime trees does something to compensate for the endless traffic. Across the way lies the charming cul-de-sac of Foster Place, lined with more trees and classical buildings built on an imposing scale. Not even a new Starbucks lurking on the corner can dent the pleasure of the scene too much. All in all, then, College Green manages to raise itself, lumberingly and in spite of its unpromising surroundings, from being a mere cacophonous intersection raked by traffic morning, noon and night; it becomes something a little different, for those with a chance to pause and to glance around. There are even plans to ban traffic from the area in the future, which would change the character of this space remarkably, and for the better.

And best of all the buildings and features that fence this open space are the grand colonnades and sweeping curves of the Palladian Bank of Ireland building that faces Trinity on the north side of College Green, and that helps to lend the area a distinctive class and dimension of grace and surprise. This beautiful building is as impressive within as it is without and would appear, moreover, to be an amazingly grandiose home for a bank. It turns the mundane business of lodging a cheque or the humiliating business of applying for an overdraft into something resembling a treat. As you climb the stone steps towards the long wooden doors that are recessed into the imposing colonnade, clip down the long corridors and through spacious lobbies, passing uniformed attendants and carefully tended fires in sparkling fireplaces and so at last into the beautiful double-height banking hall in the centre of the building, nothing, in the midst of this splendour, seems so very bad. Even as you check your bank balance and blanch, even as the bank manager refuses your request for a loan – even so, amid marvellous surroundings, life comes into focus a little more.

Banks, of course, love nothing more than to spend their customers' money on lavish corporate headquarters for themselves. The truth is, however, that this great building was not custom-built for the Bank of Ireland. The corporate world arrived a little later, for this sweeping building is the eighteenth-century Parliament House for Dublin and for Ireland. It was the first purpose-built bicameral parliament building in Europe; one of the finest and most coherent pieces of architecture in the city, and the focus of an emergent and energetic national politics in eighteenth-century Dublin. As for the bank – well, that was something of a johnny-come-lately.

The city's new Parliament House symbolises the altering allegiances and political debates and historical ironies of these years. The Irish Parliament, as we have seen, was responsible for a flood of penal-oriented legislation issuing from its doors. As the century rolled on, however, it also came to represent an altogether different politics: one that stood for reform, a shifting sense of identity and the possibility of achieving a different relationship between Ireland and Britain. These debates ran alongside each other for most of the eighteenth century – and the Parliament House housed them both, sealing in the process its ambivalent position in Irish history.

The reforming lobby in the Parliament was not after plain political independence for Ireland. It was nothing so simple or so complex as this, but rather a form of gradual economic independence that would rectify the situation that had developed in the country in the years following the Cromwellian settlement, in which the Irish economy became dependent on, and distorted by, the influence of Britain. The Woollen Act, shepherded through a docile Irish Parliament in the early years of the century, has already been mentioned, as has its devastating impact upon a nascent Irish weaving industry. Other industries too, including tanning and the manufacture of glass, were similarly penalised by legislation that forbade the import of such goods from Ireland. The aim was simple and protectionist in nature: to preserve evolving trades in Britain, at this crucial moment at the very onset of an industrial revolution, from being undercut by cheaper and hungrier industry in Ireland. And in broader and more general terms: to keep the island of Ireland as a whole well under the thumb of a colonial authority.

It is possible to trace back the creation of the new Parliament House in Dublin to this particular context, and to see a response in its design and rapid construction. As historians always note, this building – at once marvellously original and rooted in classical design – was imagined and then created within a matter of a few years following its foundation in 1729; and the Irish Parliament was sitting in its new palace while the Westminster Parliament was still meeting in its grotty and disintegrating Whitehall quarters. (And there it is again, incidentally – the Irish parliamentary building was better than that of London, to the infinite satisfaction of all.) A more potent symbol of national authority it is impossible to imagine.

Of course this overstates the matter. The Irish Parliament was no great reforming chamber – far from it; its members were to a man members of the Established Church who owed their position and authority to the patronage and benevolence of the Crown, and that was that. But there did exist a spirit in the eighteenth-century city that was dedicated to the protection of Irish interests, a spirit most usefully exemplified in Swift's *Drapier Letters*. And this spirit found expression within the Parliament itself, in the form of a faction that became increasingly dedicated, as the century wore on, to the notion of carving out for Ireland a space for manoeuvre, politically and economically. Eventually, this faction won concessions from the Crown, although the victory was brief enough. Viewed in hindsight, then, it is understandable that the new Parliament House should come to symbolise this new tide in Irish affairs, when Dublin moved from being a mere colonial centre into a political capital in its own right. It is useful symbolism too, as far as it goes.

By mid-century, affairs had taken on a momentum of their own; Parliament was by this time meeting annually, and by 1779 the reform element in Parliament, led by Henry Flood and Henry Grattan, had secured a repeal of the restrictions on the woollen and glass trades, and had won the right for free trade between Ireland and other British colonies. Even more significantly, in 1783 the Renunciation Act was passed in Westminster stating that, henceforth, Ireland owed its allegiance not to another parliament but to the British monarch alone. This legislative independence attained by the Irish Parliament seemed to initiate an entirely new era in the relationship between the two countries, with a colonial era replaced by what Burke called 'a natural, cheerful alliance'.

These were heady times and heady measures, and the building on College Green became an important focus of legislative and national energy. But the assembly remained, in many ways, as unreformed as ever; and it is important to note that the reformist faction was not by any means democratic. It approved of the measure to extend the franchise, in a very limited way, to include Catholics, but was certainly not in favour of extending it any further. Rather, the franchise would be based, as it always had been, on the man of property. The parliamentary reform agenda – the meeting of minds of Protestant, Catholic and Dissenter – was principally economic in its focus and aspirations. It was still significant for all that, marking a sea change and the bracing bite of modernity in Ireland's political culture – but it is as well to emphasise its limits.

The electrified political scene abroad, exemplified in the French Revolution and its aftermath, put paid to this modestly changing agenda in Ireland, and the role of the reformers and of the Irish Parliament itself were sidelined by more direct action. The last decade of the eighteenth century was a remarkable one for Dublin – remarkable, that is, for the sheer energy in the air. The building of the city was continuing apace, and as rapidly as ever, even as the political temperature was rising and the backlash against the French Revolution was radicalising a new generation of Irish reformers. In this sense, it is possible to see the situation in Ireland mirroring, and responding to, the new political and cultural situation across Europe. The new Society of United Irishmen, which first met in Belfast in 1791 and which was rapidly established in Dublin, was strongly influenced by the principles of the American and French Revolutions. It was founded upon principles of national unity and inclusion, irrespective of religion, and was dedicated to independence for Ireland and to the elimination of the last vestiges of the Penal Laws.

This was not at all a wish list designed to appeal to the British authorities at Dublin Castle who were, at that moment, reacting sharply to the revolutionary events taking place in France; and throughout the 1790s this reaction played out in ways that would reverberate in Irish history. The United Irishmen went underground from the middle of the decade and feelers were put out to the French authorities to assist in a revolt against British rule. A French fleet was stormbound off the south coast in 1796 before retreating in disarray, and the British authorities responded to this close shave by cracking down brutally against all dissension in Ireland. The eventual United Irish uprising in the spring of 1798 was broken by the British and its leaders were exiled or killed. During this period, the authorities used the Royal Exchange (now City Hall), on the perimeter of the Castle itself, as a place of interrogation in which information could be extracted by torture, when 'the screams of the sufferers might have been audible in the very offices where the Ministers of the Government met to perform their functions'.

The final act of this drama was played out in the Parliament House two years later, on 15 January 1800. The rebellion of 1798 had persuaded the British authorities that Ireland's Anglo-Irish elite could no longer be persuaded to run Ireland safely and well, and a new dispensation now became inevitable. The Irish Parliament was convened once more on College Green, this time to vote for its own abolition and to approve the merger of the British and Irish states into one United Kingdom. After close to a century of legislative energy and excitement, however, this debate was less than glorious. A first vote narrowly failed, and it is recorded by contemporary sources that the second vote, the one that secured the Union, was bought by bribes and the promise of peerages. Some things, clearly, never change. Grattan hauled himself from his sickbed to speak for two fiery hours in opposition to the notion, but to no avail – the motion was passed by 158 votes to 115. On 1 January 1801 the Irish Parliament ceased to exist. The Bank of Ireland took possession of the now forlorn Parliament House two years later, under the proviso that the building be restructured so that it could never again be used as a seat of parliament.

It was a miserable end to such a fiery chapter in the history of Dublin. For its parliament to abolish itself, for the city to fall overnight from being a national capital to being a mere provincial population centre, for a flight to begin of capital and power from Dublin to London – it was a startling change in fortune. What can also be said, however, is that not all was lost – the power may have gone, but its political and physical legacies nonetheless remained; and the ideas explored and debated in these years could not be bottled up again.

PART THREE

The Liffey twists inside its stone confines,
heedless. It has long since abjured protest,

saving images of nothing
but the rains and whimsy of a city sky.

It gains a wider heaven at the bay perhaps,
but at its own expense.

'Sunday' Caitríona O'Reilly[1]

PART FIVE

Chapter 13

THE GREEN

If you climb up onto the roof of my apartment building late in the afternoon on this, the last day of October, you will see the last colour dying back: the climbing hydrangea is yellowing and the hostas are yellow too and fading, and the dahlia tubers must be uprooted soon and left upside down to dry, before being stored for the winter. Across the road in the little park, the trees are not quite bare, not yet, after our long, surprisingly stretched autumn weather, but certainly beginning to show their winter lines. The beeches are stripping themselves down; the chestnuts are hanging in valiantly, though knee-deep now in their vast, damp leaves and glossy fruit.

When I was up here on an evening in midsummer, with a glass of well-chilled white wine clutched greedily in my paws – only a couple of months ago, although it feels like a century distant on this murky afternoon – I leaned out over the rail into the warm air and listened to someone playing bagpipes in the park. Someone, but I never saw who it was through the thick screen of tossing leaves; and they played for half an hour, maybe, before they packed up and vaulted over the sharp iron railings and headed off into the summer twilight. After every bagpiped tune, I could hear someone clapping – and I clapped too. Not that I like the sound

of bagpipes (not at all, not in the very least) but I could appreciate them on that fine, still evening.

I lean out over the rail now and look out into the autumn view.
The light is failing, the oncoming winter in the city a little more
distinct in its shadows and dulling colours. But the line of those
plum-blue hills is still clear and I can see the tall steeple of the
Catholic chapel away in Ranelagh, a mile or so to the south, glint-
ing bright even on this dark day; and closer at hand, the sober
spire of the Anglican church at Leeson Park; and to the east the
square tower of St Mary's, handsome and ornately Victorian, on
Haddington Road. I can see now too the leaf-strewn grass of the
park through the thinning trees and beyond them – but close at
hand – I can see the line of the Grand Canal too, Roman-straight
as it zips from east to west in front of me. The barge that moors
permanently on this stretch of the canal has already undertaken
its seasonal morphing from nightly party venue into floating
restaurant. Too late in the year now to huddle on the narrow open
deck in coats and scarves, but the intimate, long cabin below looks
pretty good (I've thought as I've picked my way along the towpath
on dark evenings and peeked enviously through portholes at the
polished fittings and warm orange light) and the menu looks not
half bad either. Come Thursday evenings, though, and the barge
still puts on its party dress of fairy lights, even as winter draws on,
and undertakes its weekly cruise; into the lock it goes and the lock
gates shut behind it and it sinks down and out of sight and away
off in the direction of the canal basin a mile away – to return a
couple of hours later, its happy diners a little more flushed and
well fed than when they departed.

Standing up here on the roof and looking out at the city, I avert
my gaze from the still-empty development site next door. Maybe,
if I don't think about it, it will go away – the building that is
doubtless being planned at this very moment on some computer
in some office in the city, the construction work, the vast pit in the

ground that will house a two-storey subterranean car park – and that's before the building even begins to go up. But no, not likely. Dublin has expanded massively throughout the twentieth century and development continues intensively today too, as developers snatch at little parcels of land and build on them; and so it will happen here too.

In spite of this expansion, though, the centre of Dublin remains as that small area contained within the ring canals – the Royal Canal that curls around the north and the Grand Canal that curls around the south and empties into the Liffey a mile away to the east. Look at a map of the city of Dublin and these two canals instantly bestow on the city a sense of cosy intimacy. It is an odd description to peg to a map but true all the same, for the sleek, sleepy curve of the two waterways wrapped around the city centre has always reminded me of a cat slipping its tail around itself to stay warm. On the ground, in the corporeal, flesh-and-blood Dublin, of course, the canals are rather less sleepy. Today, traffic roars up and down alongside both waterways, and they are far from being watery idylls.

The Grand Canal was completed in the middle years of the eighteenth century, the Royal early in the nineteenth. Both stretch west from the city across the flat midlands of Ireland to connect with the line of the river Shannon; and both part of an ambitious system of inland waterways created across the entire island in those years. Instead of a long and unpleasant overland journey to and from Dublin, it became possible to slip along in a certain style – albeit a slow one, for it took a full 12 hours to travel from Dublin to Mullingar in the centre of the country at a stately three miles an hour. The food, alas, was nothing to exclaim over, 'a leg of mutton, nearly raw – a piece of carrion salt beef – a small bit of good bacon – three fowls – the port bad – the cider like vinegar, the porter was good',[1] although happily, wine was served by the pint.

By virtue of the traffic on their waters and the lives lived along their banks, these twin canals stood witness to the changing texture of Irish society in these years – the gradually rising political unrest that preceded the Union, the tension that would build after it, the periods of hunger and of famine. Attacks on the barges that ploughed up and down the canals were not uncommon, and attacks on the very fabric of the canals themselves caused frequent ruptures to their banks. Troops were frequently stationed along the water in the nineteenth century in an attempt to limit damage, but to no avail. Clearly, we can glimpse the rising frustration of the canal managers early in the nineteenth century, as it becomes apparent that the authorities are either unwilling or unable to halt these attacks, which not infrequently took place within hailing distance of Dublin itself:

> On the night of Sunday 16 [1823] instant a laden boat on her way to the interior was scuttled and sunk by a tumultuous mob within ten miles of Dublin ... [T]o us it would seem to be a very reasonable expectation that any perpetration of a crime so vitally affecting the public welfare should be instantly followed by a general hue and cry, an active cooperation in the cause of public justice and the proclamation of adequate rewards ... [U]nless the government helps, the canal is hastening towards utter destruction.[2]

The waterways also point to the changing economics of Ireland and to a belatedly gathering environmental agenda. They were scarcely completed and swung into service before their time had passed, for they were rapidly supplanted first by the railways in the nineteenth century and then by the roads in the twentieth, with the result that they came close to disappearing entirely. Photographs taken in the 1960s paint a picture of miserable neglect: in the western outskirts of the city, abandoned locks and water channels have turned the waterways into nothing more than long, thin stretches of rush-choked swamp. The harbour basin at Portobello had already been infilled by the early years of the twentieth century. The harbour at St James's Gate, where the Guinness barges would moor and load up, was filled in 1974 and today the new lines of the LUAS trams run in its place. The nadir of this phase in the canals' history came with proposals to infill the Royal Canal and turn it into a motorway, and to drain the Grand Canal, lay a sewer in its bed and then build another roadway on top. Difficult to imagine in these days, of course – but both notions were seriously considered and only energetic lobbying stopped them from being passed.

Later, as the value of the canals became apparent, a process of restoration was undertaken – the last section of the Royal Canal is even now being fixed up. Today they are part of a system of inland waterways, impressively restored, with tentacles spread once more across Ireland. The canals, in fact, have become part of a political process. Acting, as they do, as channels both practical and symbolic connecting the two parts of Ireland, they benefit from both Irish and British funding. It is possible today to sail from Dublin to Limerick on the west coast, first on the Grand Canal and then on the broad Shannon; and with the impending restoration of the Ulster Canal now on the cards, it will soon be possible to go by inland waterway all the way from Dublin to the north coast. These canals appeal to the romantic in all of us.

The Grand and the Royal Canals are boons to Dublin specifically, and of all the manifold blessings bestowed on the city by such modest waterways, the most important are these: firstly, that water-girdled enclosure that they bring to the centre of Dublin, an element in that breathing intimacy that has always been the city's principal trademark; and second, the current of green, of light, of air, of cascading water that they channel through into the city. They influence and stir the mood of passers-by – and not merely through the familiar sight of a brood of tiny fur-ball ducklings on the water in the spring, or scarlet-legged and scarlet-beaked moorhens darting panicked across one's path in the summer, or enormous swans laid out asleep on the very towpath in the winter. One can sense the influence the water brings from a simple crossing of the narrow black-and-white painted bridge over the lock at Baggot Street, where there is space for only one person to cross at a time. A moment of striking grace – otherwise so rare – as one pedestrian waves another across with a brief grin and answers a 'thank you' with an old-fashioned inclination of the head. It must be the positive ions released by the falling water. And today, there is even an occasional organic market on the towpath on Fridays and regular clean-ups of the banks by the Friends of the Grand Canal.

The waters and environs of the Grand Canal are thick with literary associations. In *Seven Winters*, her memoir of a Dublin Edwardian childhood, Elizabeth Bowen describes her 'beat' as a child, up and down the towpath from her winter home on Herbert Place as far as Leeson Street Bridge and back. My section of the canal and hers too, although she had a governess to accompany her perambulations and I do not. 'One joy,' she writes:

> complete with the ingredient of terror, was to watch a barge go through a lock. The barge sank down intrepidly with the waters into a sucking pit I was not allowed to approach. The gates could be felt straining. Then the barge slowly appeared again, with the black standing man on it still impassive, nothing further written upon his face. We would walk along in admiration beside it as, negligently dragging its slow ripple, it now continued upon its way.[3]

Bowen writes too of the waters of the canal reflected on the high ceilings of her family home on Herbert Place, rippling in pale Dublin winter sunlight through the storeys of the high, narrow house.

Until comparatively recently, Parson's bookshop sat perched on Baggot Street Bridge, acting as a magnet to all and sundry: to Frank O'Connor and Liam O'Flaherty who lived here, in this very building; and to Patrick Kavanagh, who nipped in and out of the bookshop on a daily basis. Kavanagh famously understood the value of this water – and here, now, as I lean out from the roof and look down onto the canal that is dark on this dark day, I can see him, reclining in bronze on his seat by the towpath. Starbucks understands this too, as I noticed a few hours ago when I called into their new branch just over the lock, to see what all the fuss was about, you understand. The macchiato and frappuccino and the coffee both Fair and unFair are just as they would be in Seattle, naturally, and the firm has already rolled out its Christmas products too, all neatly packaged in red – so all is as it should be in Starbucks World.

The café, though, has gone some little way to bend to its local environment: Kavanagh's 'Lines Written on a Seat on the Grand Canal, Dublin' is emblazoned on a wall beside the canal-facing window. It is touching, I think, in spite of myself. I feel a little less frosty, I unbend a very little – though to be sure, it doesn't seduce me into buying a gingerbread-flavoured latte.

I go back home a little later on, and as I cross the lock, the water that rushes beneath the damp timbers still roars Niagarously. The water is dark on this dark day and not green as it was for him – but in the gloomy autumn light, I see the white splash of a pair of swans, a hundred metres away. I pause beside Kavanagh and pick a few yellowing and sodden leaves from his bronze hat. History rushes on, but it is well sometimes to stop, to take stock and a deep breath, and look at the falling water and the greenness.

— ◄◦► —

Hallowe'en comes and goes, bringing its usual harvest of exploding firework burns. And terrified domestic animals: the red setter, for example, clearly hysterical, that rushed past me last night in the darkness on Baggot Street. A cold front slides silently south across the island, bringing frost in its wake after this long, cool, still October. Suddenly, there is ice in the air.

It is still calm as I walk home from town through St Stephen's Green in the fading light, with the last of the day's cold sunshine gilding the tops of the trees. The park is still full of colour, but autumn seems now to hang by a thread; the leaves and the helicopter seeds from the sycamores are crisp and dry underfoot, and a few hours of strong winds would strip the trees and bring winter, definitively, at last. There are two girls by the edge of the lake (willow-fringed, romantic, rustic stone bridge and all); one is crouching on the edge of the water and watching the ducks, another stands, arms folded, a few steps back.

'Look at them,' says the first girl. 'Aren't they lovely?'

'I hate birds,' says the other.

'You can't hate these birds – look at them. Look at the colours!'

'You just wait 'til you catch avian flu from them,' her pal says balefully, staring at the fowl before her. 'You'll hate 'em too, then.'

I swerve away a little from the edge of the water, as the hairs stand up and crackle on the back of my neck. I walk on, over the stone bridge and through the formal parterre of the Green, with its flower beds and fountains.

As I approach the great nineteenth-century gates on the south-eastern corner of the park at Leeson Street, I stop as usual for a moment at the sculpted fountain nearby. *The Three Fates*, set in bronze on a granite crag, are measuring and cutting the thread of man's destiny, while water gushes and curls around their feet and fills the stone-edged pool surrounding them. The fountain was a gift to the Irish state by the government of West Germany, in gratitude for assistance given in the dreadful aftermath of the Second World War; it is my favourite piece of sculpture in the city. But somebody has emptied detergent into the water and now a bursting mountain of foam covers the feet of the impassive *Fates*.

This miserable bottle of detergent, upended last night by a passing witch, maybe, or a vampire, or an Osama bin Laden lookalike, beard and all – this bottle serves to tick, neatly, another little box in my head. In fact, this November day has been filled with little such boxes. Take the article I read in the paper this morning, which announced that the Gulf Stream is slowing down. It stopped completely, in fact, for nine days in the summer of 2004; and nobody knows why, though it's a fair bet that the melting of the Greenland ice sheet had something to do with it. If it stops again, I'm told – and it may very well – we in north-western Europe will be plunged into everlasting winter. It will be 'like living in Canada', somebody said breathlessly – although this doesn't sound to me like a vision of Armageddon. Perhaps we'll get perfectly regulated Canadian-style lifestyles and public health service as a result? Tick.

I also read in the paper that, far from lowering its carbon emissions in the aftermath of Kyoto as it should have done, Ireland has actually increased these emissions by 23 per cent in ten years. That's one of the highest increases in the industrialised world. Tick. A new motorway is planned that will slice through the hinterland of the Hill of Tara, the ancient seat of the High Kings of Ireland. A new terminal building at Dublin Airport has just been granted planning permission and should be up and running within a couple of years, increasing a thousandfold the number of planes arriving and departing the city. Meanwhile, President Bush has confided to the White House press corps that he likes to use 'the Google' to look at aerial views of his ranch at Crawford, Texas. Tick, tick, tick. And, while all these straws have flown in the wind, I have just paid to be horrified at the cinema by Al Gore and his *An Inconvenient* [and terrifying] *Truth*. Now, I walk through the gloaming, through a darkening Green foaming with detergent.

The world is coming to an end, as it seems. But no. Be comforted, for at least the Green will always be around, even if we're not there to see it.

So they say, anyway. This is the thing about great, set-piece city parks the world over: they are designed to lull citizens into a false sense of history and security. And so it is in Dublin too, where St Stephen's Green – with its fine stands of mature trees, its lake, its lawns and old stone bridge – was always here, will always be here – enjoy it. All nonsense, of course. Time and the authorities giveth, and time and the authorities can taketh away too; and we should take nothing for granted.

The Green holds a particular status in Dublin. We do not have a city centre blessed with abundant green space – no great green lung of a Central Park or Hyde Park or Englischer Garten for Dublin, more's the pity; and on a hot summer day, the extravagantly stretching expanse of the Phoenix Park is too far away from the central city to count. This lack of parkland is especially noticeable north of the river, where you would have to walk quite a distance to find an expanse of green. Arrangements south of the river are a little better, since the streetscapes and squares that come along with the Georgian city bring a little space in their wake: the park at Merrion Square that is today open to the people, the park at Fitzwilliam Square that is good to look at (but please do not touch). Add to this the playing fields and park behind the railings at Trinity; and the almost secret oasis of the Iveagh Gardens, hidden behind its grey stone walls; and St Stephen's Green, still lined in part with its eighteenth- and nineteenth-century buildings – and you have your quotient of southern parkland. Bracket them all together, and count your blessings.

The Green is an impressive space. I step away from its easy familiarity, sometimes, and look anew at the immense, surprising scale of this marvellous city square. Its perimeters are beech-lined, its walks lined with tall and gnarled limes, its central spaces home to those water birds that have murder in mind, those fountains, playgrounds and summer concerts. An average Dublin day has been captured by many artists over the years, James Malton's eighteenth-century depictions of aristocratic leisure giving way to contemporary urban images displayed, alfresco on the park railings, by painters on Sunday afternoons. And the Green's scale and weight also anchors the south city centre. The ancient city arteries of Leeson Street and Baggot Street run into it from the south and east; the shops of Grafton Street beckon on its north-west corner; the museums and parliamentary district are a stroll away to the north; weighty hotels and all manner of lofty institutions line up along its edges; and one of the city's new and gleaming tram lines terminates on the western edge.

As in Merrion Square, the park is sprinkled with bronze busts and statuary innumerable: the *Fates* in the south-east corner of the park compete with Wolfe Tone, set against a rough hedge of granite in the north-east corner; James Joyce's head is set on the southern side of the park, facing his former university haunt; Constance Markiewicz, Anglo-Irish aristocrat turned Irish nationalist who was second-in-command of the Irish Citizen Army contingent that occupied the Green in the Easter Rising and who went on to become the first woman elected to the British House of Commons and then the first female Cabinet minister in Irish political history – she is set close to the centre of the park. And so on. You could spend a long afternoon poking around the memorials established in the Green and still not see them all.

The Green, though, long predates those other squares and parks with which it is so easily bracketed. It has been practically and symbolically significant in the history of the city for centuries, ever since it was first noted in the records of medieval Dublin. In this first glimpse into its history, the Green is a common, to be used freely by all citizens as a grazing land and pasturage – free to all, owned by all, and in this way very different in its genesis to the park, say, at Merrion Square, which never was freely owned and which is not freely owned even today. And this ghostly history echoes in modern Dublin, because the Green is always more lively, more agreeably informal and more bustling than Merrion Square ever is; more democratic, maybe, in deference to an expansive past. The medieval period also saw raucous public hangings on this old common, of course, a tradition that lasted until the end of the eighteenth century. We shall say a good deal less about this, though, lest it undermine our cheery portrait of the place. The same goes for the name: the old common was named for St Stephen's leper hospital that stood nearby. Not, then, altogether salubrious.

The history of the Green as a formal city square, however, only began in 1663, with the decision of the Corporation of Dublin to enclose the common. It was a move that was economically motivated; in those sluggish days, at the beginning of the slow transition from colony and enclave into capital city, the civic authorities needed to do something to bring in revenue and jump-start the economy. Enclosing the old common and flogging the land around it in lots would, it was felt, do the trick. And it did too — building work began in the following year and money began flowing into the city's coffers.

The enclosure of the Green achieved what the act of enclosure always brings in its wake: it took land that had been held in common ownership and silently changed its position. Ostensibly still public land, the Green was in fact now under private control, and its use was, as a result, now strictly on sufferance. It was a sufferance seldom exercised, of course, for people are rarely ejected rudely from city parks – but it was a crucial change just the same. From now on, others – those who truly owned and controlled this land – would decide the form and destiny of the park, which had now become much more tangibly a useful economic asset.

The development of the Green at this point in the seventeenth century is also interesting in terms of the particular vision that was implemented. For one thing, the space was laid out as a square and this was in itself highly significant, ushering in a style of city planning that would become a specific Dublin trademark in the years to come. It also branded the city's development as explicitly European in style, for the urban square as theorised a little later by Palladio was crucial to correct urban development: it functioned as a space in which paid-up citizens might meet, greet, live, do business and pursue a genteel style of leisure. It acted as both focus and urban adornment, thus bringing into play in Dublin the twin assets of industry and pleasure.

Moreover, the Corporation was concerned from the very beginning to attract the right kind of residents to its new city scheme. The plots that were to be let and developed along the perimeter of the square were more than usually generous in scale; and the houses that slowly rose on these plots were consequently larger and more elaborate than had been seen previously in the city. Even before Dublin's massive eighteenth-century building frenzy had begun – even before Marsh's Library was built, or the Royal Hospital, or any of the city's signature buildings appeared on the scene – a blueprint for the city's future was being laid out on the site of this old medieval common.

Development proceeded slowly enough, in spite of these grand plans – but by 1740 or thereabouts, three sides of the square had been built up, and the south side was under way. These new elevations were far from uniform, consisting instead of a hotchpotch of styles and standards that were a far cry from the sleeker lines of later developments. At the same time, the gardens were being laid out. The new residents of the Green were required to plant a certain number of trees as part of their contract of ownership, for example, and broad and fashionable promenades had been laid along the edges of the new park. And of course, the usual comparisons with London followed, as night will follow day: the Sunday promenade in the Green was as agreeable as a stroll in

St James's Park, so it was said, and St Stephen's Green itself beat Lincoln's Inn Fields, on the glamour and dimension stakes, hands down.

The Green would never wholly lose its air of agreeable pleasure, even if the nineteenth century saw its temporary aura of exclusivity sloughed off in favour of a more expansive sense of possession. By mid-century, the gentry was being replaced in these great town houses by men of trade, and the park was becoming a little scruffier than it was in its posh days. Visitors complained of seeing cattle set to graze the grass, of the occasional dead animal tossed in the park ditches, of the gloomy shadows cast by the now mature sycamores and limes – and in all, it was high time for another vision of the park to be implemented.

In the 1870s, then, the Green assumed a new form. Sir Arthur Guinness, who occupied a town house on the south side of the Green, was the driving force behind this latest and more influential development of the park. The lake was excavated, ornamented with its antique stone bridge, filled with water from the nearby canal and stocked with wildfowl. Willows were planted to provide the necessary touch of romanticism and the park was subdivided into tree-studded lawns and wide avenues circling a central parterre. Bandstands were created for concerts on summer afternoons and, in short, the park assumed the form it still possesses today, give or take a bust or two. Not that everyone was altogether impressed; in *A Drama in Muslin*, George Moore acidly describes 'the weary, the woebegone, the threadbare streets – yes, threadbare conveys the moral idea of Dublin in 1882. Stephen's Green, recently embellished by a wealthy nobleman with gravel walks, mounds and ponds, looked like a school-treat set out for the entertainment of charity children.'[4]

Moore might have been better pleased with the scenes that accompanied the Easter Rising, when the set-piece tranquillity of the park was interrupted by the men and women of the Irish

Citizen Army digging trenches across its lawns. They would eventually realise the inadequacy of their situation – wide-open grassy parks and urban warfare do not mix well, trenches or no trenches – and would hole themselves up in the Royal College of Surgeons on the Green's western edge. The British army, meanwhile, took up positions in various other buildings overlooking the park and the two sides settled down to a good deal of urban warfare before the final surrender. Evidence of this warfare is clearly evident even today: the porticoed front of the College of Surgeons is still riddled with bullet marks, for instance, as is the granite Royal Dublin Fusiliers' Arch, established in 1907 on the north-western corner of the Green to commemorate the Boer War.

On the first day of that sunny Easter week, according to Elizabeth Bowen, afternoon tea carried on in the Shelbourne Hotel regardless. We must take these recollections with a grain of salt, naturally – there being more than a touch of the stiff upper lip in them. But there is something undeniably fascinating in the image of well-heeled patrons returning from the races at Fairyhouse outside the city to find Constance Markiewicz, fully aware of the theatricality of what was unfolding, parading up and down in front of the hotel's vast windows with her rifle on her shoulder.

This practice – fascinating to many, for lady colonels were rarer then than now – she was to continue for several days of what became by degrees the siege of the Shelbourne. The fact that British troops were moving into position all around the Green, ready to shoot from houses or along confluent streets, did not apparently for some time deter her. It is the stern opinion of some of the hotel staff that 'the Countess took unfair advantage of her sex'.[5]

The theatricality would subside as the week progressed. The Countess would vanish and the coffee-drinkers retreat to safer quarters at the rear of the hotel; and the army would haul a machine gun up to the roof of the hotel, the better to rake the park below. This, for a week, was deadly earnest.

Today, it is Moore's embellished and despised Victorian Green that has stood the test of time – the most hard-wearing incarnation of an ostensibly eternal and immutable square. The Guinness restoration was an indication, however, that the form of this precious green space has been ever-changing and in the gift of others; it was only the latest assertion of ownership by a governing city oligarchy. It may seem a rather heavy-handed affair, to theorise in such terms the possession of what is in other ways one of the most cheerfully democratic spaces in the city of Dublin. But consider: this square of parkland, this Green that we are naturally tempted to consider permanent and unchanging, yet that has changed constantly over the centuries, the form of this park is now under assessment once more, and will most likely be drastically altered at the wish of those same authorities that have controlled it down the years.

This present threat is bound up with Dublin's chronic traffic congestion and the plans now under way to solve it, once and for all. The area around St Stephen's Green has long been pivotal in these city-wide plans, because a major public transport interchange is planned for the area, one that will help to integrate properly the city's presently pitifully organised transport system. I should say this interchange is planned for under the area, for the scheme involves digging a vast hole in the ground to house a large station that would be – so runs the rather fanciful description – Dublin's answer to Grand Central Station. And here's the rub: it seems more than likely that a decision will be made to sacrifice a large chunk of the Green – 25 per cent – to the process of excavating, tunnelling and constructing this great interchange. This phase in the park's history would be temporary, naturally, and the damage caused by the building work would be set right. But excavations would be considerable and lengthy, and the damage that would be inflicted on the park's fabric would be – well, it would be not quite irreversible, but trees do not grow back overnight.

A necessary evil? If so, then it would be a shame but understandable, for cities develop and sacrifices must occasionally be made to their fabric in order to construct a bigger picture. But it is more appropriate to label this projected chewing up of a section of the Green as an unnecessary evil. Many engineers think so, at any rate, for there is a very great deal of street space on the west side of the Green – space where the tram lines now terminate – that might be constructively used to build as large a station as is required. Perhaps it is not actually necessary to interfere with the park at all. But don't bet on it, for the decision has probably already been made.

Taken in a large historical context, the evolution and present state of St Stephen's Green offer certain salutary lessons: namely, that not everything is necessarily as it appears to be, and that the privileges granted to the people of a city – the 'charters' of William Blake – take away more than they bestow, removing authority and control from the people in the name of the public good. Like the remains of the Georgian city, Dublin's green spaces are gifts that have been bestowed by history, rather than rights to be taken for granted. And ironically, perhaps this means that it is even more worthwhile striving to preserve them intact.

I feel crowded around, then, by gloom on this frosty evening in November. A little like *The Three Fates* must feel, maybe, surrounded in their fountain on the edge of the park by a malignant pool of foaming bubbles. Will the Gulf Stream stop in its tracks? Don't know. Will the Greenland ice sheet melt completely? Don't know, but probably. Will St Stephen's Green always be here, with its lake and great trees and broad avenues? It all depends.

Chapter 14

CLEAR WATERS

The Green might be Dublin's principal city centre park, and it might come laden with symbolic and practical value, with statuary and flower beds and gushing fountains galore, with affection and love and now a measure of foreboding as well – but the Phoenix Park will always beat it into the dust when it comes to sheer scale. Seen on Google Earth, say, the park shows up as a circle with a tail stretching south-east towards the city centre, an enormous space that encompasses the whole north-western quadrant of the city. And before Dublin's twentieth-century expansion, of course, this was exactly the case: the park took up an expanse of land that was essentially as large as the city of Dublin itself.

Consider the following and see for yourself why, to statisticians and maintainers of useful lists of facts and figures, the Phoenix Park's vital statistics will eclipse those of any other Dublin park. So, it covers some 8 square kilometres of undulating land on the north bank of the Liffey, north and west of today's city centre. That's three square miles – or, if you prefer, 700-odd hectares. Or, if you are still imperially minded, 1,750-odd acres, or 16 kilometres (10 miles) of fully walled circumference. Add to this the 78 acres of the adjoining Farmleigh estate, bought by the state in 2001 from the Guinness family, and you get one of the biggest urban parks in Europe. Hurrah!

And the most satisfying crowning glory in this litany of useful facts is of course that the Phoenix Park is bigger than London's Green Park, St James's Park, Hyde Park and Regent's Park all combined. I have read this statistic so very many times, in fact – in this book and that book and another book, endlessly, over the years – that I decided I had to check it for myself. I did a sum and added my figures together. And it's true, the Phoenix Park is bigger, a good deal bigger, than all these other parks combined. Does it matter? Of course not. Not in the very least, in fact, but I thought I might as well keep the old traditions going strong, and cite it too.

Anyway, the crucial thing to remember about the Phoenix Park is that, like outer space, it's big. So extremely big, in fact, that you have to wonder how on earth a moderately sized city like Dublin ever happened to acquire such a vast expanse of land in the first place, much less hold on to it intact as the centuries rolled by. The answer, of course, lies in Dublin's history as an ecclesiastical centre and as a colonial capital: two threads that have entwined here and in the process contrived to preserve the park intact.

The origins of the park, which takes its name, incidentally, not from the mythical bird but from the Irish *fionn uisce*, which translates as 'clear waters', can be traced back to the city's own shadowy medieval past. Once the whole sweeping demesne encompassed land both north and south of the Liffey, and was in the possession of the Knights Hospitaller, the ruins of whose priory can still be seen in the grounds of the Royal Hospital. With the Reformation, the Knights were suppressed on the orders of Henry VIII and their lands confiscated by the Crown; thereafter the park would become a hunting ground for the monarch's representatives. The ghosts of this period can still be seen in the sturdy surrounding walls, which were designed to keep secure the deer with which the park was stocked. As one strident tour guide put it to me, the park became 'somewhere to house the king of

England's deer, where he could come over and hunt and have, kind of like, lavish hunting parties and, like, shooting parties in the summer months'. The southern portion of the park – much the smaller portion, happily – was carved away to provide land for the Royal Hospital. It was only in 1747, meanwhile, that the remaining land was opened to the people of the city, and its future as open land secured.

It was beginning to be understood that the Phoenix Park was a prized asset of the Georgian city now unfolding to its south and east. As the new Dublin treasured its expanding stock of precious civic buildings and wealth, so it treasured also the massive asset of nearby parkland. This evolving attitude had much to do with changing fashions, ideologies and tastes, for by the middle of the eighteenth century the notion of urban parkland was coming to be valued. New notions of public health meant that such a great expanse of green land was better appreciated, for it kept the populace healthy, vigorous and exercised and their lungs free of the pestilence that, so it was thought, seeped as a foul miasma from the city streets and houses. Better by far to go to a park and keep disease at arm's length.

It is an attitude neatly exemplified by William Ashford (1746–1824) in his striking painting of *A View of Dublin From Chapelizod*. Ashford romanticises the city, to be sure, offering us a view of dreaming spires and domes galore, the sea and hills far away and the Liffey, complete with waterfall, flowing through the midst of it all. Nevertheless, it is clear that Dublin is at its best when viewed from a happy distance, with nostrils and eyes unassailed by the stench and sight of urban poverty. Pride of place in the painting, therefore, is given to a large stag, generous of antler, which looms in the foreground as he munches his way through a notably sylvan Phoenix Park. Ashford, however, also manages to contextualise his park and city: behind the stag, a group of soldiers make their way up to the Magazine Fort, which is manned and hung with military banners; and the Royal Hospital and brand-new Kilmainham Gaol figure largely to the south. The rural idyll, therefore, is cut through with the cold, military reality of a colonial city – but equally, the park's beauty and worth remain intact.

At this same time, the future of the great park was also being settled by other means. It became the setting for a scattering of buildings that provided homes for the chief figures in the colonial administration in the burgeoning city of Dublin. As early as the beginning of the seventeenth century, the viceroy – the British monarch's representative in Ireland – had taken up residence in the 'Phoenix', a house lately built on a high bluff of land overlooking the Liffey, close to where the Magazine Fort stands today. The viceregal association with the park was at that time temporary, for within ten years the official residence would be moved to nearby Chapelizod, there to remain for the next hundred years or so. But a precedent of sorts had been set. By the middle of the eighteenth century, it was decided that the viceroy was in need of a still better refuge from the city and from the ceremony and state of Dublin Castle, and eventually the park was chosen as an ideal location for a summer residence. The viceroys would eventually be joined in the park by successive chief secretaries (essentially the prime ministers in the colonial administration) and by under-secretaries (the heads of the civil service) and both of these offices enjoyed the use of equally agreeable summer residences nearby.

All of these positions – viceroy, chief secretary, under-secretary – shared the identical aim of underpinning and securing British colonial control over Ireland, of course, but there was frequently tension between them. The viceroy, for instance, was in the happy position of having endless powers of patronage at his disposal. He could, if he was so minded, bypass the chief secretary's administration in Dublin Castle in order to fulfil his own agenda, thereby laying the entire administration open to disruption and confusion. Not always a happy relationship then, and it is amusing to think that the residences which the viceroy and chief secretary would come to occupy would be, even in the immensity of the Phoenix Park, so close to each other. Even in times of discord and strain, it seems, there could be little escape from government business.

The building fixed upon to house the viceroy had been built by Nathaniel Clements, close to the northern boundary of the park, and completed in 1754. Clements is an interesting character in these energetic years: as amateur architect, entrepreneur, and general mover and shaker, he was instrumental in the development of Henrietta Street and was the holder of a clutch of titles – Deputy Paymaster-General in Ireland, Deputy Vice-Treasurer and others – which brought power and patronage in their wake. To this portfolio was added, in 1751, the title of Chief Ranger of the Phoenix Park (a post for life) and Clements lost no time in building himself a residence in the highest area of the park, with fine views across the fields to the southern mountains.

Clements' house was an agreeable affair: sturdily built but with Palladian influences plain to be seen in the sweeping curved external walls that echoed the new Parliament House on College Green. Inside, the house was pleasant enough, featuring good plasterwork and top-lit vaulted ceilings that also reflected – even if they did not equal – the detail woven into the many fine buildings then being constructed down the road in Dublin. In short, then, little wonder that the colonial administration, following Clements' death and that of his wife, should negotiate for possession of the house, nor that his son Robert should eventually agree to sell the building to the Crown for £10,000.

Lord Carlisle was the first viceroy to occupy the new residence. As is the way with these sorts of arrangements, he almost immediately began to tinker with the house, making repairs, adding stuccowork and sundry other improvements. This was not enough for his successor, Lord Portland, who disliked the house and who attempted to rid himself of it by offloading it onto Henry Grattan, ostensibly in recognition for the legislative changes and independence that Grattan had helped to win for the Irish Parliament. Such a poisoned gift, needless to say, was refused. As a result, viceregal tinkering was instead continued year by year, with plasterwork added and removed, entrances inaugurated and fronts improved, wings added to celebrate royal visits (Victoria visited twice), gardens laid out and improved and disimproved, and the house generally and endlessly mucked about with as the years marched on. Some of its inmates would hate the residence and its relative isolation, some would relish its seclusion, bosky delights and distance from Dublin Castle and Dublin generally, and would eventually come to spend longer and longer periods of time in the Park, longer and longer periods away from the city itself. And so the house itself can be seen to be a cockpit of sorts through the stormy years of Irish history, witnessing deals done and broken, competence and incompetence, scandal and cruelty and ceremony enacted within its cool white walls.

The most famous or infamous of these episodes occurred, if not quite within those walls, then certainly within screaming distance of them, on the evening of 6 May 1882. The newly arrived chief secretary, Lord Frederick Cavendish, together with the new viceroy, Earl Spencer, had attended a meeting at Dublin Castle earlier in the evening. Spencer then set off by carriage for the Phoenix Park, while Cavendish, accompanied by the under secretary, Thomas Burke, decided to walk up from the castle through the city and the park to the Viceregal Lodge, where he was due for dinner later in the evening. Spencer had scarcely arrived at the Lodge when he heard screams coming from the other side of the palings and then a man was seen racing through the grounds of the residence calling, 'Mr Burke and Lord Frederick Cavendish are killed!'

They had indeed been killed, and in a most brutal manner too, their bodies cut and slashed with surgical knives. The killings had been carried out by the so-called Invincibles, a radical political splinter group. One of the group's members, James Carey, subsequently turned informer, and a year later six of the group were hanged at Kilmainham Gaol as a result of the information he had passed. Twenty more received life imprisonment and Carey himself was pursued and killed on board a ship off Cape Town in the following year.

The Phoenix Park murders had repercussions that rippled across the Irish political landscape and were instrumental in preventing the imminent introduction of Home Rule for Ireland. The British authorities could not be seen to be granting a form of autonomy to a country in which revolutionary acts could occur with seeming impunity. And there was a personal connection too: Cavendish was the nephew by marriage of the British prime minister and principal proponent of Irish Home Rule, William Gladstone.

Following Irish independence in 1922 the line of the viceroys came to an end. After a long period of uncertainty and in one of those strokes of masterful irony in which Irish history specialises, the Viceregal Lodge became the residence of the presidents of Ireland and was renamed Áras an Uachtaráin (the house of the president). Those centuries of mucking about have left their trace in the rather muddled interior and odd circulation spaces of today's house. But the porticoes, white walls and formal gardens of the residence's exterior present an agreeable sight as one walks or drives along the central avenue of the park. The careful planting that otherwise screens the Áras and its grounds are cut down at one point to allow a vista across the gardens to the south front; and when Mary Robinson became the first female president of Ireland in 1990, she utilised this view of the building as though it was a painting in a frame – and placed a light in a window where it could be seen from the park: a symbol to the Irish diaspora that it was not forgotten in Ireland itself. A pleasant house, then, rather than an immensely impressive or grandiose one. And so, perhaps, fully appropriate to the small state that is modern Ireland.

The former chief secretary's residence nearby is now the home to the American ambassador to Ireland, its private grounds today taking a substantial chunk out of the public parkland that surrounds it. It was here in the park, too, that Pope John Paul came in September 1979 to tell the assembled multitudes, 'Young people of Ireland, I love you!' The spot upon which he held his mass is now marked by a vast cross. Over one million people came to Dublin to see the Pope on that momentous day, and the event rather overshadows any other single episode – the murders included, maybe – in the history of the park. The Irish police service has its national headquarters in the Phoenix Park too, as does the Department of Defence, Dublin Zoo, the Ordnance Survey of Ireland and a good many more bodies besides – all nibbling sections out of the public space in the process. The former Guinness house at Farmleigh – dull and mediocre as it is, with nothing to recommend it either inside or out – has today become the State Guest House, lodging a variety of very important people for the duration of their visits to Dublin. Its pleasure grounds and associated buildings play host to all manner of exhibitions, farmers' markets, concerts and free public entertainments throughout the year.

The Phoenix Park, though, amounts to a good deal more than this clatter of facts and buildings, of presidents, viceregal lodges and popes. It is so connected to Dublin that it features repeatedly in the city's literature, used by Joyce and Kinsella and many others; and by Paul Durcan, who in his poem 'Making love outside Áras an Uachtaráin' imagines the Park as a place of sexual and social liberation, of rebellion against a repressive past – as an elderly and irascible President Eamon de Valera bears down on a young couple lying on the grass, bawling at them to desist from making love on the grass outside the Áras.

The park features too in episode after episode of civic history. Some of these – the Pope's visit and the political murders – are as electric as could be hoped for, while others instantly evoke the atmosphere and texture of an era. During the Second World War – Ireland's 'Emergency' – the city's stashes of coal and turf were stacked here, in great hills dotted across the parkland. The roads and lanes that criss-cross the park became heavily rutted by the wheels of lorries that ran through the grassland to take delivery of the precious fuel; these same lorries not only played havoc with the landscape but also damaged the roots of the park's long avenues of trees so that they slowly died in succeeding years. Great areas were given over to allotments, to enable the people of the city to feed themselves throughout these years of rationing. Other episodes are no less representative of the culture of the city – from the robbers and highwaymen that haunted the seventeenth- and eighteenth-century parkland to the preying muggers and the occasional murderers of today.

Approached from the city, the Phoenix Park appears stately, almost grand in appearance; the dourly enormous obelisk of the Wellington Testimonial stands close to the principal entrance gates and the central ceremonial avenue, still lit by gas lamps, stretches away up the hill and out of sight. Viewed from across the Liffey in Kilmainham, the park appears as a miraculous expanse of countryside, now open, now heavily wooded; there might be no city encompassing it at all. Once inside, the scene breaks down: an old man whistles for his recalcitrant dog by the lake in the People's Garden; a younger man bears an imposing toy boat down the steps to sail it on the water; a pair of women, clad for the weather, sip coffee outside the little kiosk by the zoo entrance.

Today, as one lies on the grass or strolls or jogs or saunters through its immensity, or walks purposefully by night, for the

Phoenix Park is also one of the city's main cruising grounds for sex, it is an easy matter to forget the surrounding city. For sure, the central avenue is usually busy with traffic – too busy, these days, for comfort; for sure, the zoo is filled to capacity during the summer months and cars are parked bumper to bumper around its entrance; for sure, summer rock concerts regularly bring swelling multitudes. But more often than not, the park can absorb these crowds with cool ease. Wander among the crossing lanes and paths and through heathland or woods, take in the air of unmani-cured shagginess, the herds of deer grazing just off to the left or the right, glimpse the sun shining on the threaded system of lakes on a frosty weekend morning or piercing through a summer canopy of leaves – and it becomes very easy indeed to imagine that the enveloping city has peeled away, somehow, never to be seen again.

Chapter 15

RIVERRUN

On a bitter afternoon late in November, I take an unaccustomed bus through the north inner city and out north and east, towards Clontarf and the hill of Howth in the distance. To the right of the bus lie the waters of Dublin Bay and then, a few hundred metres beyond, more land that rises up from the shoreline in a straight, keel-like, stone-edged bank: land belonging to the Port of Dublin and topped with gleaming new office buildings wrought of glass and steel. Beyond this again the candy-striped twin towers of the Pigeonhouse power plant puncture the sky.

This – this road, the land on both sides of the road, the new ground beyond that narrow channel of water protruding from Dublin Bay – this is all reclaimed land. Flat polder land, slowly taken from the sea over the course of a millennium, backed and walled by sea defences and then built on, densely. I know that between those glass-and-steel office buildings in the distance and the towers of the Pigeonhouse behind lies a tangled land of docks, dotted with cranes and stacked with containers painted in blue and white and cherry red and brought here from all over Europe – and then the channelled mouth of the Liffey itself. Today, a few yachts will lie at anchor in the mouth of the river, close to shore; maybe the looming ferry has come in from Wales and pulled smoothly into the North Wall, ready to disembark, or is just pulling away again, maybe, to make the fast crossing back again, churning up the sea as it goes. From my history and my research I know that this was all sea a thousand years ago; and common sense tells me that it might be sea again, one of these days.

The nomenclature betrays the elemental history of this part of Dublin. The North Wall and the East Wall, which have given their names to old working-class districts of the city, have always been heavily influenced by the sea and by labour, and criss-crossed with watercourses and railway lines and deep-delved harbour basins. Now, today, they are being pulled apart again and rebuilt as elements in Dublin's future as a newly packaged Docklands. They are lined and stacked, not with containers, but with apartment buildings and corporate headquarters that overshadow the existing tight networks of terraced houses. Today, there are no more boats decanting cargoes of Indian tea in the old harbours; instead, waterskiers cross these same basins, and new cafés dispense their lattes from waterfront sites.

As the bus makes its way along the seafront, I think of the corresponding land on the southern bank of the Liffey. On the maps, and in my mind's eye, the curving shores of Dublin Bay here becomes chunkily, extravagantly artificial, pushing out into the bay in large squares and rectangles that were also created by human hands to house the city's sprawling docks. The desolate road that runs down to the Pigeonhouse, for example, exemplifies this landscape, lined as it is with more containers that are piled like so many Lego bricks. Eventually, though, this road curves around to meet the sea once more and the natural shoreline begins to assert itself on the accumulated sands of Sandymount Strand, where beach and bars of sand stretch for miles at low tide and lonely walkers pick their way through pools of standing water, far out on the stretching shoreline. And above all of this, a vast sky that silently puts everything else in its place.

As I imagine this shoreline in my mind, the coast road bends around gradually and enters the seaside suburb of Clontarf – pleasant, well heeled, with a grassy promenade stretching away north and east before me, into the distance. The reclaimed land on the opposite side of the channel abruptly comes to an end and sea takes its place, but only momentarily; Bull Island picks up where the office buildings and keel-like sea wall stop, and cuts out the horizon. The shoreline of Dublin Bay is nothing if not complicated.

The bus decants me after a few more moments and I cross the busy coast road and step out onto an odd wooden bridge, picturesque in its rickety lines and hollowness. I shrug further into my collar and scarf and step out with the chill wind at my back, across the bridge, along another artificial shoreline. To my right – to the west and south – the water frets and chops against a smooth stone bank; to the left – to the east and north – Bull Island stretches out as dunes and undulations, all stitched together by coarse grass. The wind blows in visible, silver-green waves through the tussocks as I walk south along this straight-edged coastline. I feel as though I am walking out to sea, and so, in a way, I am. This straight coastline, this straight path – this is the Bull Wall – one of the two great sea walls that stretch out across the mouth of the Liffey, which seem, on the maps, to hold the sea and the river in a pincer grip.

The wind picks up as I walk. Bull Island to my left ends in the wide stretch of Dollymount Beach, where one or two hardy individuals are flying their kites in the snapping wind. And then suddenly I have the sea on both sides and the wind hurries me along and sings past my ears. I pass one person, two people; one or two more were walking their dogs on the beach, but it is too cold for crowds. I pass little bathing pavilions to right and left, which look as though they have been sculpted out of the stone. The progeny of the 1950s, from the look of them, and weathered now, but still useable. Stone steps lead down into the water; some are for 'gentle-men' and others for 'ladies'; and I am reminded – though I can't think why – of James Bond and of Princess Grace of Monaco. It must be the faint sigh of 1950s lidos and glamour that these fading bathing pavilions still exude, although I am willing to bet a good deal of money that Princess Grace of Monaco never picked her way down Dublin's Bull Wall to swim from the ladies' bathing place.

After walking for another ten or so minutes, the Bull Wall comes to a sudden end in front of my feet. It seems to sink down into the water, in fact, for the line of the wall continues its sub-terranean way out into the sea; it is marked, Loch Ness Monster-like, only by a line of jagged rock breaking the waves. But the public path ends here. It too is marked, however, and in a most characterful way: a three-legged plinth, maybe 18 metres (60 feet) high, rises on the end of the breakwater. This plinth is topped by a statue of a female, crowned by 12 stars. Is it a statue of Princess Grace of Monaco? Or a prescient symbol, maybe, of the European Union? No indeed, this lady is the Virgin Mary herself. The Star of the Sea. This statue, however, is gazing not east, not to protect those in peril on the sea – but inland, towards the city of Dublin.

I linger for a while in the chilly wind, taking in the complicated view before me. Straight ahead is the cheery brick-red of the Poolbeg Lighthouse, which marks the tip of the South Wall – the second of these two pincers protecting the mouth of the Liffey. Beyond this again is the southern half of the city of Dublin: white and brightly coloured seaside terraces, block-like office buildings, television transmitters and a flecking of yachts close to the great sea walls of Dun Laoghaire harbour on the southern side of Dublin Bay, and all backed and completed by the line of the moun-tains. To the west lies the reclaimed land and the cranes and towers of the Port of Dublin. Behind me, the stretch of Dollymount Beach and of the dunes and grasses of Bull Island. A wide, commanding and exhilarating view; and it is difficult to believe that so much of this wide shoreline exists as the direct result not of natural processes but of centuries of human intervention and labour.

— ◄o► —

Dublin, like every city the world over, has altered its natural environment to suit itself and to enable itself to grow and survive. The reason that these endless human interventions were necessary in the first place is that the bay and the harbour at Dublin were never perfectly designed to suit the needs of a capital city. For centuries, indeed, shipping entering the bay bound for Dublin faced an ordeal of shallows and shoals and contrary tides and winds in order to enter the mouth of the Liffey, and so along to the quays of the city. Rather than imperil themselves and their ships indeed – and you can't blame them – many preferred to offload their cargoes at the old harbour on the north side of the hill of Howth, or at the superior chain of little anchorages around Dalkey village on the south side of the bay, and bring their goods up to Dublin by road, regardless of the additional expense involved.

In the medieval city itself, there had been tentative public works intended to create a tolerable anchorage for shipping. The Liffey in its lower stretches began to be narrowed and channelled progressively: wooden walls were driven into the bed of the river and the spaces behind them filled with earth and rubble that were compacted and then built upon; and in this makeshift manner, the Liffey itself began to be slowly tamed, narrowed and deepened, and precious land reclaimed for building. But these were, at first, only small works of engineering and limited to the beginnings of the areas we now know as Wood Quay and Merchants Quay, lying directly below and in the vicinity of Christ Church. The rest of the river, as it began to widen out at its shallow mouth, was more or less untouched. For centuries the people of the city, and those unlucky enough to have to navigate up to its quays, were obliged to grin and bear the vagaries of the Liffey.[1]

With all of these inferior harbours and small harbours, sand-bars and gravel shoals, and roads flooding at each high tide – the wonder of it is that people persevered in building their settlements in the Liffey valley, and did not up in disgust and move somewhere less aggravating; or that Dublin did not take its maritime destiny squarely into its own two hands hundreds of years ago. In fact, it would take until late in the seventeenth century before the author-ities belatedly agreed to establish a harbour in the city itself and to cut out the need for the plethora of middle-harbours that it had largely relied on until then. The result of this decision was momen-tous, leading as it did to the river and bay that we know today and establishing the economic supremacy of Dublin once and for all.

It was with this consolidation of the city harbour in mind that work began in 1715 on the building of an embankment on the southern shore of the Liffey estuary, with the purpose of effec-tively channelling it. The embankment was supported and braced by piles driven into the bed of the river, and although it did its job well enough, it was clear from the very beginning that it could only be a temporary measure. The action of wind and wave end-lessly swept away the foundations of the piles and the embank-ment was subject to an endless round of maintenance and repair. As a result of this looming reality, therefore, it was decided to replace this bank with a wall, the South Wall, which would run east and out into the middle of the bay, to be capped by a light-house. The granite blocks needed to construct this vast piece of engineering were quarried in the Wicklow Mountains and then ferried across Dublin Bay, while the timber used in the construc-tion process was brought in from Poland and Sweden. The Wall took most of the eighteenth century to complete; in 1767 the Poolbeg Lighthouse was lit (with candles) for the first time, and the breakwater was then carried eastward to meet the mainland.

The South Wall was finally completed in the final years of the century, and it was and remains a marvellous feat of engineering. In building and completing this breakwater, however, the city was beginning the process of creating an entirely new coastline, fencing in the old community of Ringsend in the process and blocking its access to the sea. Today, the village centre of Ringsend lies a kilometre or more from the open sea, its former maritime flavour and history expunged by the workings of progress.

The South Wall's companion breakwater, the Bull Wall that is crowned today by the Virgin Mary atop her tripod, was not completed until 1824, after a survey of the harbour entrance by one Captain William Bligh suggested further improvements that might be made. Bligh's adventures on and off the *Bounty* have done little for his reputation, but there is no doubt that his charting of Dublin Bay remains a great feat of marine cartography and was instrumental in the growth and consolidation of the Port of Dublin. In one respect, however, Bligh got it wrong: he had proposed the construction of a parallel breakwater to the South Wall, thus forming a narrow and well-defined channel in which the Liffey would meet the sea. It became evident that such a narrow channel would play havoc with the sandbars and shoals of the bay and, as a result, it was decided instead to build the new breakwater where the Bull Wall stands today – slanting south and east into the sea from Clontarf, with a subterranean section extending a little further into the water. These two great breakwaters, it was reasoned, would contrive to introduce a flow of tide-borne water into the mouth of the Liffey and out again, acting as a scourer and keeping the seabed deep and free of impediments.

And so it came to pass: the depth of water was slowly increased and, in the meantime, the river itself was continuing to be channelled and embanked and generally improved for commerce. It took a long time to work out, perhaps, but by the middle of the nineteenth century the city had a modern harbour and could deal properly with what the Irish maritime historian John de Courcy has called 'death-dealing Dublin Bay', with the rotting hulks of 100 foundered ships lying on its seabed. Remember the *Prince of Wales*, for example, and the *Rochdale*, lost off Blackrock and Seapoint on the ferocious night of 18–19 November 1807, with the loss of over 300 lives between them. This was a disaster that led to the creation of the great harbour at Dun Laoghaire on the south shore of the bay, enclosed within its two massive granite piers. Or remember the mailboat *Leinster* – the second to bear the name – that was sunk by a German U-boat at the Kish light on 10 October 1918, with the loss of a staggering 500 lives.

A pleasing element in this long story of construction and human engineering lies in the part that nature, in the form of winds and tides and currents, continues to play in the formation of Dublin Bay and its shorelines. South of the South Wall, in the angle between the breakwater and the coast, lie the tangled sands and pools of Sandymount Strand – today one of the city's greatest assets. Behind it lies a nature reserve, formed of landfill spawned by endless works of engineering, long piled up on the seashore and grassed over and planted within the last 20 years. There are few better walks in the city on a windy day than to set out from the seafront at Sandymount, skirting the edge of the nature reserve and hugging the coast as it bends around to the line of the South Wall, and then to set out along the breakwater towards the Poolbeg Lighthouse, with the water slapping on both sides and the spray flying. I remember that the last time I did such a walk on a windy, choppy day, there were mad little flotillas of yellow plastic ducks – the sort you might find in a child's bath or ranged in the bathroom of an ironically luxurious modern Dublin hotel – floating amid the hard squares of granite at the foot of the wall. Dozens and dozens, some of them beached by the tide, others floating free. Not a clever artistic installation – presumably – but a container fallen overboard from a cargo ship and split on the shallow seabed.[2] I read recently that a container full of millions of Lego bricks had gone overboard off the south-west tip of England; they were confidently expected to materialise on the other side of the Atlantic shortly. Our yellow plastic ducks were a little less intrepid.

The existence of Bull Island, with its grasses, kite fliers and abundant birdlife, meanwhile, is owed wholly to the existence of the Bull Wall. At the end of the seventeenth century, the island did not even exist; at the time of the Act of Union, say, it consisted of a restlessly prowling and shifting sandbar in the waters off Clontarf. Today, it is a marvellous asset: an island some five kilometres (three miles) long, a United Nations Biosphere reserve, a bird sanctuary of world renown and home to the Royal Dublin Golf Club, one of the great Irish links courses.

As the nineteenth century progressed and the city's suburbs began to roll north and south along the edge of the sea, so the role of Dublin Bay in the life of the city began to change too. This changing role has been partially recorded by artists, as the years have passed, with paintings coming down to us that capture aspects of life on the seashore. The proximity of the sea is, after all, one of the great pleasures and characteristics of Dublin life, with bathing places galore: from the beaches at Killiney and Dollymount, say, or from the bathing steps on the North Wall and South Wall, or – most famous of all – from the Forty Foot, just up the coast from Bullock Harbour. Guarded by a Martello tower and yet another Dublin locale immortalised in *Ulysses*, it is one of the few places in the city where nude swimming will not land one in the gallows, and has been patronised by the people of the city for centuries. It was until fairly recently, in fact, patronised by gents only – a state of affairs portrayed in motionless and primitive detail in Harry Kernoff's painting of *The Forty Foot, Sandycove* (1940), with its harshly contrasting blocks of shade and colour and its self-absorbed yet watchful male bathers. The ladies, at last, arrived in the 1970s, consigning Kernoff's motionless bathers to history, and today it is thronged by all of humanity on summer days. Today also, the waters of the bay are cleaner than they have been for centuries: state-of-the-art treatment works at Ringsend have ended the vile practice of dumping the city's sludge in the sea beyond the Bailey light. And so today there is less chance than ever of picking up a nasty virus as one paddles in the water.

Before then, swimming in Dublin Bay – said to be therapeutic, although it is difficult to imagine why it gained such a reputation – was largely the preserve of the moneyed classes. Sturdy bathing houses appeared at points along the coast – at Sandymount and Dalkey – and these were frequented by those who could afford the subs; they were, however, unfrequented by those who could not, and who instead made their independent way down to the seashore in order to bathe *gratis*.

—— ◄o►— ——

And what of the river Liffey, all this time? As the city struggled through the Middle Ages and then began its belated expansion in the middle of the seventeenth century and continued to expand in the centuries that followed, what was the Liffey up to? Flowing quietly along, one might say, along its mere 120 kilometres (75 miles) from source to sea; providing the city's lifeblood, maybe; minding its own business. Not as simple as this.

The presence of the sea, the tempting proximity of the east coast, of Britain and Europe beyond and the convenient convergence of the country's ancient road system in the locality – these are all reasons, as we have seen, why Dublin was founded in its present location, and why it grew to achieve its present pre-eminence. But the greatest reason of all, though, is this river flowing through the heart of it all. The Liffey has always been Dublin's raison d'être, providing food, sustenance, opportunities and sanctuary from the earliest times. It has been at the heart of the city's economy, its identity and its imagination; and the dialogue between the Liffey and the city has been constant since the first Stone Age inhabitants – those prehistoric settlers, who have left little trace – settled on the shores of the river long ago.

It is also true, however, that in the process of sustaining the city, the Liffey has itself been altered beyond all recognition. The river's source, 'a shy gasp of waters in the gorse,' is up in the highlands, near the Sally Gap.[3] From here, it turns west and drops down and out of the hills before curving east again in the direction of Dublin. In these few miles and powered by the slopes of the mountains and the rain that falls there, the river manages to attain considerable strength – and it is for this reason that it has long been subject to human interventions. As early as the beginning of the seventeenth century, the city authorities were being petitioned for money to make the river navigable by means of a series of locks – an idea doomed to failure by the force of the river and the unsympathetic topography. It was this failure to create a properly navigable Liffey that resulted, indirectly, in the building of the canals instead.

Having failed to tame the river by means of lock building, the city set out to control it by other means. The results of this can be seen today: the river has already been dammed – not damned, not quite – three times in its short length, at Poulaphouca, Golden Falls and Leixlip, before ever it reaches Dublin. In the process, the city has been provided with valuable hydroelectric power, and the occasional flash floods that were a feature of the river are now a thing of the past. This damming and engineering, however, also significantly alters the nature of the river well before it approaches the city.

Take the Liffey as it enters the city itself, at a point where the southern edge of the Phoenix Park falls steeply in wooded slopes and ridges, down into the river valley at Chapelizod and at Islandbridge, where long ago the Vikings buried their dead. Where the Park meets the Liffey, the rowing clubs of Trinity College and

University College maintain their boathouses, while on the other side of the river lie the War Memorial Gardens. Here, lawns give way to austere stone memorials to the dead of two world wars, flanked by sunken rose gardens – the most stirring park in the city and, most of the time, probably the emptiest too. This is the Liffey at its most tranquil, flanked by parkland and riverside paths and rowers cutting smoothly through the water on fine mornings. But this is the Liffey engineered too, for here at Islandbridge is the weir of the river, below which it becomes tidal.

Below Islandbridge, the city gathers and encroaches ever more forcefully. The city bridges – named and then renamed and renamed again, as the political context changes – line up in ever-quickening succession. The river's potential for violence has already been removed by means of upstream dams; its very mouth has been engineered by the city. And now, in between source and mouth, the waters of the river are progressively chartered and channelled, its flow altered, its banks dictated by human hands. Today, then, the Liffey would appear to be the very tamest of rivers, bound up with the city, its story and mythology told by the people that live on its banks: Joyce, for example, who imagines the river embodied as Anna Livia Plurabelle in *Finnegans Wake*; or Patrick Collins, whose *Liffey Quaysides* paints a ghostly impressionistic ensemble of quays and bridges and river, all clad in grey and silver and white.

It is understated as it makes its way quietly through Dublin, but beautiful too. Stand on a city bridge late in the afternoon or at sunset and look west and the beauty is clear to be seen. Stand at the riverside house in which Joyce set 'The Dead' and look west at the vast bulk of the Wellington Testimonial and the Phoenix Park beyond. Stand on the quays and watch the city's shadows fall on the lamplit water and see the city's silhouette – the spires of churches high in the Liberties, the towers and stacks of the Guinness Brewery beyond – reflected in its flow. Even the most hackneyed view, the one that takes in the arching span of the Ha'penny Bridge, is no less beautiful simply because it is overused. At Grattan Bridge, which joins Capel Street on the north side of the Liffey with Parliament Street and City Hall on the south, sailing ships would tie up until late in the eighteenth century, when the Custom House and the South Wall were completed and the harbour moved downstream. Today, the bridge has been re-engineered a little and equipped with kiosks and glass-backed benches that – nice touch, this – help to break the winds that sweep up and down the river. Further east again sits the Custom House itself on the edge of the water, constructed here to set the seal on the new harbour of Dublin and to finish once and for all the old city-centre anchorages. Further on towards Dublin Bay and the river widens a little and begins to lose its identity to the encroaching sea, and the sky seems to spread out in response and become grand. A beautiful river, then, and characterful and endlessly changing. The earliest settlers would scarcely recognise it as the same stretch of water.

If the Liffey is as much a work of human hands as it is of nature, there are increasing signs that these human hands are beginning to recognise the river's virtues. For decades, the Liffey was profoundly disconnected from the city surrounding it. This, for the most part, was the result of the sorry state of the city quays; long years of neglect had resulted in a state of architectural dilapidation and many of the once-fine buildings that lined the quays were in poor repair or altogether derelict. The river also received untreated effluent until the early years of the twentieth century, turning its lower reaches into a foul-smelling sewer; and there would have been little reason to linger nearby. The attitude towards the Liffey – as with the canals – had become so unenlightened by the middle of the twentieth century that a proposal was seriously considered to pave over the river as it passed O'Connell Bridge in order to build a vast car park. And the Liffey and its associated rivers can occasionally bite back too, even if floods no longer rage down the valley from the mountains, but instead come in from the sea. In one nineteenth-century tidal surge that followed a storm and a high tide, for example, the waters of the Liffey and its tributaries backed up to such an extent that a female servant was drowned – in a vile mixture of storm waters and sewage – in a deep cellar on Grafton Street.

In recent years, traffic levels along the river have spiralled, with nowhere to put these increasing numbers of cars. As a result, the quays – always the principal route into and out of the city and its port – have been clogged with cars and clogged even more with heavy vehicles thundering towards the docks (on the north quays) or away from them (on the south quays). With footpaths that are perilously narrow and with roads that are perilously busy, it is little wonder that the people of Dublin have tended to flit across the bridges at top speed, hardly pausing to look at the Liffey flowing below.

Today, the quays are as busy as they ever were, but better times may be in the process of being engineered. The Dublin Port Tunnel, long in the delving and expensive in the creating, is now open. It is intended to take all of the heavy vehicles from the quays, funnel them into Dublin's ring road and so direct them into this long connecting tunnel towards the city's docks. Whether this stated objective will be achieved is open to question – persistent reports claim that the tunnel may not be high enough to take some of the vehicles destined to use it; and it seems that only time will tell. At the very least, however, the worst of the infernal traffic on the city quays will be banished and so the latest stage in the city's progressive aim to connect itself to the river will – we hope – be achieved.

Much has already been done. The river still smells bracing at low tide, of course, but it is the rank smell of seaweed, of organic matter, of the sea itself that now assails the nostrils of the populace.

A healthy smell – there is nothing much one could do about that and nobody seems to mind too much. New projects have been undertaken in recent years, some of these, like the slender Millennium Footbridge, are good; others, like the signature Calatrava-designed Joyce Bridge that looks like a split pitta pocket, less so. Some projects are chattered about but never undertaken – so that the hideous Loop Line railway bridge still scars the view across the water to the Custom House. Others are much grumbled over, like the river Boardwalk that is a touch tatty but is mighty agreeable at the same time, representing a potent part of this conscious effort to reconnect Dublin's river to its citizens. Stretching for a kilometre or so along the northern shore of the river and attached to the stone embankments by cables and wires of steel, the Boardwalk is surfaced with timber and lined by benches and little seasonal cafés dispensing those essential cappuccinos. The southerly aspect of the Boardwalk captures the best of the sun and through the summer months Dubliners and visitors alike saunter, take in the rays and keep an eye out for pickpockets. And, where the river broadens and flows through the Docklands, the authorities have widened the footpaths, installed cycle paths and benches and moored the *Jeannie Johnston* to lie quietly on the water close to the Custom House. A delicate replica of one of the many nineteenth-century sailing ships that moored along the Liffey during the Famine and in its aftermath, the *Jeannie Johnston* provides a useful reminder of the city's role as a departure point for generations of emigrants from Ireland.

— ◄o► —

Today, one has the sense of the river, the harbour and the Docklands as existing in a truly post-industrial age; increasingly, they are together being marketed as a leisure opportunity. Some time ago, for example, Dubliners, web surfers and global citizens with too much time on their hands were treated to a new press release. So, an email lands in my inbox on a fine autumn afternoon purporting to be from the Wasaki Global Corporation and advertising the luminous charms of the Dublin Coastal Development. Never heard of it; I narrow my eyes. I click on to the website – only to find a proposal to build a motorway along the South Wall to three new artificial islands in the mouth of Dublin Bay. I sit up straight in my chair. On these new islands will be built a central business district, which will itself be a 'hub of commerce and industry' consisting of 'exclusive restaurants, amazing indoor malls, off-shore casinos and designer shopping districts'. Gosh. I sit up even more straight. It sounds like the gateway to Hell itself.

It takes a little while, of course, for the penny to drop. It doesn't drop when I read about the 42,000 new homes planned for the three artificial islands in the shape of a shamrock – this simply makes my eyes open even wider – and it doesn't drop even when I read about the 'off-shore casinos', the idea of which simply makes me squeak with indignation. The website now invites me to 'register an interest' – but only if I earn more than €100,000 per annum. And so on. Yes: it takes an embarrassingly long time to realise that the Wasaki Global Corporation, um, does not exist.

A hoax, then – but with a sharp edge. The megalomaniacal plans of the Wasaki Global Corporation are not a million miles from other, genuine and rather breathless plans proposed for Dublin Bay. In recent times, the call has gone out for the Port of Dublin to relocate in its entirety to a greenfield site north of town and for the vacated land to be given over to clusters of high-rise apartments, together with their attendant cafés, restaurants and cultural life. Nothing intrinsically wrong with this, of course. This plan has been floated many times before – density is after all the way of the future; and indeed, this plan might well prove to be the perfect solution to the city's pressing housing needs, if it really is more than hot air.

Proposals such as these, however, encapsulate the growing tension between the wish to exploit the margins of Dublin Bay and the need to conserve what already exists here. A plan is well advanced to build a cycle path and footpath, for example, along the entire edge of the bay, from Sutton to Sandycove – a marvellous idea and well overdue. But can the bay be intensively used without compromising its integrity? Can the bay's wildlife – seals, oystercatchers, gulls and all – coexist happily with an exploding human population housed in a new city quarter built on the site of the former docks? And, in an age in which global warming is already balefully upon us and where eastern Ireland will be, more than anywhere else in the country, prone to its effects – in such an age, is it a good idea to develop lands intensively that were, after all, reclaimed from the sea only recently? Nobody knows the answers to these questions – not definitively – but they are worth asking all the same.

Imagine, a few years from now, a teenager rollerblading her way along a new and marvellous coastal cycle path that bends its way around Dublin Bay, from north to south. The summit of Howth is behind her, the candy stripes of the Pigeonhouse before her. She glides past a couple strolling hand in hand through the sunny afternoon, a few couples queuing for their coffee at one of the new kiosks set up on the seashore, children jostling and calling in the new waterside playground. The white sails of yachts are thick on the sea.

Now imagine those Vikings again, rounding the same hill of Howth a thousand years ago to face these unknown waters; or the captains of seventeenth-century sailing ships, maybe, manoeuvring through the shoals and contrary winds of Dublin Bay, into the river mouth and slowly, painfully, all the way up the Liffey to moor on the quays below Grattan Bridge; or the herring fishermen of Ringsend scratching out a bitter living on their precarious spit of land. The engineers laying the first vast granite blocks of the

South Wall; or the keepers lighting the first mass of candles atop the Poolbeg Lighthouse. Dubliners all, or would-be Dubliners – but what a difference a millennium makes.

This air and green and water, then – this is Dublin too, its past as well as its present. And perhaps the city's natural environment encapsulates the city's story as well as any straightforward narrative ever could.

PART FOUR

And the bare bones of a fanlight
Over a hungry door
And the air soft on the cheek
And porter running from the taps
With a head of yellow cream ...

'The Closing Album I: Dublin' LOUIS MACNEICE [1]

Chapter 16

CONSUMPTION

Christmas is coming, and Grafton Street begins to resemble a rugby scrum. Crowds mill and thicken throughout the day, as the holiday creeps nearer and blood pressures creep higher. By mid-morning, the area is already dense with anxious shoppers embarking on a gruelling day. In the swarming afternoon, choirs stand at the southern end of the street, sing carols, shake buckets of coins under chilly noses, as the red, faux-Edwardian Grafton Street Christmas lanterns swing overhead. Darkness falls, winter-early, and they are still at it, and the owners of the pubs and cafés that cluster in the side streets light their lamps and lick their lips.

Grafton Street, as every Irish person knows, is one of Dublin's principal shopping strips. Running, crooked and crack-like, between Trinity College and the bullet-marked Fusiliers' Arch on the north-western corner of St Stephen's Green, its scale is curiously modest and it bears the traces of its age and previous incarnations more visibly than do other notable Dublin thoroughfares. Although it is recorded that the Wide Streets Commissioners gave Grafton Street something of a makeover in the nineteenth century, it would seem that the gentlemen's minds weren't really on the job, if the street's almost medieval dimensions are anything to go by. But it is these dimensions that give the street its distinctive stamp and character today. Intimate in an already intimate city, it is a place to meet and to greet – a natural promenade through the south city centre.

Or would be, if the crowds would only go away. If I have no actual business to transact on Grafton Street in the weeks leading up to Christmas – and I make it my business not to have – then I stay far, far away. So too does any sane person, for the alternative is to shuffle up or shuffle down the suddenly and monstrously too-narrow street, hampered by the crowds, by the buskers and street performers, by those charity-collectors-on-a-commission that jump like a velociraptor into one's path, who snap and bite against an absence of charity, against such unpromising conditions. But today, alas, I have presents to buy on this frosty Friday just before Christmas, and so I trudge reluctantly through the park, under the arch, across the road, and past a man in a Mexican sombrero, who is playing 'Silent Night' on a trombone.

'Just a minute of your time!' says the nearest of the charity per-sons (a girl, in Santa Claus-red today). She delivers her line with that curious long-practised mingling of good cheer and savage aggression. 'In aid of –' something deserving.

'No thank you,' I mumble. (Not even one bloody minute. Not for the most deserving cause in the world. I've bought too many charity scratch cards in my time, and I've have never – not ever – won so much as a euro on any of them. But I only think these un-festive thoughts; I don't actually speak them aloud.)

'Well, thanks anyway,' the girl trills, skilfully dumping a load of guilt for good measure. 'You have a good day anyway.'

'I will!' I say; and to hell with the orphans.

So – no. Steer clear of Grafton Street at all costs, unless you have no choice. Better instead to swing into Dawson Street, with its bookshops, its generous dimensions and its merciful absence of crowds. Its delightfully broad pavements make charity dodging so very straightforward and guilt-free.

As for Grafton Street itself – it began its existence as a mere alley, twisting and bending its modest way between Trinity and the evolving St Stephen's Green. And, while the local landowners were creating Dawson Street, Molesworth Street and Kildare Street in the early years of the eighteenth century – broad, elegant and much praised by contemporary commentators; posh, we might say now – nobody gave much thought to widening that rather crooked lane to the north. But, and without being widened or extended or fussed with in any way, Grafton Street nonetheless rose in the world, evolving by reason of its location into an upmarket residential area; and, later, as Dublin was engineered, bridges built and new north–south routes created through the cityscape, into an important artery and commercial zone.

In the nineteenth and twentieth centuries, Grafton Street developed into a fashionable shopping area, taking on the commercial importance it retains today. Key Dublin institutions – Switzers and Brown Thomas department stores, Weir's jewellers, Bewley's Oriental Café with its glowing stained glass – set up shop on the street, together with a host of other, largely locally owned, shops and enterprises; and by the middle of the twentieth century, Grafton Street was in the business of providing something of a respite from what had become a drab surrounding city. To the east, Dawson Street was always more explicitly fashionable, and Molesworth Street was anchored by the great pile of Leinster House; to the west, a grid of narrow streets stretched up towards the Castle, with the granite mass of Powerscourt House crowded into the midst of all. Grafton Street, meanwhile, with its cinema and cafés and long strip of good shopping, offered pure entertainment.

Today, it presents something of a conundrum, being both a reflection of a new and glittering twenty-first-century Dublin and also a symbol of the perils of globalisation. We are told – breathlessly – that retailers are queuing to establish a 'footprint' here;

that the street is now, in terms of retail rental prices per square metre, the sixth most expensive shopping zone in the world; that only the likes of – scream it – Fifth Avenue, Bond Street and the Ginza outstrips it. Brown Thomas department store, now foreign-owned, still anchors the street, by far the most expensive and luxurious store in the city. It is a place I seldom venture for fear of the eye-popping prices, the whirling blizzards of Hermès scarves and battalions of Vuitton and Chanel bags, the disdainful staff and the toilet attendants who remind me obscurely of those charity collectors as they crack crisp towels through the air, enveloping customers in clouds of designer scent and expecting tips as lavish as the surrounding store. Skin consultations are carried out by white-coated assistants on laboratory-like stools set against the store's cold-gleaming ground-floor plate-glass windows. I could press my cold red nose against the glass and watch raptly from an inch away, through a spreading cloud of condensation, as unguents are applied and removed and expensive advice proffered and accepted. I could, if I wanted to – not that I would ever want to do such a thing. The store represents Dublin's present consumer-oriented hyper-reality, in other words, a world in which people willingly put their names on a waiting list for that Vuitton hand-bag that represents happiness. And the store also stands for a potent vulgarity, for surely the expensive treatment areas should be tucked well away from the plate-glass windows, or at least slipped discreetly behind a potted plant? Not here, alas. Here it's like being on TV.

A few local shops remain on Grafton Street: Weir's still dispenses its jewellery; you can still buy coffee under the sign of Bewley and drink it in the ruddy light of its stained glass, even if the Bewley family no longer own the place. Brown Thomas has established another bridgehead on the street too, and it in turn is home to a piggybacking Starbucks franchise. But nearly all the other, locally owned shops – these are long gone. Brown Thomas itself swallowed Switzers in the 1990s and moved across the road into its much larger building, while its old premises were taken over by a chain store. Branches of other, mainly British high-street multiples, together with fast-food joints, mobile phone shops and – latterly – shops dispensing Chinese herbal remedies have proliferated up and down the street, so that Grafton Street has in recent years become more and more anonymous and bland. Indeed, the very pedestrian bricks that face the road are characterless and banal, they might be seen surfacing any windswept suburban shopping precinct.

Ireland is, so we are told, the most open economy in the world – whatever that means – and hence the most exposed to the sweeping influence of globalisation. Perhaps it is the case that Dublin's principal shopping street simply reflects this fact, with all its many facets and truths. And so you can buy your Vuitton bag here, in other words, if that's what pulls your chain. But understand the trade-off, which is that in other shopping streets all over the world, people will be buying the same bag, purchasing identical designs in identical shops. And that's life. But having said all this, those awful red bricks, the ones that pave and cheapen the street, that's an issue that the city authorities really could address – really could change, if they were so inclined.

The roads that surround Grafton Street, maybe, present a more vital and textured version of Dublin. Today's Dawson Street remains measured and handsome, with bookshops clustered close to Trinity at its northern end, the Mansion House in the middle, the trees of the Green waving to the south. Not even the cluster of gigantic bars near the Green, all outdoing each other in gold leaf, palm trees and manic frescoed ceilings, can wreck the area entirely. Molesworth Street is home to a handful of galleries and Leinster House still rises solidly to the east. West of Grafton Street, the roads and laneways are still tightly bunched, although today they are filled with energy by day and night: small shops, locally owned cafés, bars and tapas joints draw in passing trade; the second-hand Secret Bookshop survives against all the odds; and the punters sip coffee beneath the glazed roof of Powerscourt, which is today an upmarket shopping centre. Dublin even has its own super-deli anchoring the top of Wicklow Street, in the shape of Fallon & Byrne – or Falon Gong, as I have sometimes heard it called – in which it is as possible to buy dragon fruit, sweet-smoked Spanish paprika and blue corn chips as it is to buy an apple and a piece of good Irish cheese. And this, as I occasionally, reluctantly, rustily try to remind myself, clambering down from my high horse to seize a dragon fruit from the teetering pile on display – this is all part of globalisation too. And not all character is lost, you just have to poke about a little in order to find it. Grafton Street can be seen, then, to represent the very epitome of the present Irish age of splurge, to some best avoided, to others the very stuff of life. It can epitomise and encapsulate the present state of the city and of the country, both good and bad; and it can symbolise the breathtaking changes that have taken place in Dublin in recent times. Fifteen years ago, ten years ago, after all, you would be hard-pressed to find a Hermès scarf along Grafton Street – or anywhere in Dublin, come to that.

It is as well to sometimes stretch out this fabric of time a little. Rather than simply take the state of Grafton Street as a sort of modern yardstick that measures this new city of recent years – useful though this may be, to be sure – it can be even more instructive to make broader comparisons. To imagine instead quite another Dublin – the Dublin of 200-odd years ago when the street ran crookedly, much as it runs today; when the roadways, lanes and institutions that surround it were, for the most part, already in situ. The Dublin of the nineteenth century, which is associated so deeply with the shades of famine and of political chafing and turmoil, when not so much as a single dragon fruit was to be seen gleaming in the markets of the city.

So the year is, say, 1803 or thereabouts. Imagine yourself at the north end of Grafton Street, close to where the old Viking Thing once loomed and where today the statue of a busty Molly Malone stands for the benefit of the tourists. Trinity is at your back, College Green and the Parliament House to your right, Grafton Street running away to your left. The scene is busy, for this is the very heart of Dublin, then as now. Up to the north, an all-new Westmoreland Street has opened up a wide vista to the river and on to a marvellously wide and grand Sackville Street beyond. Closer to hand, the Parliament House, so recently abandoned and only just occupied by the Bank of Ireland, is accustoming itself to its new commercial role. But the mica in the granite of Trinity's West Front catches and sparkles in the morning light; Joyce's description of the 'grey block of Trinity ... set heavily in the city's ignorance like a great dull stone set in a cumbrous ring' has yet to be set down on paper. Carriages and pedestrians move up Dame Street towards the Castle and more carriages make their way along Grafton Street south towards the Green and the southern suburbs. There are signs of a military presence – not indeed the lines of soldiers massing on College Green as the final vote was taken to extinguish the Irish Parliament, but soldiers enough, for Robert Emmet's abortive rebellion of 1803 has come and gone, crushed before it ever got going.

Life and commerce, then, notwithstanding this military presence, is continuing as normal. Much as normal, at any rate; maybe, if you stood long enough, you might hear a trader complaining about a fall-off of business and certainly a beggar or two, vexingly, would come along. The Act of Union has passed, but it seems that life goes on. Or does it?

— ◄o► —

The general sense of Dublin in the years after the Act of Union is that it was a city very much down on its luck. And this is true, although it is not the whole truth. Certainly, the loss of the Parliament, of the paraphernalia of a capital city, the loss of pride and buoying feelings of importance, the diminishing and creeping reality of provincialism – these were bitter blows. And some of the economic capital was seeping away too. The money that spilled into the city from the countryside when Parliament was in session, for example, had vanished. The army of administrators and civil servants that was resident in Dublin and the function of which was to support the country's legislature, this was suddenly, at a stroke, unnecessary. Put in purely economic terms, there was less money in circulation, there was less business to be transacted, there was less business altogether. Reality bites – and this reality would have bitten hard into Dublin.

The great mansions and town houses – all of them still essentially brand new – that littered Dublin city centre no longer had much of a use. We can still see these great buildings, many of them at any rate, in the modern cityscape, and so perhaps it is inevitable that the history of these times concentrates on the decamping of their inmates to England. What is less visible and less palpable and therefore more easily forgotten, however, is the hardship that the Act of Union would have visited on those silent administrators and civil servants, not to mention on the craftspeople and artisans – the silversmiths and goldsmiths and glassmakers and importers of all manner of luxury goods – who depended on a steady business from a moneyed oligarchy and who saw that business shaken and gradually diminished in the years after 1801.

But none of this happened overnight. Dublin's aristocracy did not simply up sticks all of a sudden, as is sometimes imagined, and move to London en masse. Instead, the loss of power and economic vitality was a gradual affair; and it is worth noting, for example, that the building of the remainder of the city's Georgian squares continued apace into the nineteenth century, indicating that the appetite for large, grand houses was still there, and that so was the means to pay for them. The Napoleonic Wars were still ongoing for 15 years after the Act of Union and this fact also helped to stave off any recession. Irish corn and other agricultural produce were still in great demand, much of it was funnelled through the Dublin docks for export; and it only was with the coming of peace to Europe in 1815 that Dublin, in common with much of Ireland and Britain, was struck by recession. And besides, the loss of the city's capital status did not mean that all power was stripped and summarily removed to Whitehall. Far from it, for Dublin Castle remained a centre of administrative activity with all the financial implications that this carries.

Other building and development also carried on regardless in the years that followed the Act of Union. Most significant of these – and most ironic given the fact of Dublin's apparent economic desolation – were two of the city's key structures. The first was the now-iconic General Post Office (GPO) on Sackville Street, designed by Francis Johnston and completed in 1818; imposing and grand behind its tall neo-classical columns and later to play such a pivotal role in the modern history of Dublin. The second – one of a throng of Liffey bridges to be created in these years – was the graceful arch of the Wellington Bridge, also built in 1818 and named in honour of Arthur Wellesley, Duke of Wellington, the Irish-born British soldier and politician. Wellesley was famously touchy about his Irish roots, noting tartly that 'being born in a stable does not make one a horse'. The Irish authorities must have been less touchy, however, because the bridge was named after him anyway. It would later be rechristened, less provokingly, as the Liffey Bridge; and today – such a layer of names – it is of course better known as the Ha'penny Bridge.

And, before either the GPO or Ha'penny Bridge came into existence, the Nelson Pillar had been constructed in the central island of Sackville Street. The Pillar, raised in 1808 to 1809 in the aftermath of the Battle of Trafalgar, and standing almost 37 metres

(120 feet) high, was constructed of granite and was topped by Admiral Nelson himself. While it was desperately unpopular, naturally enough, among the majority of Dubliners, its very existence served as a reminder of the political climate of those harsh days: Britain was in the throes of a bitter war with Napoleonic France, the civil liberties of its own population had been savagely curtailed and so the British government would certainly not stand for any more trouble emanating from Dublin at this time. Hence the erection of the Pillar, which made this harsh attitude perfectly and abundantly clear. The monument would always generate strong feelings, right to the end, for it was blown to kingdom come by the IRA in 1966, in as bracing a statement of opinion as can be imagined.

This new wave of construction was mirrored in the changing society of these years. There continued to exist, in Dublin as in any other city in this new United Kingdom, an army of professionals with the means to spend money and the will to do so. There would always be shopping to be done, carriages to be kept, houses to be bought and sold and public entertainments to be attended, and there was a large enough constituency in the city to keep these activities going. In other words, Dublin was continuing its evolution: it needed modern communications and a modern infrastructure in the form of general post offices, bridges and (later) railways, just like every other modern European city – and it got them.

And so, although a sense of a creeping economic hollowness would certainly have been palpable in certain quarters, it is not quite the case that Dublin suddenly slid, lock, stock and barrel, into the poorhouse. As we stand in the early years of the nineteenth century, in fact, and look south towards Grafton Street and north across College Green towards the river, where presently the GPO would rise on Sackville Street, the threads of continuity are plain to be seen. Dublin was a consumer society, then as now;

fashions were followed and purchased, and Grafton Street was a place to be seen. The vitality of such consumption would stretch and droop in the aftermath of the Act of Union but it would not vanish altogether. So yes, with political change came hardship; but life did indeed go on, in an altered state.

Chapter 17

A SKY FOR THE FAVOURED

It is not overstating the matter – well, not too much, at any rate – to say that the story of city governance in nineteenth-century Dublin resembles a game of Risk: monumentally long-running, bitterly fought and with the glittering prize of absolute global domination awaiting the eventual, ruthless, winner.

First of all, it is here that we can locate the rise to power of Dublin's middle class, a process that would have repercussions for the whole city. The bourgeoisie, of course, give the impression of having been rising for all eternity. Certainly in Dublin they had been rising since well before the Act of Union, their confidence generated by the steadily changing nature of the city's population, by an expanding and diversifying economy and by the gradual dismantling of the Penal Laws. It is not simply the case that in Dublin they expanded to fill some vacuum left by a decamping aristocracy, although it could be argued that the Act of Union certainly made their progress a little smoother than it otherwise would have been. Rather, this expansion and empowerment of the middle classes was a consequence of a greater and more complex development in European history: economic supremacy was shifting as it would have shifted in any case, from the country's aristocracy towards the bourgeoisie. And, although the Protestant middle class was still very much present in the life of the city, increasingly the Catholic middle class was also rising in the world.

This middle-class impact upon Dublin, its society and economy, was profound, even if it took some time to develop. Naturally, the city was buoyed up by rising habits of investment and consumption, but it was impoverished too, as middle-class choices began to impact directly upon the development of Dublin, and specifically as the upwardly mobile began progressively to abandon the central city for new homes north and south of the canals. This certain hollowing out of Dublin's built environment and its economy continued and expanded throughout the nineteenth century, and its traces are clearly evident in the lines and development of the city even today.

Eighteenth-century Dublin, as we know, had already begun to be clearly demarcated into fashionable districts (mainly in the east) and unfashionable ones (mainly in the west). This existing template began to be further applied in the nineteenth century, as the city spilled out beyond the new ring of canals and into new suburban developments in the countryside beyond. There is, of course, nothing altogether exceptional in all this: nineteenth-century British fiction, for example, is full of instances of the professional classes decamping for the suburbs, as any reader of Elizabeth Gaskell, for example, will happily tell you. Industrialisation, as in *North and South*, is always the principal reason for this process of fleeing the city; who would choose to live next door to a factory in the midst of a smoke-belching urban hellscape when they could live in a nice house with a nice garden in the suburbs instead?

But the circumstances of Dublin are different in a number of ways. For one thing, the city never did transform itself into some smoke-belching urban hellscape. As was the case in most of Ireland in these years, there was little in the way of systematic or thoroughgoing industrialisation to speak of. Only in Ulster did the

Industrial Revolution come calling to any great extent, resulting in the establishment of shipyards, textiles factories and a famously productive linen industry. In Dublin, however, economic expansion was rather more sluggish. Occasionally, this has been translated into a sense that there was no process of industrial expansion at all in the city – and this was not the case, to be sure. Industrialisation did indeed occur, but it came in the guise of a curate's egg: good only in parts.

First of all, of course, come the economic success stories, and first among these is the story of Guinness. Up on that long ridge above the river, where James's Street runs west to Kilmainham, lies St James's Gate and this remains Guinness territory. The very name of the district speaks of its antiquity, for the gate in question was one of those unusual disembodied gates of medieval Dublin – gates without any city walls attached – which were used throughout the period as forts and rallying points in their own right in the event of an attack on the city suburbs. Following the Cromwellian settlement, with Dublin no longer threatened by attack from beyond the Pale, these old fortress-towers were dismantled, and today only their names remain as traces of the past. And it was up here, on the ridge of the hill, that the Guinness family first established themselves in the city.

The presence in the city of the Guinness brewery, so dominant as it was, so established even at the beginning of the nineteenth century and already in the business at that point of spreading its aroma of roasting barley far and wide over the rooftops, certainly gives the impression of industrial activity and virtue. Arthur Guinness (1725–1803) had begun his brewing career in 1755 at Leixlip, in the valley of the Liffey west of Dublin, before handing this nascent business over to his brother a few years later and turning his attentions to the city itself. He took a 999-year lease on a piece of land at St James's Gate in 1759 and established his new brewery on the site. It was not considered a wise move: the land

and the ramshackle brewery which occupied it had been on the market for years without anyone showing much in the way of interest; and besides, the city was already groaning under the weight of breweries large and small. But Guinness was a man of considerable vision. Before long he had ceased brewing ale and instead put his energy into the production of porter – dark, strong and produced by the roasting of barley. The brewery could tap the Irish countryside for unlimited supplies of barley and the river for unlimited water supplies – and before long, the Guinness brand was on its way to civic domination.

Arthur Guinness was also a politician no less than he was a brewer: he backed Grattan's Parliament in those tempestuous eighteenth-century days, seeing advantages, opportunities and a less punitive tax regime in legislative and economic independence for Ireland; and like Grattan, he favoured a measure of Catholic emancipation. And he was also, in a very precise way, quite the family man, channelling a generous measure of his prodigious energy towards peopling the world with Guinnesses. His wife Olivia – whose thoughts on the situation are not recorded – bore him 21 children in the course of their marriage, of whom ten survived to adulthood. These descendants of Arthur and Olivia went on to carve out many a reputation for themselves both in Ireland and overseas.

Good management was the order of the day at Guinness. By 1810 the brewery was already the largest in the city, after 1833 it was the largest in the whole of Ireland and by the turn of the twentieth century it was the largest in the world, selling its products now throughout Europe, North America and the British Empire, and threatening and devouring competitors in the process. The business became increasingly land hungry, expanding in 1873 from its small four-acre site into its present sprawling expanse on both sides of James's Street and down to the river. And by the last years of the century it was producing a million barrels a year and forging ahead in the export trade. At the height of operations, cargo was loaded onto the dedicated Guinness railway line and transferred down to Kingsbridge (now Heuston) Station for distribution or loaded onto barges at the private Guinness harbour on the Grand Canal, and so down to the Liffey for export abroad.

The components in this vast Guinness complex, which sprawl today on both sides of James's Street, are notable for their bulk and height in a city that features little in the way of vast, sky-scraping buildings. One of the Guinness buildings – the Storehouse topped with a bar boasting a 360-degree vista – has become one of Dublin's modern tourist meccas. The brewery site, even today, still possesses the characteristics of a city in its own right, with its own road infrastructure, place of worship and medical, sporting and leisure facilities all on site for employees and their families. It is a curious mixture of the public and the inscrutable: great doors and gates, all emblazoned with the Guinness trademark harp, open up the length of this main thoroughfare, hinting at the other city working silently behind the façades. But the buildings and the work and the industry itself, these are secreted away behind these multiple Guinness logos, hardly to be glimpsed except when one of these gates opens and a truck emerges, laden with keg after keg of the black stuff. You need to visit the Storehouse and pay, alas, the rather steep entrance fee to gain an insight into the workings of the company. And, although Guinness has now been swallowed up by an even larger international conglomerate, and although the aroma of roasting barley no longer permeates the city air, the name and image and logo continue to resonate in Dublin. A cliché, certainly – maybe the ultimate cliché of Ireland – but no less potent for that.

There were other industrial success stories too. Like that of the Jacob's biscuit factory, which by century's end was exporting prodigious amounts of biscuits to the four corners of the world. It was a success that must surely have been founded upon that other

Irish cliché of a propensity to down gallons of tea hourly. (Sadly, one cannot readily lay one's hand on any research that could prove this theory – but it certainly feels true.) While the Guinness behemoth and a few other success stories contributed so much to the industrial development of the city in these years, the presence of such dominant industries in Dublin disguised the difficulties that other occupations faced.

Other, smaller industries there certainly were: cotton mills and glue factories that had set up shop along the South Circular Road; an ancient, domestic and male-dominated trade in silk that still existed in the Liberties; a printing trade growing up on Dame Street; and metalworking too, based in and around Blackhall Place. But none of them flourished. The limited shipbuilding facilities that existed around the old docks at Ringsend, for example, gradually withered and died as the shipyards of Belfast expanded through the century; the small cotton factories were undercut and diminished by the booming Ulster textile trade. As the years crept on, in short, many of these Dublin-based industries struggled to compete and then to survive, an extinction that can be laid at the door of a failure or inability to mechanise. Gradually, they died, or at best shrank to cater to the luxury end of the market, in which profits might be good but were never to be relied upon. As a result, jobs – consistent employment, a necessity for social progress – were less abundant in Dublin than in other similar-sized European cities; and the effect of this situation was evident to any observer at the time.

Such industry as existed in Dublin, however, especially when coupled with the growth of professional and administrative occupations and with other social, demographic and political changes, provided more than sufficient impetus to fuel the growth of the city suburbs. The phenomenon of suburban growth is like a vortex that, as it tentatively begins to spin – powered by middle-class aspiration and the creation of modern communications – becomes next to impossible to stop. As better roads and railways developed in and around Dublin, for example, as it became easier to get around and to get in and out of the city centre, so new districts became increasingly agreeable to the professional classes. Just as the Earl of Kildare, proclaiming that 'they will follow me wherever I go', had pulled new populations into the marshy green fields south of the Liffey a century before, so now neighbour followed trailblazing middle-class neighbour into the countryside. As a result, it would become more attractive to landowners to indulge in a little land speculation, and increasingly this speculation would pay off.

In the south-eastern quadrant of the city, the lands of the old Pembroke estate around Merrion and Fitzwilliam Squares would maintain their social position. George Moore fictionalises his Merrion Square at century's end as faded, ramshackle and possibly dangerous, 'melancholy Merrion Square! Broken pavements, unpainted hall-doors, rusty area railings, meagre outside curs hidden almost out of sight in the deep gutters – how infinitely painful!'[1] But the cooler eyes of Elizabeth Bowen remember the intricate fanlights and glossy Georgian front doors of her childhood, 'freshly painted – crimson, chocolate, chestnut, ink-blue or olive-green. One barrister friend of my father's had a chalk-white front door I found beautiful.'[2] She remembers too the polished windows of these same houses around Merrion Square inhabited now, at the turn of the century, by a 'second society' of judges, doctors and lawyers, 'the great staircases possibly better swept and the high-ceilinged double drawing-rooms heated and lit for conversazioni'.[3]

And beyond these Georgian neighbourhoods, the new, red-brick suburbs were spreading out into Donnybrook, Ballsbridge, Ranelagh, Rathgar and Rathmines – areas knitted to the city by main arteries like Baggot Street and Leeson Street that crossed the canals on sturdy hump-backed bridges. We see the results of this new speculative development today in the fine terraces and residential streets of Donnybrook, say, which maintains its position even now as one of the most expensive areas of the city. And, as new districts became fashionable, so previously agreeable neighbourhoods began slipping down the social ladder. This process too was part of the vicious circle. As the old aristocratic houses began to lose their sheen, so the pace of the movement away from them quickened and so the sheen was stripped more and more quickly. Houses like those on Henrietta Street, for example, previously the pinnacle of Dublin society but now too large, too cold, too expensive to maintain and a good deal too close to poor districts of the city, were the first to lose their place. They were followed, as the nineteenth century wore on, by other parts of the old Gardiner estate north of the Liffey.

It was not inevitable, of course, that this growth of suburban Dublin should result in a crisis for the city – and that it did was largely the result of political, and not economic, factors. In the early nineteenth century, the area under the authority of Dublin Corporation covered only the relatively small and confined space within the ring of canals; a hundred years later, this situation had not changed. This small district, of course, encompassed some wealthy and opulent parts of Dublin – the main shopping streets, the centre of government power in Dublin Castle and the areas around Merrion and Fitzwilliam Squares – but it also covered the tenements and squalid housing of the Liberties and those formerly prosperous areas now sliding slowly into decay. And crucially, it did not cover the areas of new wealth – the new suburbs south and north of the canals. These districts remained beyond the reach of the Corporation, retaining a form of autonomy and paying no taxes, in the form of rates, to the city. As a result, Dublin's financial base shrunk progressively as the century wore on. As the supply of cash dried up, so the infrastructure of the city declined and came to need increasing investment, which was not forthcoming, and so on it went in a downward spiral.

In the early, unreformed years of the nineteenth century, Dublin Corporation had been largely oligarchical, and hence wholly unrepresentative of the people of the city. Daniel O'Connell (1775–1847), whose career would later profoundly impact on Irish affairs, called it 'a beggarly corporation'. (As a result, he was obliged to fight a duel with an outraged city councillor, which he won, fatally wounding the unfortunate gentleman in the process.) Moreover, in those early years, the Corporation shared responsibility for civic government with a million other boards, authorities, commissions – quangos, as we would call them today. The result of these unsatisfactory arrangements was that joined-up thinking was an alien concept, and that nothing was done very well.

But these systemic problems – financial, economic and administrative – were not unchanging, not written on tablets of stone. The nineteenth century in Europe was, after all, a time of profound social and political change, and Dublin was certainly not immune to the reforms of these years. This thread of steady progress is visible in the legislative advances that were enacted at Westminster once the fear of and draconian reactions to the Napoleonic Wars had receded, and that would impact directly on Ireland. Nor did Ireland wait passively on the receiving end of this legislative change. Rather, much of the energy that fuelled the spirit of reform in Britain – a sort of hesitant grasping at modernity and democracy symbolised by the Reform Act of 1832 that abolished the rotten boroughs and extended the franchise – was generated in and transmitted from Ireland. O'Connell was, for example, instrumental in the passing by the Westminster Parliament of the Catholic Relief Act of 1829, which extended the suffrage to a wider range of propertied Catholics across the United Kingdom. The oligarchic Corporation of Dublin reacted to this threat of reform in terms that were distinctly medieval, its members appealing to their English co-religionists to defend the religious orthodoxy of the city against the assault of 'damnable' papist 'idolatry'. Such language as this being bandied about, even at this point in the nineteenth century, highlights the tension that was still unmistakably present between modernity and politics.

Later, in 1840, came the Municipal Corporations Act that reformed local government in Ireland. Thereafter, Dublin Corporation would be a little more (though not too much, mind) representative of the population it was designed to serve. And in 1849 the Dublin Improvement Act would, at last, grant to the Corporation greater powers of self-government and sweep away certain of those quangos that had so long cluttered and complicated city governance.

The result of these reforms was that, as time passed, an increased number of Catholics were rendered able to vote and to sit on the Corporation – always providing, of course, they were male and held an extensive property portfolio; and the city was then able to regulate its affairs differently. It was a limited form of democracy, although better than none at all, and it meant that henceforth the Corporation would always have a Catholic majority and become increasingly marked by a specifically nationalist character. This quickening and changing political climate generated new possibilities and new debates, and in the specific context of Dublin and Ireland, new national imaginings too. It is not that civic life would thereafter be dominated by a national debate. In a city with as many social and economic problems as Dublin, social and economic questions and issues would always press. But the story of the nineteenth century in Ireland is indeed marked by an evolving national discourse – that Dublin would necessarily take the lead in developing.

Into this thickening debate stepped O'Connell, who had devoted his very considerable energies to the cause of Catholic Emancipation and to the repeal of the Act of Union. 'No person knows better than you do,' he had written to a clerical friend in 1831, 'that the domination of England is the sole and blighting curse of this country. It is the incubus that sits on our energies, stops the pulsation of the nation's heart and leaves to Ireland not gay vitality but horrid the convulsions of a troubled dream.'[4]

O'Connell was a Kerryman but visible in Dublin – he kept a house on Merrion Square – and he was a potent national leader, harnessing both the frustrations of poor Catholics and the latent power and resources of the evolving Catholic bourgeoisie, and offering to all a giddy possibility of change. It was a heady combination for Irish nationalists and, for a brief period, it seemed possible that a good deal might actually be achieved. It was a sign, for example, of changing times and possibly yet more changes to come when, in 1841, O'Connell became Lord Mayor of Dublin – the first Catholic Lord Mayor of the city for 150 years and an election made possible by the reforms of 1840 that had brought into being this hesitant civic accountability. His vision was specifically focused; it was Catholic and constitutional, it sought independence for Ireland under a British monarch, and it abhorred violence.

O'Connell's importance in Irish history lies less in the formation of a radical politics, then, and more in the sense that he was able to provide inspirational leadership to the country's Catholic majority, using his charisma, his common touch, sharp intellect and oratorical powers to build a truly mass appeal. He was tremendously media-savvy, pitching his calls for reform ostensibly at his immediate audience, at public meetings or in the chamber of the House of Commons, but in reality over their heads at the newspapers and at public opinion. Moreover, he was able to act directly and in ways which addressed Catholic grievances directly: in moving, for example, to have repealed that remnant of the Penal Laws which made the Catholic funeral rite difficult and humiliating to enact. Glasnevin Cemetery – in essence a national cemetery, regardless of religious belief – was opened on the northern outskirts of the city in 1832 as a consequence of this campaign. And it has gone on to receive a long line of notables, including O'Connell himself.

By 1841, Catholic Emancipation was a settled matter, but so too was the Union of Britain and Ireland, and O'Connell knew he could channel popular disaffection into effecting its repeal. He began his so-called 'monster meetings', travelling the length and breadth of the country and drawing crowds that today seem extraordinary. At any one time 100,000 could be relied upon to turn out to listen to him speak. His famous rally at the Hill of Tara in August 1843 reputedly drew – like Pope John Paul in the Phoenix Park 130 years later – an audience of a million people. The culmination of these monster meetings was to have taken place at Clontarf, on the north Dublin seafront, on 8 October 1843. The location for the meeting, like that of Tara before it, had been chosen carefully for its symbolic resonances. As Tara had been the seat of the High Kings and so the location of a historical unified Irish nation of yore, so Clontarf was the scene of what, in an evolving nationalist historiography, had been a famous victory of the native Irish over the Viking invaders – although of course the truth in both cases is a little more complex.

Still, truth or no truth, the size and energy of the Tara meeting put the frighteners on the British administration. On 7 October, it prorogued the Clontarf meeting; and O'Connell, fearing the violence that might ensue, refused the government challenge. He was arrested for sedition just the same, convicted, jailed for three months, and on his release it became apparent that the energy he had harnessed was dissipated, and he retired to his family home in Kerry. He died in Genoa, on 15 May 1847, as he was on his way to Rome on pilgrimage. His heart, as he had requested, was dispatched on to Rome, while his body was returned to Dublin for burial. It was interred, witnessed by more vast crowds, at Glasnevin.

— ◄o► —

Throughout the nineteenth century, then, a most striking situation was developing in Dublin. O'Connell is of course a significant figure for all sorts of good reasons, but in the present context he best symbolises the blurring that took place in these years between the local and the national in Dublin – a state of affairs that contributed to the stunting of the city's development throughout the century. The local government reforms ironically exacerbated the problem, because now a Catholic-dominated Dublin Corporation would be consistently at loggerheads with the British administration in Dublin Castle. The Corporation's various attempts to assert its authority and flag its changing identity – such as its attempts to change the name of Sackville Street to O'Connell Street, for example, which was not finally achieved until 1924 – is a good example of this ceaselessly waged war of attrition. The gradual petering out of the tradition of rotating the position of Lord Mayor between Protestants and Catholics, a notion propagated by O'Connell himself and still followed occasionally today in Northern Ireland, was another. The centenary in 1875 of the birth of Daniel O'Connell was marked by vast crowds, triumphal banners and great processions through the city. The spectacle was vividly evoked by Charles Russell (1850–1910) in his panoramic canvas of *The O'Connell Centenary Celebrations*. Such displays of power, coupled with the church-building programme undertaken by the Catholic Church at the same time, did very little to mend the breach, or to reconcile the suburban Protestant population to the reality of the new power in the land.

The relationship between the two, between city and suburban 'townships', was deeply dysfunctional, characterised as it was by a sort of mutual municipal hostility. This was in spite of the proximity between the two entities, their countless economic, cultural and family ties, the endless coming and going between the two, the wholly symbiotic relationship. The more the city authorities agitated for control over the city suburbs, the more the suburban authorities fought, and for a long time successfully, against any such measures. There were endless quarrelsome turf wars fought over such issues as rates, water supplies and other infrastructural questions – prosaic but deeply important and all founded on the issue of power and who was to wield it. And the result of this dysfunction was that Dublin remained confined and impoverished within the canals and estranged politically from its own hinterland.

The relative financial standing of these 'townships', in comparison to the city itself, can be deduced from the quality of the municipal buildings that survive from those days. Dublin city – in sharp contrast to similar-sized English cities – is noticeable for a relative dearth of good, sturdy Victorian civic buildings, the result of that narrow tax base and an inability to invest properly in its infrastructure. The 'townships', on the other hand, preserve today some of the finest Victorian and Edwardian buildings in the city. Joyce describes in *A Portrait of the Artist* the 'trees and the scattered light of the villas', the 'air of wealth and repose', as the 'voice of a servant was heard singing as she sharpened knives' in a lamplit kitchen. Elizabeth Bowen remembers the 'red roads' full of well-heeled residents in their large mansion-like red-brick houses hidden behind dense shrubberies – so very different from the austere Georgian terraced house that was her winter home. And classy folk bred classy shops:

> where white cotton coats were worn these were chalky clean, and sweet dry sawdust covered victuallers' floors. Everyone had not only manners but time: we nearby residents made this our own village. Unfamiliar faces seldom appeared; kind smiles came over high counters at me, and almost everyone knew my name. A few red shops and large red hospital had had places cut for them in the facades of grey [...] Stretching across the roof lines of Upper Baggot Street I see a timeless white sky, a solution of sunshine in not imminent cloud – a sky for the favoured.[5]

Handsome Church of Ireland churches and quietly agreeable squares and terraces abound in these neighbourhoods even today, and the elaborate public library and tall tower of the fine town hall in Rathmines, for example, are prominent landmarks in the area, recalling the expansive means, generous income and well-heeled and predominantly Protestant population of those nineteenth-century days. South, in Dún Laoghaire (Kingstown) – another township that had prospered following the completion of its great harbour and by the arrival of the railway in 1834 and another suburb that kept a strict distance from the city itself – the distinctive façade and handsome tower of yet another town hall has welcomed generations of travellers from its prominent position beside those pincer-like harbour walls.

Not that it was all posh shops and elaborate brickwork in these districts. The authorities of Rathmines seem to have been a good deal more concerned with maintaining low rates of local taxation than in investing to any great extent in the township's infrastructure. When gas streetlamps were introduced into Dublin city in 1824, for example, the authorities in Rathmines declined the offer to establish a similar lighting system throughout its jurisdiction on the grounds of expense, with the result that, even late in the century, its streets were plunged into darkness after nightfall. They were also reluctant to invest in a proper fire brigade until the need became pressing – and even then it was clearly inadequate. In Kingstown, meanwhile, a lack of a proper sewage system resulted in a large amount of raw effluent being discharged directly into Dublin Bay – especially embarrassing to a township marketing itself as a tourist attraction.

The suburbs also went to some considerable lengths to maintain a certain social homogeneity. Their residents could relax in the knowledge that the authorities would do a good deal to make sure that undesirable elements, including members of the 'labouring classes', did not come to settle in these areas in the first place – and that if they did, would soon be rooted out. One house on the Ranelagh Road in Rathmines, for example, had its water supply disconnected in an effort to drive out its tenants. And it is remarkable that, in an age when the Catholic population of the city and country was rising steadily, the number of Catholics in Rathmines, for example, actually fell in the second half of the century.

In the neighbouring Pembroke township, we see the inevitable consequences of this kind of social engineering. Unlike Rathmines, Pembroke was obliged to deal with a large resident – and poor – Catholic population, who lived in the old maritime villages at Ringsend and Irishtown, close to the mouth of the Liffey. The contrast between the elegant terraces of Pembroke, Elgin and Raglan Roads on the one hand and these miserable, low-lying cottages and cabins at the other end of the township was stark, and in the end impossible to ignore, with even the Establishment-oriented *Irish Times* damning the disgrace of it all: 'Not even on the west coast of Africa,' it thundered, 'are the natives worse than are the humble residents of Irishtown, Ringsend and Ballsbridge.'[6]

This sense of the townships as inhabiting an alternative *Upstairs, Downstairs* universe is further emphasised by the suppression of Donnybrook Fair in mid-century. This large, noisy and prosperous fair had been a staple of Dublin life for over 600 years. From its medieval origins as a summer fair trading animals, wool and various odds and ends for a week in August, Donnybrook Fair had developed into a two-week extravaganza famed far and wide for its fights, hedonism, profligate drunkenness, sexual immorality – truly, the works. The tales have doubtless grown in the telling, especially since the Fair was first scaled back and then abolished in 1855; but it is small wonder that the word 'donnybrook' had by that point edged its way into English dictionaries to mean 'a place of uproar'. The abolition of the Fair was the result of a terrifyingly potent combination of a tightening Victorian moral code, the disapproval of an ever more powerful and authoritarian Catholic Church and the dismay of the

Pembroke township at having to play host to such an annual exercise in hedonism.

Erskine Nicol (1825–1904), in what would appear to be a touching but poignant tribute to this Dublin institution, painted his vast and elaborate canvas entitled *Donnybrook Fair* in 1859, four years after its abolition. The tents, the revellers, the placards advertising various freak shows (including a canine fortune-teller) – all debauched human life is here, though delightfully leavened by the presence of a tent manned by a temperance order, pitched woefully in the midst of the disorder. Seeing this canvas, one can but sigh in bitter grief that such a corrective to corseted Victorian Dublin was ever allowed to pass away. Today, Donnybrook Fair is remembered in the city only in the name of a chain of delicatessens – albeit a giddyingly upmarket chain and therefore hedonistic enough, maybe, in its own way.

This urban–suburban relationship is even more odd given the volume of traffic passing between these various entities. The good denizens of Pembroke and Rathmines would have travelled daily into Dublin: the gentlemen on business, the ladies to shop in Switzers, maybe, or in Pim's department store on South George's Street. By mid-century, they might have gone into town again, this time for a comfortable evening at the Star of Erin Music Hall – now the Olympia on Dame Street, with its Victorian tiered interior, all plush seats and elaborate stained glass – to partake in a comfortable evening of light opera, sketches or minstrel shows. At century's end, the bourgeoisie were coming into town to visit one of the new picture houses, maybe to visit Ireland's very first cinema show, screened at the Olympia in April 1896; maybe even to visit the short-lived Volta Cinema, established in 1906 by a certain Mr Joyce on Mary Street. Well heeled and all as they were, the suburbs had nothing like such a range of delights to offer; and the existence of such civic jollities also, incidentally, gives the lie to the notion that the city centre in those years consisted of little more than a ruinous, pox-infested landscape.

Such a civic relationship, so extremely odd and at once remote and necessarily intimate, could not ultimately be sustained – especially after a natural expansion of the municipal boundary of Belfast in 1896 resulted in a doubling in the size of that city, rendering it at a stroke more populous than Dublin. It was too grievous a blow to civic pride and altogether too absurd a situation to be further tolerated, and the city of Dublin was duly, and belatedly, extended into its natural hinterland. Only up to a point, however, and still grudgingly – the two most prosperous suburbs of Rathmines and Pembroke held out as independent entities as late as 1930. But the impact of what had been a supremely troubled relationship persisted and can still be seen in the fabric of the city of Dublin today.

Chapter 18

⊗

'PART ELEGANT AND PARTLY SLUM'[1]

On the northern bank of the Liffey, as the river begins to widen in its approach to the sea and close to the end of the new Sean O'Casey footbridge, stands a sculpture ensemble: a group of human figures, cast in bronze, razor-thin and rather taller than life-size. They make a striking sight, their impact enhanced further by their position opposite George's Dock where concerts take place in the summer months and markets at Christmas, on a floating stage. In autumn, during the Theatre Festival, the Spiegeltent sets up shop on the water and offers an evening of 1920s decadence inside its mirror-spangled walls. The dock has been earmarked too as a site for a new Abbey Theatre and it marks in general a gateway to the city's docklands – or rather Docklands, now taking off as a zone of urban regeneration and enterprise. To one side of the harbour is the Stack A building – striking of design if not quite of name – built by John Rennie in 1821 as a tobacco and wine warehouse, and now decked with sparkling fairy lights, rebranded and redesigned as an exhibition space with cafés, wine bars and other zones of cheerful consumerism attached. Beyond, the main Docklands drag is lined with new apartment buildings and restaurants, cafés, new hotels. It is all part of a sustained effort to stretch Dublin's commercial centre beyond its traditional heart and east, into these spacious, watery areas. The contrast, meanwhile, between the sculpture ensemble and its surroundings – whether intentional or not – could scarcely be more marked and more painfully pleasing. This set of figures, after all, is the city's Famine Memorial, remembering a time when Dublin – and this Dublin too, in this very specific locale – had rather more to think about than wine bars.

The history and consequences of the Great Famine of 1845 to 1849 have been much picked over in Irish history, and it remains an area of great contention. Whether British policies exacerbated the effects of the Famine, whether they turned a shortage into a disaster, whether those policies were sins of omission or of commission, have and will continue to be much discussed. What is certainly the case is that the swelling population of Ireland had already been dangerously dependent on the potato crop in the years leading up to the catastrophe; that in the summer of 1845, the potato plants were seen to be rotting in the fields, the potatoes themselves coming out of the ground as a soft and stinking mass; that this horror of potato blight repeated itself in successive summers; that up to a million people died in Ireland from famine in these years; and that between a million and two million people emigrated during and immediately after the Famine. It is also clear that the experience of famine in Dublin itself both mirrored the experience in the rest of the island but also diverged radically from that experience.

Although the city of Dublin had long since accustomed itself to accommodating a steady influx of newcomers from the countryside, the scale of such immigration in the Famine years threatened to overwhelm it. The city's workhouses, not filled in 1845, overflowed in 1846 and again in the following year, as the Famine tightened its dreadful grip. The prisons filled too, as desperate people committed crimes in the hope of admittance to jail; inside, they would at least be fed, although they also ran the risk of succumbing to one of any number of diseases that ran rampant in the unsanitary and overcrowded conditions. The city gained rapidly in population, as did other cities – Belfast, Cork, Derry – as the starving and dispossessed fled the countryside in search of relief or, if no relief was forthcoming, in search of an emigration ship that would take them away from Ireland for good.

The spot now occupied by the Famine sculptures, by summer-clad lingerers by George's Dock quaffing their Chardonnay – this spot would have seen much in the way of bitter and desperate farewells, as ships crowded into the Liffey estuary to pick up their cargo of passengers and bear them away to new lives in the United States and Canada. *An Emigrant Ship, Dublin Bay, Sunset* (1853) by Edwin Hayes (1819–1904) captures, albeit with rather jarring romanticism, a typical scene in the waters off Dublin in the post-Famine years. The ship in question looms in the foreground, as a rowing boat filled with emigrants makes its way out to meet it; the waters in the background are choked with yet more tall, three-masted sailing ships. A scene of considerable industry but glowering and sad under a vast and melancholic sunset.

Not everyone had the means or the inclination to emigrate, however, and those that remained added to the pressing housing shortage in Dublin. The city's population would continue to rise in the years after the Famine, even as the population of the rest of the country spiralled ever downward. And, if the first half of the century witnessed a steady growth of the city's slums, the years after the Famine saw this problem develop into a scandal. Industrial-scale soup kitchens became a prominent feature of city life until they were abruptly shut down in 1847; thereafter the utterly destitute and starving wandering the streets of the capital were a common sight. And meanwhile, in another indication of the cleavage between the two sides of Dublin society, the social life of the governing class continued each winter, with balls and concerts galore, and even, in 1849, a royal visit by a still youthful Victoria.

In some of the last glimpses we have of O'Connell, he is pleading in the House of Commons with increasing desperation for an adequate British response to the ravages of the Famine:

> I have shown you our distress. I have shown you that there are no agricultural labourers, no peasantry in Europe, so badly off – suffering such privations as do the great body of the Irish people. [...] There are five millions of people always on the verge of starvation. I have shown you from Government documents ... that its [Ireland's] people are threatened, that they are in the utmost danger of fearful famine, with its concomitant horrors. [...] I call upon all the members of this House to join in the most energetic measures to stop the impending calamity. You cannot be too speedy, you cannot be too extensive in your remedies. [...] death to an enormous amount will be the consequence of neglect.[2]

This broad context – not just of famine with its attendant horrors, but of famine combined with political chafing against colonial rule – was to consolidate the sense among the country's Catholic majority that their British masters were at best indifferent to Irish affairs, at worst malicious in intent. 'God sent the potato blight,' so the contemporary saying went, 'but the English caused the Famine.' And, while debate and argument may still rage over the Famine, over its origins, its consequences and the reactions to its predations, there is little doubt that it progressed a changing mood in Irish affairs. It encapsulated and advanced that mood, or tide, or energy, for change that had been waxing in the country as the century wore on.

— ◄o► —

Disorder and political and financial insecurity, whether originating in famine or in some other cause, always impact first and most directly on the lives of the poor, and so it was in Dublin too. The result of the horribly potent combination of mismanagement, political jockeying and financial chaos in the nineteenth century was acute deprivation, even before the Famine took hold of Ireland and certainly in its aftermath. Dublin very rapidly acquired the unenviable reputation of having some of the worst – that is to say, most visible – levels of urban deprivation in western Europe; and it is largely as a result of this ostentatious poverty that the nineteenth century in the city is imagined to be one of unremitting gloom and grief. As the suburbs spread rapidly and bedded down to stay, so too did the slums of Dublin – and not only in those places that had always been slums and which could therefore be more easily ignored, but in all quarters of the city.

George Moore sketches the gathering darkness of these late century days in the most atmospheric terms, demonstrating that even the most well-heeled neighbourhoods could not take their status and safety for granted:

> And the darkness grows thicker, but the man still stands on the bridge. Around him every street is deserted. On the right murder has ended for the night; on the left, towards Merrion Square, the violins have ceased to sing in the ballrooms; and in their white beds the girls sleep their white sleep of celibacy…[A]ll but he are at rest; and now the city sleeps; wharves, walls and bridges are veiled and have disappeared in the fog that has crept up from the sea; the shameless squalor of the outlying streets is wrapped in the grey mist, but over them and dark against the sky the Castle still stretches out its arms as if for some monstrous embrace.[3]

Take the fine new façades of D'Olier Street, which had been laid out by the Wide Streets Commissioners and which was an integral section of that stately channel of streets from the Castle to Sackville Street; behind them, in the nineteenth century, lay some of the worst slums in the city, squeezed into the space between Trinity College and the Liffey embankments where the Vikings had once established their Long Stone. Urban renewal is well under way in this part of Dublin today. There are a good many gleaming new apartment and office buildings, and yet even so it remains an odd part of town. Horrendous structures such as hideous Hawkins House, togged out with stained grey brick and buckling aluminium windows, look out over narrow streets; Pearse Street, which runs east from the city centre towards Lansdowne Road stadium, is largely stripped of businesses these days and traffic-snarled from morning to night; and, since the fine old Theatre Royal was demolished in the 1960s, only the Screen cinema and Mulligan's pub provide much in the way of cheer.

Alleviation is on the way today – or so they say at any rate. Over many years, Trinity slowly bought most of the houses on the south side of Pearse Street, sealed their entrances and opened the rear of each building to the grounds of the College instead. Good for the campus, but disastrous for Pearse Street, which was slowly stripped of its life and commerce. Now, the College intends to reverse its engineering works, and maybe a less dismal future is in store for Pearse Street as a result. But perhaps the area's previous history has left a mark on the streets and buildings, like a shadow on a lung. In ages past the home of the Lazar's Hill leper hospital, the area added to its unpleasant reputation first in 1754 with the arrival of the hopelessly named Hospital for Incurables, which provided a home – if a dreadful one – for the crippled, the deformed and the otherwise medically challenged. The intention of the hospital, frankly, was rather to remove these unfortunates from sight than to treat them in any meaningful way. Then, in 1792, the Incurables was removed to the suburbs and the Lock Hospital arrived in its place, dedicated to the treatment of venereal disease. Quite a succession. Quite a history.

The area, of course, had competition. If a punter had ventured off Grafton Street in those nineteenth-century days and, skirting the Castle, walked west towards the Liberties, the worst sights in Dublin would have been lying in wait. Here too the city's fabric began to disintegrate into slums, with St Patrick's and Marsh's famously fenced about by the very worst kinds of housing. Or north, crossing the river towards old Oxmantown; or east, in the lanes and alleys behind Merrion Square, for desolation was liberally scattered through the city. The gradual movement of the prosperous into the suburbs meant that there were always opportunities for once grand houses and their associated outbuildings to be converted to a new use. Converted – but we should say 'converted', maybe, for the word implies a thoroughgoing adaptation of dwellings to the needs of its new inhabitants, which was certainly not the case.

It did not much help matters that in Ireland, as in Britain, the contemporary orthodoxy in relation to social distress discouraged much in the way of a consistent response to these problems. The state laid only the lightest hand on what was essentially a free-market, laissez-faire economic system; it was not until later in the century that this creed would change, as society changed around it. Until that point, a clumsy mingling of public charity and private enterprise worked to alleviate social distress. Older charities such as the eighteenth-century Sick and Indigent Roomkeepers Society, still functioning in the aftermath of the Famine, were joined by new Catholic institutions such as the Sisters of Mercy (founded by Catherine McAuley in 1831) and Sisters of Charity (founded by Mary Aikenhead in 1815), which became active in Ireland and abroad. But this activity was limited even at the best of times; and at the worst of times, its limited reach and its shortcomings were laid shockingly bare.

In these slums of Dublin, conditions could be hellish. In small alleys and courts across the city, in dark cellars and basement rooms, and in once fine first-floor libraries and drawing rooms, families lived in the most desperate of situations. Many of the poorest houses and cabins were built on land reclaimed from the sea and the river and had no natural drainage. Even late in the century there was little or no running water in the great majority of houses, no adequate lighting and still no sewage systems worth the name. The Liffey was an open sewer, the yards and lanes of the city abounded with human and animal waste, and the pavements and ditches ran with filth and provided perfect breeding conditions for disease.[4]

Epidemics of typhoid and cholera were, as a result, regular features of Dublin life, and what the city did not itself generate effortlessly, it imported on the ships coming in from Liverpool. The ongoing pollution of the river and the sea led to contamination of the cockle and mussel beds in Dublin Bay, and this in turn led to even higher incidents of typhoid than would otherwise have been the case. The numbers of typhoid deaths only began to fall, in fact, following the enforced closure of the cockle beds in the early twentieth century.

As attitudes towards public health and state responsibility began to evolve, there were greater efforts made to ameliorate conditions in the city. Various Acts of Parliament were passed, most of them cobbled together badly or hastily and most them having little or no impact. Inspectors were appointed, minor fines levied, and premises threatened with closure. Some of the ameliorating measures were literally surface deep: by-laws issued in 1851, for example, stipulated that certain premises be whitewashed. Later again, with the public mood now actively shifting and with the concept of the public good becoming emphatically mainstream, slum clearance began in certain quarters of the city. It was claimed – in keeping with the Victorian emphasis on both internal and external cleanliness – that the removal of such slums from the face of the city would inevitably improve not just public health but also public morality, which throughout the century had been the subject of much official hand-wringing.

And with slum clearance came new housing – subsidised public or private. Even the suburban townships began to address these pressing problems: the house-building activities of Pembroke township picked up markedly at the turn of the century, and even the authorities in Rathmines, long subject to shrill accusations from Dublin Corporation that they were evading their social responsibilities, oversaw the construction of artisan dwellings in various parts of the township. In Dublin itself, much of the oldest and most fetid fabric of the city was swept away for good, notably the now notorious eighteenth- and nineteenth-century slums of the Liberties. In the Coombe, in the valley of the now culverted Poddle, surviving nineteenth-century public housing demonstrates a new model of social engineering: neat red-brick streets hide quiet courtyards built as an effort to give residents a respite from the congested city around them. Most private Dublin companies resisted any invitation to contribute to such schemes themselves, but a few did enter into this changing social atmosphere, notably the Guinness family. The impact and legacy of the Guinness family, in fact – socially, architecturally, philanthropically – remains overwhelmingly present in and around the Liberties.

The Guinness domination of this district of the city has historically been not simply physical or economic, of course, but psychological too. So is always the case with dominant and philanthropic families. The Guinnesses, like other immensely wealthy socially minded families in other cities – the Rowntrees in York, say, or the Cadburys in Birmingham – were involved in every aspect of their employees' lives, and in the life of the city as a whole. And the result of this philanthropy is everywhere to be seen in this part of Dublin. St Patrick's Park, for example, adjoining its eponymous cathedral, was laid out in the early years of the twentieth century to replace the horrendous slums that once flanked the cathedral walls, and its establishment was bankrolled by the Guinness Trust. St Patrick's itself was largely rebuilt and restored in the nineteenth century under the patronage of Benjamin Lee Guinness. Think of the Iveagh Market rising amid the throng of antique shops on Francis Street. It was created by Benjamin Lee Guinness to compensate the market traders for land lost in the laying out of St Patrick's Park and to provide them with a covered trading area. It is a distinctive building, though sadly neglected now, with buddleia growing in the roofs and gutters. Think of the now vanished Lying-In Hospital in the Coombe, established in 1826 in response to the number of women in the area who died in childbirth, and soon endowed by the Guinness family with a dispensary. Think, in particular, of the handsome Victorian design of the Iveagh Buildings that overlook St Patrick's Park and which bear the Guinness imprimatur. Instead of constructing small houses and cottages, as was accomplished elsewhere in the city, the Guinness architects favoured large complexes built around airy courtyards and encompassing not only accommodation but kindergartens and educational and sporting facilities. Large ideas, and specifically and emphatically part of a wider scheme of social engineering.

In many respects, these expansive and ambitious schemes were perfectly straightforward, for many working-class families were rehoused in larger, sturdier and more hygienic quarters than could ever have been imagined up to that point. And certainly it is difficult to imagine the old slums holding much in the way of sentimental attraction for anyone. But philanthropy – or social engineering, or call it what you will – is a muddy and complicated subject, evoking as it does a sense of immense and righteous control over the lives of other people. It is difficult to quarrel with its architectural legacy to the city of Dublin, but its overall impact was, and remains, rather more complex. The Guinness-sponsored buildings, for example, never addressed the needs of the very poorest members of society: instead, they and their facilities were reserved for Guinness employees and their families; and whereas their influence on health as well as on the fabric of the city cannot be doubted, their wider social effect was a good deal more limited.

Of even more dubious impact was the slow and belated entry, late in the century, of the Corporation into the field of public housing. After 1879, and in keeping with the new social respectability of such activity, the city authorities embarked on a plan of action that would see tenement after tenement condemned, demolished and rebuilt. It was a slow plan, hampered by a lack of resources and of genuine enthusiasm for what was taking place in Dublin's name. There is a distinct impression, indeed, that these schemes were forced upon the city and undertaken out of a sense of shame and public scandal that could no longer be ignored. This sense is only emphasised by the fact that there was no great social stigma attached to the ownership of the tenements, horrendous and all as they usually were. Indeed, city councillors and various professional pillars of the community were among the owners of the slum tenements and there is seldom any indication that this was seen as much of a problem.

Those first houses built in the Coombe were solid, with thick walls, adequate sewerage systems and a water supply. In true Victorian style, they were represented as emanating a very miasma of delight – issuing along with the new water supplies, from their sturdy pipes, perhaps. Their existence, it was claimed, would serve as a potent symbol of virtue to the hovels and slums that surrounded them, and that had not yet been knocked down; and their fortunate inhabitants would also serve as an example of what good and virtuous living could bring.

This, in itself, is typical enough of Victorian discourse, with its strident public narratives of purity, industry and righteousness. It was also typical, alas, that the question of what would happen to the former residents of the slums – removed so that their homes could be demolished and replaced with a new caste of the rent-paying righteous – was well and truly fudged. Contemporary commentators claimed that all would be well in the end, that the gradual renewal of Dublin's public housing would benefit all and sundry eventually, if only people would be patient for a little while longer. It was a nineteenth-century version of the modern 'trickle down' theory. In other words, like that theory, it consisted of little more than hypocrisy, nonsense and cant. By the end of the century, the *Irish Times* was noting both the injustice and the impracticality of these schemes in creating a new and pathetic subclass of the peripatetic dispossessed who simply removed to another tenement elsewhere in the city, there to vanish for another period of time from the statistics and the public eye. The newspaper commented:

> Many in Dublin cannot afford to pay even 2/-. They live in courts, lanes etc. and the poorest class tenements. These are 'unhealthy' and many of them are cleared by the Corporation [...] new dwellings are erected but evicted people cannot afford the rent of the new. They have sought refuge in the lowest class tenements and in the process of time, the districts to which they have migrated become as unhealthy as the ones from which they have been evicted.[5]

This was not a conundrum that could ever be satisfactorily resolved. Meanwhile, those happy few who inhabited the new model homes in the inner city were invited to aspire to an improving, sub-bourgeois and sub-suburban life, with competitions held and prizes awarded for the neatest houses, prettiest windows and most blooming window boxes.

With all this grime, filth and endless sweeps of disease came natural consequences. The Victorians were highly adept at denying what they could not control, as we shall see later, but they were equally good at obsessing over what they could control, and in mid-century Dublin this took the form of a specific attention to cleanliness. It is unfortunate for the city's population that this did not take the form of comprehensive public works – adequate running water, say, or sewage schemes. It was nothing so ambitious as that. Instead, Dublin witnessed the rolling out of a series of Turkish baths across the city. Such baths are hardly synonymous with Dublin – not any more – but in fact they formed quite a feature of city life in the second half of the nineteenth century. And of Irish life too, for they were something of an Irish invention. Referred to in Europe as Roman–Irish baths as a result of their mixed genesis, they were connected explicitly with cleanliness and relief from a variety of ailments. The first one was founded by Richard Barter at St Anne's in Blarney, County Cork, in 1851; thereafter, they cropped up in various locations across Ireland from the middle of the century onwards. Barter went on to incorporate them into his workhouses, which were not, God knows, in any other way the luxury spas of their time. Even animals were given treatments in these establishments, for the sake of their health and hence for good, sound, economically productive reasons.

The distinctiveness and importance of the Turkish Bath Movement, in Britain at any rate, was not simply an indication of the increasing Victorian fascination with dirt and cleanliness, but a sign too of a genuinely working-class movement to improve living and sanitary conditions, to import foreign methods of stamping out illness and disease and to create institutions specifically tailored to their needs. David Urquhart's movement in England itself stemmed from his observation of Barter's set-up at Blarney. Urquhart took back to England his knowledge of Irish methods, with the result that his Turkish Bath Movement took off – sometimes in the face of considerable opposition from the medical establishment – from the 1850s on. In Ireland, however, the situation was rather different. Although Barter's work was successful, the baths movement in general was more philanthropic in nature and so, as was the situation with Dublin's new Victorian public housing, this air of philanthropy served to complicate the situation. Handed down as they were from above, tainted by an air of middle-class do-goodery, and never wholly owned by those that were supposed to use them, the specifically working-class baths never took off in Ireland in the same way.

Dublin possessed its own working-class baths, on Temple Street, in the north inner city. The first of the city's elaborate Turkish baths, however, opened on Lincoln Place, behind Trinity College, in 1860. Opened with a splash too, architecturally, that is, for the building was almost as thoroughly un-Dublin in its lines and design as is possible to imagine, sporting a large Ottoman or 'Saracenic' dome, 'many narrow pilasters, half-moon apertures, fretwork'[6] and – for good measure – a clutch of pseudo-minarets. It was, though, partly fronted in gleaming Portland stone, in what was perhaps a vestigial nod at past Dublin building traditions. It must have been a striking sight in those mid-century days, on a murky Dublin morning on a murky Dublin street, and it stretches the imagination delightfully to imagine what certain people, in those strait-laced days, would have made of it.

Inside the walls of this domed and minareted building, the Turkish theme was continued in lip-smacking and kitschy excess – as one client, who calls himself 'Moist Man' in his proto-blog of the time, makes clear:

... I was conducted into a large room around which were arranged little curtained pavilions about the size and shape of a four-post bedstead. The room was decidedly Turkish in its aspect and appointments, the crescent form being as far as possible given to every thing, while ottomans and other matters of oriental furniture were to be seen. The servants wore long scarlet flowing dressing gowns and Turkish slippers, and on stands were arranged trays with china coffee-cups, &c. [...] the calidarium ... was still more ottomanic than the [tepidarium], being in dim prismatic twilight, and without windows, unless the little star-shaped scraps of crimson, blue, and amethyst-stained glass, artistically inserted in the vaulted roof, could be so-called.[7]

Such a description is reminiscent, in fact, of some of Dublin's more extravagant theme bars of the present day, with their full-grown palm trees and expensively and badly frescoed ceilings. Maybe this in turn might lead to another agreeable speculation: that a love of camp is a persistent, if somewhat unlikely, characteristic of the city.

The Lincoln Street baths are the most famous of the Dublin Turkish baths, largely due to the fact that Joyce referred to them in *Ulysses* – his protagonist Leopold Bloom considered a visit to the baths on 16 June 1904. (The baths on Lincoln Place in fact closed in 1899.) But many other baths were liberally sprinkled through the city, both north and south of the river and in the suburbs too. Some of these establishments were not simply upmarket but positively ritzy. In one particularly agreeable Sackville Street bath house, for example, underfloor heating jockeyed for position with ice cream, brilliant gaslight and gleaming stained-glass windows. It is evident, in fact, that nearly all of Dublin's Turkish baths were distinctively bourgeois affairs: resolutely upmarket, with none of the hoi polloi in sight if they could be avoided. They acted as an updated version of the earlier bathing houses that lined the shore of Dublin Bay and which were also reserved exclusively for the use of the quality. It was certainly the case that, although the city's baths were open to whomsoever could pay, and although first-class and second-class bathing was available, both classes were beyond the means of the city's poor, and there was no great impetus in Dublin to change this state of affairs.

In this, then, the experience of Dublin is markedly different not simply from that of many British cities but from the wider Irish experience too. The baths symbolised a privatisation of health and hygiene in the city; that is to say, the Victorians may have been manic about cleanliness of the body and of the soul, but this mania in Dublin took an explicitly personal form. The baths at Lincoln Place and elsewhere, with their minarets and crescent-shaped fittings and fixtures and general air of easeful pleasure, in this way served as useful symbols of one aspect of the city's social life, and in the process as yet another strikingly odd and contradictory feature of Victorian Dublin's mental and urban landscape. The other pole was, as we know, characterised by the extreme deprivation and want, the filth and disease of those days. And as it happened, the city of Dublin had a prodigiously useful symbol for this feature of city life too.

For the most desperate in society – as we know from the displays occasionally to be glimpsed from the roof of my apartment building – there is always prostitution to fall back on; and so it was a happy chance that Dublin, by the end of the nineteenth century, was the proud possessor of one of the largest red-light districts in the British Empire. This striking fact owes a good deal to the general poverty and appallingly straitened circumstances in which most people in the city found themselves. It also, however, came about as a result of the very large number of British soldiers that were stationed in the city at any one time; and naturally it also drew a good deal of its economic strength from the fact that Dublin was a thriving port. Together, these factors led to the gradual formation of a red-light area popularly known as Monto – Joyce's Night-Town – in a district north of the Custom House, east of Sackville Street and west of what is now Connolly Station.

Foley Street runs through the area today, although the nomenclature here has been altered; its former name was Montgomery Street, which was changed by the Corporation in a fruitless attempt to rid the area of its livid reputation. Plans were even drawn up to insert public housing in the very heart of what the *Irish Times* called this 'loathsome locality', as a means of cleansing Monto; plans that were perforce abandoned after claims that decent families would never consent to live in the midst of such a den of iniquity.[8]

The tales told about Monto have passed into popular myth: the tunnels that led into and out of the district and that enabled various clients to pass into and out of the arms of their chosen girls all unobserved; the ferocious madams who ran the operations, each one keeping their girls in debt and in thrall; the bastard children born as a result of a million couplings, and who were wholly possessed by the system; the sheer size of the Monto operation, with up to 1,600 girls working at any one time; the slick class consciousness that prevailed even here, with certain houses of pleasure a good deal better appointed and regarded than others – and so it goes on. It was a hard-nosed business: the madams had a masterly knowledge of British troop movements, for example, sending out their cards afresh as each new regiment arrived in the city. It is even possible to piece together a roll-call of clients: not just Joyce either, but also the future Edward VII, in Dublin on military service and who apparently came a-visiting to Monto in order to shed himself of the encumbrance of his virginity – if you can believe this.

They are all highly Victorian, these tales: *Fingersmith* in its evocation of flickering gaslight and river mists; the passing gentlemen in it for the exercise and the relief; the passing policemen quick to pounce; the madams in voluminous shawls, at once motherly and savage. The carefully poised Victorian social model is all here, making a mockery of its cherished virtue even as this virtue is trumpeted from the rooftops; in this, in all this, Dublin was like any other big city in this still United Kingdom. Only when the Irish dimension is brought into account – the city heavy with a military presence and with new, muscular Catholic churches – does the scene refocus. Now it becomes even more strange and contradictory, even more reeking of hypocrisy, if possible, than any standard Victorian city. Monto would survive until the 1930s, although in diminished form, but eventually the changed political situation, the loss of its military patrons and the moral climate prevailing in the new Irish Free State came together to pronounce its end.

The existence of Monto with its subtext of disease and human deprivation, and of the city's luxurious and scrupulously clean Turkish baths – these elements of the city are as two sides of the one coin, encapsulating the divisions and contradictions of Dublin. They also underscore, in my mind, a preoccupation with a notion of hygiene that has evolved into a consistent cultural trope in the culture of the city and of Ireland. It is a thread that connects, obscurely but persistently, back to the Lock Hospital, built after the expulsion of the Incurables to the countryside at the beginning of the century. The Lock would remain on its Townsend Street site, close to the Liffey, until its eventual closure in 1952. By 1820, it had morphed into a female-only institution and become part of particularly Victorian discourse that was obsessed with a notion of female sexual depravity and disease.

And, fascinatingly, as the hospital developed and focused its operations, so another element appeared as part of its medical vision – the laundry. The cleansing and drying of garments and fabric became part of a moral treatment applied to female patients in the Lock Hospital, envisaged as it was as part of a means whereby women might be in some way treated – that is, controlled and cleaned. It is, maybe, one of the earliest manifestations of what would eventually become an infamous part of the fabric of the city – the Magdalen laundries. They were run by nuns within convent walls until late in the twentieth century, and staffed by women and girls who had, in various ways and by various means, been rejected by wider society. The taproot, the taint, the persistent cultural notion of female sexual impurity – this is one which runs and runs.

Come back to the contrasts we made earlier, between the Dublin of then and of now. The two cities – can we compare them? In a plain and practical sense, the physical and topographical threads that connect them are strikingly evident, for the lines of the early nineteenth-century city are very much those of today; the modern streets were fully formed even then, so many of the buildings remain intact and the Liffey bridged busily, extravagantly, even charmingly and with grace. The circularity of history is evident too: those new suburbs that impacted so greatly on the old city centre have within two centuries gone down a little in the world and then back up, with a vengeance. Walk over the bridge across the Dodder in Ballsbridge and look up at the gleaming new hotels. Walk through the centre of Donnybrook and glance into the electronics shops and delicatessens or at the prices in estate agents windows for all the evidence you could ever want. And the bourgeois habits of consumption, so evident on Grafton Street today – these were on show then also, in the form of elegant shops, catering to equally elegant patrons, in the form of luxurious Turkish baths, and much else besides.

So much for the consistency, the shared experiences. There is discontinuity too, of course – a flinching discontinuity between the dragon fruit on display in the city's upmarket delis and the overflowing workhouses of Dublin in the Famine. The social deprivation that characterised the nineteenth century is today a distant memory; the social problems and inequality that characterise present-day Dublin are bad enough, but they cannot equal the horrors of the old slums and the poverty and disease. But much, if not exactly identical, is certainly recognisable.

Dublin today, of course, covers a vastly greater area, and that area includes the townships that in those days lay stubbornly outside the city's control; and it is in this economic and political sense that change is evident. The city is a capital once more, for one thing, and the paraphernalia so traumatically stripped away early in the nineteenth century has been restored and augmented. But here too, change began as a process of evolution – not always steady or constant, and certainly not always smooth or peaceful – but evolution just the same. This evolution, that was part of a gathering national debate and that began so ironically with the Act of Union itself, would gather speed as the century unfolded.

PART FIVE

What Larkin bawled to hungry crowds
Is murmured now in dining-hall
And study. Faith bestirs itself
Lest infidels in their impatience
Leave it behind. Who could have guessed
Batons were blessings in disguise,
When every ambulance was filled
With half-killed men and Sunday trampled
Upon unrest? Such fear can harden
Or soften heart, knowing too clearly
His name endures on our holiest page,
Scrawled in a rage by Dublin's poor.

'Inscription on a Headstone' AUSTIN CLARKE[1]

Chapter 19

⊗

THE SHIFT

Christmas is over at last, leaving maxed-out credit cards and sleepless nights in its wake, and January is passing, mild, damp and snowless. Already, flies are buzzing jauntily against window panes. In the park, the narcissi bulbs are pushing through the wet grass; by March they will be a drift of white under the chestnut trees. On the roof, the plants have a stripped, bleached winter air, but here too life is stirring. I planted giant allium corms in October, beguiled by the photographs on the packet promising bouncing purple blooms the size of footballs, and already their green shoots are breaking the surface.

All this fecundity is unlikely, in the teeth of January. El Niño, say the meteorologists, and this may be the first year without a proper winter in Europe. A daunting enough idea, but to judge from the chatter on the radio, people seem more worried about the dearth of snow in the Alps caused by the mild weather and the impact this might have upon of our lifestyles. For after all, what would we do without our winter skiing? But, although there is no snow or frost, there is wind: gales that roar through bare branches day after day as storms move in jostling lines from the Atlantic and sweep across the country, over Dublin and out to sea again. On one such tempestuous Saturday morning – yet dry and bright with clouds scudding across the sky – I blow into town in search of a little culture.

Reaching Dublin city centre in the first place can be positively an ordeal, whether one is a traveller arriving here for the first time, or a commuter coming into work in the morning. The roads are choked, the buses slow, the gleaming new trams run on lines that do not connect with each other; the main railway stations at Connolly and Heuston may have been lately tarted up but it remains difficult and cumbersome to get from one to the other; and Dublin Airport floats in a galaxy far, far away, in another dimension entirely of space and time, of inefficiency and aesthetic hellishness.

Nowadays, workers have been forced by spiralling house prices to live 130 kilometres (80 miles) away from Dublin, sometimes, to rise before dawn and commute into the city on crowded roads or trains. The compact city centre, therefore, acts as a compensation of sorts for this daily fandango, and for me too, as all the places I want to visit on this Saturday morning are within walking distance of each other. The National Library, National Gallery, National Museum, Natural History Museum – all these cluster within a city block, edged by Merrion Square to the east, the playing fields of Trinity College to the north, St Stephen's Green to the south. In the middle of this enclosure rises Leinster House, today the seat of the Irish legislature, and government departments cluster all around.

It is an unlikely scale for a capital city; a pleasure for the stroller or tourist or a Dubliner intent on business and yet – as two sides of the one coin – tight and enclosed too. This scale and sense of enclosure in some ways symbolises the claustrophobia that this city sometimes engenders, which has driven so many Irish citizens to choose to leave Dublin for good and all. Sometimes, this claustrophobia can seem to be almost tangible. Certainly, it seems extraordinary that so many offices and foundations of the state should be squashed together so, all within a couple of hundred

metres of one other. And the inmates of these offices and foundations naturally socialise together, dine together, drink together – in
the bar of Buswell's Hotel, for example, or in the Horseshoe Bar
of the newly restored Shelbourne Hotel, where politicians have
always gathered and hammered out deals within whispering distance of Leinster House. This is how Dublin works – on a human
level, an intimate level. It is a system with inherent strengths – pri-
marily the ease of doing business. And there are inherent weak-
nesses in such a system too, most notably the tainted breath of an
easy corruption engendered by close familiarity.

The claustrophobia is made manifest in the very entrances to
the National Library and National Museum, the handsome curving porticoes of which face each other across the forecourt of
Leinster House. 'Face each other' – but maybe this is not a correct
description, for each entrance is hedged and squeezed and diminished by the security railings of Leinster House and one must
squeeze through and into each building as though through a tube
of toothpaste. It is always with a sense of relief that I step out of
these cluttered courtyards and into the respective buildings.

Leinster House and the buildings that surround it, it always
seems at such times, were badly served by the Irish state, which
ought to have left the old austere town house well alone and found
a headquarters for its parliament elsewhere. The Oireachtas
reminds me of a cuckoo, elbowing its way into surroundings never
intended for it, and wreaking havoc on what was previously an
ambitious and finely calibrated collection of buildings. Previously
the ultimate address in the city, Leinster House had been offloaded
into the possession of the Royal Dublin Society (RDS) in 1815,
and the RDS continued to own the building until the Parliament
of the new Irish state occupied it in 1922. But in late Victorian and
Edwardian Dublin, Leinster House, its forecourt and its wide
stretch of Leinster Lawn, formed a pleasing centrepiece for the
library, gallery and museums that flanked it on all sides.

I like to imagine the area today – one vast city block – had the legislature not moved in, and had the entire precinct been opened instead to the city as one large and generous public space, the various institutions inter-connecting with each other and with Merrion Square to the east and Grafton Street to the west. As was formerly the case:

> We had a choice of two routes into the city. From the foot of our steps we could turn right, then go along Lower Baggot Street; or we could turn left, take the curve round St Stephen's Church and after that go along Upper Mount Street and the south side of Merrion Square; to this route was added the charm of going through Leinster Lawn, between the Museum and the National Gallery; one then followed that secretive passage, under the high flank of Leinster House, through to the circular lawn on the other side and the gates opening on to Kildare Street.[1]

Such a walk, then, was a possibility for the gentry in Elizabeth Bowen's precisely described Edwardian Dublin. Not possible now; instead Leinster House, in common with most parliamentary complexes, has become more fortified and distant from the citizens – for fear, maybe, of yet more pesky terrorists clipping briskly through summer sunshine, Prada handbags full of enriched uranium at the ready. As a result, we are left with these squeezing and unsatisfactory entrances to museum and library, with these blocks and barriers, with a collection of buildings unable to engage properly either with each other or with the city that surrounds them.

The formation of a nascent cultural quarter for the city began in the turbulent and bitter middle years of the nineteenth century, as the Victorian mania for categorisation and collection began to seek a new direction. As early as 1836, plans were being laid for the establishment of a national library in Dublin, based on the already expanding collections of the RDS and floated with a measure of government money. The RDS and the Royal Irish Academy had also been accumulating, for years, a collection of artefacts that would form the nucleus of a national museum collection: ancient and priceless works of gold and silver, for example, that had been recovered from Irish fields and peat bogs, as well as precious objects taken as booty by Irish soldiers in colonial campaigns overseas and carried home. The result was that, when the two institutions would eventually open towards the end of the century, they would already possess sizeable and unique collections. It would take many more years, however, and the influence of events both in Ireland and in England, before these mooted institutions finally came into being.

The event in Ireland was of course the Famine, which was the cause of a trauma on a national scale and which begged a response of some kind. The event in England – a more specific and localised event – was the Great Exhibition, which was held in 1851 in the Crystal Palace in Hyde Park. The details of the Exhibition – its genesis, rapid delivery, commercial success and stunning impact on the national psyche – are of course all well known, and it is hardly surprising that Dublin was just one of many cities that had watched enviously as events unfolded in London and that resolved to repeat that city's success. The RDS – both the institution and its headquarters – formed a natural centre of the operation and it was intimately involved in the preparations for Dublin's Great Industrial Exhibition, which opened on 12 May 1853. The focus of the Exhibition was to be an imposing five-domed structure of glass and steel – not unlike the original Crystal Palace – sited on the Leinster Lawn beside Leinster House itself, and filled with all manner of economic and industrial displays.

The Exhibition in Dublin was a huge commercial and critical success in its five-month run and, pouring as it did money and visitors into the city, provided a much-needed fillip to the economy in those pinched post-Famine days. It published its own weekly newspaper, which detailed breathlessly the various economic, cultural and indeed spiritual triumphs of the Exhibition:

> now, while with triumph and banner and the acclaims of congregated thousands, the pageantry of martial attire and the gorgeousness of civic robes [...] now while all this tide of human life surges and swells, and pours along the halls which have risen as it were to the touch of the enchanter's wand, a profound emotion agitates the heart.[2]

But, in a sign that Dublin's nineteenth-century industrial heart beat fitfully at best, the majority of the goods on display were British, and not Irish, in origin.

No trace remains of the imposing crystal palace today, of course, and the Leinster Lawn has become the site of a dispiriting and ostensibly temporary government car park. The Exhibition's legacy, however, remains notably tangible today in the shape of the large and much extended building that lies just to the north of the Leinster Lawn. One of the features of the Exhibition had been a side display of Irish art, and this in turn led to the establishment of plans to supply what Dublin had hitherto lacked: a purpose-built gallery – a national gallery – for the city. Funds were raised and construction eventually began, and the new National Gallery building opened on part of the now-vacated Exhibition site in 1864. The initial collection was modest – a mere 125 paintings – but the Gallery's hoard was built up with surprising speed in the years that followed, helped by any number of bequests and good turns. As a result, the Gallery has expanded its building many times since, most recently with the opening of the marvellous Millennium Wing in 2003. The result is that the interior resembles a maze, although hardly an unpleasant one.

The National Gallery provides an agreeable passageway through the city. It can be used as an alternative route through from Merrion Square to Clare Street and so on north and west into the city centre. This, at any rate, is the way that I sometimes use the building, making my way through the passages of inter-connecting rooms, pausing to look at a painting here or a painting there, and then emerging after a few minutes into the high, illuminated spaces of the Millennium Wing, down the long flight of steps and so out into Clare Street. It is perhaps the result of this strong sense of the building as being a marvellous channel that I feel such regret that the whole of what is now the parliamentary complex cannot be used in the same way.

The Gallery has long been imagined, and used, in just such a way – as a place of respite, of change, a place in which to stop for a moment and take a breath. George Bernard Shaw famously took youthful refuge within its walls, finding sanctuary from a hum-drum provincial world outside. He claimed that he received a bet-ter education in this building than ever he did at school, and in his will he bequeathed a portion of his future royalties to the National Gallery as a sign of his enduring gratitude. Samuel Beckett spent a good deal of time here too, nipping in from Trinity and from his father's offices on Clare Street to study the Gallery's collection sys-tematically and to offer a range of comments on the hanging and display of various paintings.

The Gallery has also been around long enough by now that it has accumulated its own weight of tradition and of history. Each January, for example, a selection of Turner watercolours goes on display for one month in the Print Room. The collection was left to the Gallery with the stipulation that it be displayed only in the winter, the better to protect it from the effects of strong sunlight. In today's controlled conditions, of course, such a stipulation would be unnecessary – but the Gallery has chosen to continue this winter tradition nevertheless, turning the display into a splash or occasion; and one cannot but admire the restraint, or, rather, commercial nous of such a decision.

And the building saw its fair share of violent Irish responses to art too, as in 1935, when an aggrieved member of the public punched a hole in a Jean Lurcat landscape on display in the Gallery. The authorities had been nervous of hanging the painting in the first place as they judged it 'very queer' and apprehended that the public in those narrowly doctrinaire days might think so too. Some of the staff feared that the then director of the Gallery, Dermot O'Brien, might have 'a fit' when he saw it. When Beckett subsequently went looking for the Lurcat and could not find it, he assumed that 'O'Brien has it in a cupboard somewhere.'

The Natural History Museum nearby is fascinating in its own way, although its considerable collection, featuring all manner of stuffed mammals, butterflies petrified and framed, arachnids imprisoned within glass jars and a range of primitive creatures pickled and suspended in brine, is by no means for the faint-hearted. For all its variety of horrors, though, the Museum illustrates well the ideological and teleological drive that lay behind this creation of a substantial cultural zone in nineteenth-century Dublin. Its collection has been frozen in time as a memorial to that obsessive Victorian penchant for collection, classification and collation. The other three institutions, National Gallery, Museum and Library – these have all naturally moved with the times, but it is nevertheless worth remembering that the same instinct was responsible, partly at least, for the foundation of all four buildings.

This understanding helps to give meaning to what might otherwise appear to be an odd phenomenon – the creation, with the financial support of a colonial government, of explicitly national cultural institutions in the centre of what was becoming increasingly a contested city. As one looks at an unfortunate butterfly held within its frame inside the charnel house that is the Natural History Museum, or at a maggot-like larva of an exotic species of insect pinned under a glass slide, one is gazing at ideological control made flesh. And in founding these institutions under the aegis of scientific and artistic endeavour and categorisation, combined with a good dash of economic muscle and inventiveness, the same impulse of authority was at work.

The political context lent itself to such enterprises too. The last third of the nineteenth century and beginning of the twentieth saw the Home Rule debate gather pace both in Ireland and in the House of Commons in London. Arguably, the foundation of a series of national cultural bodies surrounding Leinster House lends itself unthreateningly to the notion of this new dispensation: of an Ireland in peaceful and flexible union with Britain.

This was one model. But there were others, for the terrain of nationalism in the Dublin of those years was fractured and contested and the various factions still had all to play for. The orderly collection of buildings to the west of Merrion Square, an unfolding monument to science and classification anchored in the cool and austerely rational design of Leinster House – this was one aspect of a gathering political debate. Up on Sackville Street, another sort of iconography and spectacle was unfolding, in the shape of new monuments to Daniel O'Connell and to Charles Stewart Parnell: potent public figures both and heroes of constitutional nationalism. O'Connell's monument, unveiled in 1882, has the great man flanked by Hibernia herself and by four winged figures representing Patriotism, Fidelity, Eloquence and Courage. The Parnell Monument, which anchors the north end of the street, portrays a figure in full oratorical flight and insisting that the march of a nation can be stopped by no man – and, so the implication must be, by no British government either.

Together, the two memorials offered a potent dialogue with and a significant nationalist iconographic riposte to Nelson atop his pillar – a monument that was, by 1900, already almost a century old and still cordially disliked by most of the city's population. This was not a polar debate; there were too many inflections and shades of opinion, too much of a ferment of ideas to be boiled down into some simplistic philosophical model. Nor was it all-consuming, for the citizens of Dublin were – as we have seen – naturally as interested in their living and working conditions as in the nature of the nation in which they lived. But there was the gathering sense of a contest in the form of bricks and mortar, in icons and engravings, in Petri dishes and on library card catalogues.

On that mild and windy Saturday morning in January, then, with the shopping crowds still relatively sparse – but thickening with every passing moment – it is not to the slaughter house of the Natural History Museum I am heading, nor to the gold-filled mosaiced spaces of the National Museum, nor to the crimson- and green-wallpapered rooms of the National Gallery. Instead, I turn onto Kildare Street, pass Buswell's Hotel on the left and the railings and glass security boxes of Leinster House on the right. I squeeze into the National Library, pass through its echoing rotunda and down the steps to the exhibition rooms, to look at other angles on the national question in those vexed and impassioned years.

The exhibition in question is on W. B. Yeats; it acts as part of the Library's commitment to long-running shows focusing on key figures in Ireland's literary history. I come down the stairs to the sound of a voice chanting 'Sailing to Byzantium' and join a little group of visitors to listen to a short medley of Yeats's poems as an image of the Lake Isle of Innisfree is projected onto the walls in front of us. Filled as it is with context and letters and detail, the exhibition satisfies – even if one cannot help but cast a cold ear on the voiceover artists who occasionally, who more than occasionally, play fast and loose with the poet's words.

It is difficult, of course, not to look pruriently on aspects of this Dubliner's life: on the mysticism of his middle years, the Fascist sympathies of his old age and the devotion to his muse, Maud Gonne, who proved to be, as one contributor to the exhibition puts it, not the 'six-foot virgin' of his imagination but a woman who managed, amazingly, to keep secret the fact that she had two illegitimate children living in France. Once I manage, however, to keep my eye on the ball, the exhibition begins to hint at the debates and ideological flexibility of those end-of-century times. It begins to illustrate the sense in which the national form was up for grabs, and in particular the extent to which the theory and practice of a Dublin-centred nation predated by many years the formation of the state itself.

This is a country noted, of course, for the number of its artists who left its shores, never to return. In this crucial phase in the history of Dublin – these last years of the nineteenth century and opening years of the twentieth – the same syndrome is present, with Wilde and then Shaw and Joyce and later Beckett all departing for England and for Europe. Their impact abroad, of course, is well known, although it is worth mentioning again that these artistic waves are echoed in the politics of the time, in which Ireland and Irish affairs ran out in ripples, coming to dominate and to dog for decades the work of the British Parliament. But this period is also characterised by the presence of artists, activists and intellectuals who left Ireland before coming back to Dublin to stay, to put their new ideas into practice, to imprint them on the city.

Yeats, that suburban Protestant Dublin boy, is the best example of this movement home; his spells in London characterised by dislocation and by the gradual realisation that Dublin could best offer what he sought. Bite-sized chunks of Dublin at any rate, for Yeats continued to be a great traveller all his life and the city's Janus face of intimacy and claustrophobia would have been even more evident then than it is now. Yeats was, in his turn, a long-time friend of Constance Gore-Booth, who was born of Anglo-Irish stock at Lissadell House in Sligo. She trained as a painter in

London, marrying the exotic Casimir Dunin-Markiewicz, a Polish aristocrat, before returning to Ireland and becoming active in nationalist circles. And Augusta Gregory, Yeats's long-time friend and collaborator, similarly spent much time abroad, before coming back in her turn to Ireland and embarking on a political journey from her Anglo-Irish roots to a new – if ambiguous – understanding of her Irish identity. Yeats and Gregory and Markiewicz and others too – they were aware of the impact of their own characters and personalities in the project on which they had embarked.

Indeed, although history cannot any longer be taught as one long linear parade of kings, queens and political leaders, it is difficult not to see Irish history in this period as being precisely personality driven, for Yeats, Gregory and Markiewicz were joined by a succession of other equally significant characters who would direct the course of this unfolding history of Dublin and who were aware of their own performance in this history. It is, perhaps, all part of a Dublin tradition that begins with Jonathan Swift, who in any case believed that personality – and specifically his personality – might be brought to drive and direct action decisively on the ground.

Such ideological journeys should be set against a wider context of philosophical expansion and debate. Organisations such as the Gaelic Athletic Association (GAA) and the Gaelic League (Conradh na Gaeilge) were founded in these years to promote and encourage interest specifically in Irish sport, language and culture; and Douglas Hyde began to expound his theory of the necessity of the de-Anglicisation, not by means of returning the country to some notional Celtic twilight, but by fusing ancient language and cultural tropes with the reality of a modern, industrial world. Hyde would eventually give up his leadership of the Gaelic League, shunning its increasing political edge, and was replaced – in a sign of changing times and tides – by Eoin McNeill and the altogether more radical Patrick Pearse, who was co-opted on to its executive in 1898.

This was a heady time in Dublin, characterised by this stewing mixture of idea and argument, and it is therefore worth under-scoring the fact that this 'revival' was by no means a coherent philosophy. Instead, this ideology contained as many contradictions and oppositions as the next one, reflecting the many currents of opinion and ambiguity that flowed within society at large and, frequently, within the heart and soul of the protagonists themselves. Take, for example, Gregory – the Augusta, Lady Gregory, who in 1897 felt able to protest against Victoria's Golden Jubilee celebrations by refusing to light a celebratory bonfire on her estate at Coole. (Yeats had marched in Dublin, in company with Maud Gonne and many others, behind a coffin bearing the words 'British Empire' on its lid to protest against the same event.) The Gregory who sought to write in an Irish peasant-inflected idiom that can today make us blush with embarrassment and who anxiously reinterpreted the history of her aristocratic family to bring them closer to the rebels and heroes of a recent nationalist past. This was the same Gregory who was nevertheless a landlord and was determined to preserve her Galway estate intact for her son.

Or take Gregory's nephew, the scholar and art collector Hugh Lane. Lane amassed a substantial Impressionist art collection in the course of his art-dealing career, and his frequent visits home to Ireland – including many visits to Coole – had made him a major proponent of contemporary Irish art overseas. It was this interest that prompted Lane to organise the first ever exhibition of Irish art at Guildhall in London in 1904; and it was this interest too that led him to found in Dublin the world's first municipal art gallery, which opened in temporary premises on Harcourt Street in 1908.

This was not, however, to be a straightforward success story: Lane left elements of his collection to the city on condition that suitable premises be found to house them. The Corporation was to drag its feet over this stipulation to such an extent that eventually, and in high dudgeon, Lane changed his mind and left the collection to the National Gallery in London instead. Following his death in the sinking of the *Lusitania* off the Irish coast in 1915, and at the instigation of Lady Gregory, Lane's desk at the (Dublin) National Gallery was searched and a codicil to his will discovered. By the terms of this codicil, the entire Lane collection was to be left, after all, to the city of Dublin. The codicil, alas, was unwitnessed, the result of which was a struggle across the Irish Sea for control of the Lane legacy, a struggle that was eventually resolved only in the 1960s with an agreement to rotate the display of the collection works between London and Dublin.

The impact of such a welter of ideas on the city's fabric and on its cultural life was considerable and is nowhere better exemplified than in the creation of the Irish Literary Theatre. The notion of a national theatre in Dublin – an Irish theatre for an Irish people – had been first discussed by Yeats and Gregory at Coole in 1897; and after a long gestation, the Literary Theatre came into being in 1899. In 1902, *Cathleen Ni Houlihan* was staged for the first time; ostensibly from the pen of Yeats, it was in fact largely the work of Gregory, although at the time the latter was happy, more or less, to give Yeats the credit for the piece. In fact, she took herself off to Venice before the production even opened.

That Gregory wrote *Cathleen Ni Houlihan* in the first place, however, adds another layer of strangeness to what we would today probably call her profile. The play encapsulated one version of a national story and it caused ripples of excitement through the city. Cathleen herself, played by a Maud Gonne who had the auditorium filled to capacity night after night, exhorted her audience to step away from everyday life and do what was needful, even unto death, in the cause of national liberation. And this from the pen of a woman who would also do what was needful to collect her rent from her tenant farmers at Coole. It is no wonder, in short, that Gregory was content to leave the credit for the play at Yeats's door, for it was altogether too incendiary a piece of work to feel entirely comfortable with – not for Gregory, not in the circles in which she moved. And it was only later, once Dublin and Ireland itself had settled into a different sort of reality, that Gregory can be glimpsed mourning the lack of appropriate acknowledgement she had received for her work.

Christmas 1904 saw the Abbey Theatre, the successor to the Irish Literary Theatre, first open its doors to the city from its premises on Middle Abbey Street. That the new theatre managed to secure such a site – a few steps from Sackville Street and in the very heart of the city – was the result of good luck and, specifically, of generous financial backing. The location, however, would serve the theatre well, given its explicitly political genesis and aims: it was as close to the dreadful slums of the north inner city as it was to the generously proportioned spaces of Sackville Street and could therefore not be seen – as some of its detractors would have it – to be inhabiting its own contained world.

As for those financial backers: Yeats, Gregory and others had provided the creative energy that brought the Abbey into existence, but the cash for the infant theatre was supplied not by forces within Ireland itself, but from outside – and principally by one Annie Horniman, who was an English tea-heiress, feminist, theatre-lover and philanthropist. An ironic state of affairs – but a pleasing irony too, underlining the fact that economic reality will always cut to the chase. Maybe Gregory was aware of the irony of the situation too; she and Horniman never got on too well and eventually, once the theatre was established, Horniman was edged out.

The Abbey in those early days was explicitly a national theatre for a national people, but one look through its books and its various projects illustrates the nationalism it projected. It was no narrow institution, mingling as it did its early theatre with forays into the European avant-garde and various forms of bold experimentation. It was to be an arena of debate, passion and flexibility, in which the shadow of 'anglicisation' might be countered by a range of other influences and in which a variety of national ideas might be tried on for size. A bold vision, then, and a building in which various influences might not simply jockey for position but actually meet in the first place – no mean feat in what was still a socially stratified city and society.

The most famous feature of those early years at the Abbey was the public disturbances that greeted the first performances of John Millington Synge's *The Playboy of the Western World*, in January 1907. In simple terms, *Playboy* was written by a young Protestant playwright who had gone off to the Aran Islands to gather information and to listen to the patterns and inflections of speech among the Irish-speaking peasants of the west of Ireland. In this journey or pilgrimage to the western coasts, Synge was echoing what a good many other Irish artists and writers – including Augusta Gregory herself – were doing at the same time: migrating from an urban or an intellectual context, mediating between written and oral cultures and working between languages, the better to understand and to help fix the form of the nation that was in the process of being created. Then, this information gathered, Synge had returned and dramatised the results of his research on the Abbey stage – results that would subvert some of the national myths then in play and that would thus contribute to the staying power of his writing a hundred years on. All well and good, then, but for the fact that the political ferment of these years did not permit plays transmitting such cultural representations to be viewed impassively. And this is but one example of the tensions that existed in this broad church of Irish nationalism during these years.

The disturbances – 'riots', if you will, although they were not riots as we would understand the term today – have been fetishised over the years and transformed into a founding and cherished myth of the Abbey itself. And, like all good myths, the facts have become obscured along the way. In the first place, the disturbances were far from unique; on the contrary, they form part of an honourable tradition in a history of Irish theatre that abounds with such episodes. Audiences routinely smoked, drank and chatted their way through productions, occasionally emerged on stage themselves to challenge the actors and thought nothing of throwing fruit at them as a matter of course. As far back as the mid-eighteenth century, meanwhile, the Castle authorities had maintained a narrow-eyed gaze on the explicitly political activities of such theatres as Smock Alley, in Temple Bar; and riots – true lip-smacking riots, which resulted in substantial material damage to the venues concerned – were far from unheard of. Thomas Sheridan, father of Richard Brinsley Sheridan, had been at the centre of one such disturbance in 1754; his production of Voltaire's *Mahomet* had tapped into the contemporary patriotic mood and brought about a full-blown riot at Smock Alley, leaving the theatre a smoking ruin. Against such a context, therefore, the Abbey unrest of 1907, reputation or no reputation, appears positively tame.

With hindsight, indeed, the only surprising aspect of the disturbances of January 1907 is that they did not take place even sooner. After all, the Abbey had entered the production well prepared for trouble, after a 1903 production of Synge's *In the Shadow of the Glen* had led to murmurs of unrest. The National Council, the forerunner of Sinn Féin, had been formed in that year and its founder, Arthur Griffith – as well as many others, including Maud Gonne – had decried the play for its representation of

Ireland's peasantry, its degeneracy and its openness to foreign, and therefore undesirable, influences. Yeats had responded with a series of choice comments, excoriating both the narrowness of certain national visions and also the pragmatism of politicians who rejected those ideas they could not immediately turn to their own ends.

The *Playboy* disturbances and their context symbolise very well the chafing between ideologies that characterises these years – in this case, the vision, ambiguous though it was, of the Abbey's founders rubbing against an explicitly political nationalism. It also exposed a tension: the relationship between Protestant and Catholic, a faultline that was never going to simply go away. Certainly, Yeats made no effort to hide his dislike of what he felt to be Griffith's opportunism and narrow provincialism; and Griffith, we may be sure, took exception to Yeats's Anglo-Irish hauteur. And in any case, it is clear that the Abbey, on the eve of the production of *The Playboy*, expected trouble. It probably relished its delicious possibilities, being well aware that a good riot offers more in the way of publicity than any number of glowing reviews. The theatre had also brought more variety into its audience by introducing cheap seats in the 'pits' – close to the stage – that were duly filled by a rather different class of punter than normally attended Abbey shows. Following the initial unrest, Gregory had summonsed a collection of students from Trinity – Unionist, Protestant, representing everything that the crowd in the pits did not represent – to balance out the situation. It was not, perhaps, the wisest decision Gregory ever made, for in so doing, she created a positively incendiary situation. And so the scene was duly set.

The ostensible trigger for the disturbances – the reason dwelt on subsequently – was the presence of the word 'shift' in Synge's script. 'Shift': a word for a female undergarment; and so a riot erupted at the immodesty being paraded on the Abbey stage. The more general explanation was that, as was the case with *In the Shadow of the Glen* earlier, the behaviour and general conduct of Synge's characters in their west of Ireland shebeen did nothing to portray the plain people of Ireland in a good light. The accounts of the strife which followed – the police stationed along the edge of the pits, the trouble and strife erupting as different audience factions challenged each other, the actors bawled from the stage, the Trinity students breaking into a rendition of 'God Save the King' and the musicians all the while playing a selection of light airs – are pure farce; and it is no wonder that the situation should have passed into myth.

Taken all in all, this story hints at a large cultural reason why the Abbey should have risen in disorder on that week in January and why, in the end, the hated Dublin police were called into the theatre to quell the disorder. They hint at the faultlines and the issues that remained in play in the course of this national debate; and they hint too at how, when faced with trouble and pressure, the various players in this debate were tempted to revert to type. After all, the very fact that Yeats and Gregory were quick to call in the police to quell the disturbances demonstrates vividly that while they may have lived in a world of evolving cultural nationalism, they also lived in a world of bourgeois and aristocratic authority, and that these two worlds, at moments of stress, could not mix.

Nor should the *Playboy* disturbances be viewed, one hundred years on, through some prism of hindsight, in which a metropolitan sophistication is set against its uncultured opposite. It is the case, after all, that the disturbed Abbey punters were genuinely offended by what they saw – these strong, sexualised and fresh-tongued women and these feeble men, an absence of traditional images of Catholic and rural virtue, the language that was as coarse as it was lyrical – and moreover, they were entitled to be offended, according to the mores of the time. It is the case too –

lest we be tempted to boil the whole episode into some notional clash of civilisations – that *The Playboy* was as disturbing to Gregory, for example, who had her own and very different take on the Irish peasant, as it was to those Abbey audiences. And it is the case too that these audiences knew full well what was at stake. Here was the new national theatre, demonstrating an image of Ireland at a time of flux, of change, when the identity of that same nation was up for grabs. The disturbances, these riots, were therefore symptomatic of the extreme politicisation of Dublin society – at all levels – in these years. They can be seen, then, as a normal event; maybe it was exactly what a national theatre, at this moment in history, ought to have been doing.

The Abbey would be omnipresent in the violent and traumatic years that followed, as commentator, witness and dramatiser of events. In the lobby of today's modernist Abbey building, built to replace the first theatre that burned down in the 1950s, is a plaque to those members of the Abbey staff who actively engaged in the events of Easter 1916. Sean O'Casey, initially a political activist and later disillusioned with the course of events, would produce a trio of plays – *The Plough and the Stars*, *The Shadow of a Gunman* and *Juno and the Paycock* – which interrogated versions of the Rising, the War of Independence and the Civil War that took place on the theatre's very doorstep; all three were premiered on the Abbey stage. This close relationship between nationalism and cultural politics is a symptom of the fluidity of those crucial years in Dublin, when a previous political dispensation was visibly dying, when the city teetered on the edge of a new era, and when the meaning and substance of that new era remained to be defined.

— ◄o► —

The National Council that was formed in Dublin in 1903 and that was the forerunner of Sinn Féin, the Abbey Theatre that opened its doors at the end of 1904, the Westminster elections of 1906 that saw the Liberals returned to power with the intention of returning once more to the question of Home Rule for Ireland: these movements and many others formed part of a radical, class-based political scene in Dublin in the years leading up to the First World War, one that was different and distinctive from the omnipresent and familiar sectarianism and nationalism. James Connolly, who hailed from working-class Scottish stock, arrived in Dublin in 1896 with the intention of organising a socialist party in the city. Connolly is a useful illustration of the variety of opinion that existed in nationalist circles at this time. His own views and interests were expansive: he was a founder of the Labour Party of Ireland but he was also deeply engaged in Scottish politics and in international affairs in general and was a student of Esperanto. And he is significant in the history of international socialism; nationalism was all very well, Connolly declared, but it needed socialism too, and if a genuinely socialist republic in Ireland was not founded, then:

> England would still rule you; she would rule you through her capitalists, through her landlords, through her financiers, through her usurers, through the whole array of commercial and individualistic institutions she has planted in this country and watered with the tears of our mothers and blood of our martyrs. England would rule you to your ruin ...[3]

The contrasts between Connolly's internationalist and socialist philosophy and that of the fervently Catholic and nationalist Pearse are very marked; and it is just as apparent that Connolly would never be invited to take tea with Lady Gregory at Coole.

The period also saw the foundation of the Irish Transport and General Workers' Union (ITGWU) by Liverpool-born Jim Larkin. The creation and development of the ITGWU was as a response to the consistently bad and now steadily worsening economic and social conditions in the city, knowledge of which provides a useful practical counterweight to the discourse of ideas and of cultural nationalism of these years. As the Abbey, for all its plans, could not function in those early days without a generous injection of cash from its English tea-heiress benefactress, so Dublin's working class could not eat, could not live, on rising nationalist sentiment alone. Specifically, they could not eat as long as prices of basic foodstuffs remained prohibitively high. And they were high – conditions in the countryside were improving, farmers could ask higher prices for their produce and the result was that for the urban poor conditions became impossible. The birth of a trades union, as a result, was hardly a surprise.

It was also almost inevitable, however, that the creation of an organised labour movement would spark a savage reaction – and the Dublin Lockout of 1913 ranks as among the most bitter of all labour disputes. The ITGWU had rapidly, by this point, developed in numbers and authority and the response came in the summer of 1913 when William Martin Murphy, one of the city's principal employers, 'locked out' some 24,000 from their jobs, resulting in tremendous hardship and destitution for some of the city's poorest citizens. Larkin formed the idea of sending some of the workers' children temporarily to England as a means of relieving the burden on their families – but this in turn brought down the wrath of the Catholic hierarchy upon the union's head. A combination of corporate and ecclesiastical power is not one to be resisted by any force known to man, and, as a result, the dispute eventually collapsed.

The lockout was highly significant in labour terms, notably for the sense of collective class identity the ITGWU helped to foster through a combination of workers' solidarity and various cultural activities. It also reflected both the new radical mood abroad in the streets of Dublin in those years and the extent to which at this point political and cultural issues had fused. Yeats's 'September 1913', for example, was written in response to the events of the lockout (Was it for this the wild geese spread/The grey wing upon every tide:/For this that all the blood was shed ...) demonstrating that what Lady Gregory had termed 'the intellectual movement' was aware of the politics on the streets too. The lockout also led to the formation of the Irish Citizen Army (ICA), created as a means of protecting the workers from police violence and initially armed only with bats and sticks. In the following year, the ICA was reformed; Connolly assumed the leadership following the departure of Larkin to the United States in 1914 and began to reorganise the ICA as a more purposeful and drilled militia.

The political and social tension of these years, in fact, is best exemplified by the presence of militias in Irish life: by a range of independent, occasionally overlapping and fragmented organisations of various shades and complexions that sprouted around the country like mushrooms. The ICA was not alone in fostering a purposeful vision: it was joined by the more secretive Irish Republic Brotherhood (IRB), a nineteenth-century society that had been reinstituted from about 1910. Headed by a group that included Pearse, Sean MacDermott and Tom Clarke, the IRB drilled and acquired a few weapons, but its main strength lay in the realm of ideas.

The vision of rapidly approaching Home Rule, meanwhile, had the effect of radicalising elements of the Protestant population in Ulster too, in this case in their rejection of the possibility of Home Rule. The Ulster Volunteers were formed in 1912 and the Ulster Covenant – undertaking to defend the place of Ulster in the Union, by force of arms if necessary – was signed by over 250,000 Ulster Protestants in the autumn of that year (with another 250,000 women signing their own declaration, which was shorter and decidedly less martial in tone). In April 1914, as part of this militarisation of Ulster, some 20,000 rifles and millions of rounds of ammunition were landed at the port of Larne and other harbours on the north-east coast – under the noses of the police and the army, which made no attempt to stop the landings or to arrest those responsible.

Yet another militia, the Irish Volunteers, was formed in response to the situation in Ulster. The Irish Volunteers were dedicated to the implementation of Home Rule throughout the whole of the island of Ireland, and their first meeting was convened in November 1913 amid the cosily bourgeois surroundings of Wynn's Hotel on Middle Abbey Street, a few doors up from the Abbey. The Ulster gunrunning of the following year boosted the numbers joining the Irish Volunteers, and also made it desirable that they should have a stash of arms to call their own. As a result, yet another gunrunning incident took place when, in July 1914, the yacht *Asgard* sailed into the old harbour at Howth in broad daylight, with 900 German rifles on board – considerably less than the amount previously landed at Larne, but not to be sniffed at all the same. (A smaller consignment was landed later at Kilcoole on the Wicklow coast.) A group of Volunteers marched out from Dublin to take delivery of the cargo and brought the arms back into the city in safety – this, despite the fact that it was stopped by an army detachment on the way. Later, on their empty-handed way back to their barracks at Arbour Hill in the north inner city, the soldiers fired into a crowd of jeering Dubliners, killing several in the process. These killings had the inevitable result of causing a further swelling in the numbers enlisting in the militia.

This proliferation of militias drilled, paraded and trained openly – or at any rate not in conditions of secrecy. Such secrecy would have been impossible in any case, given Dublin's size, given the security apparatus that was in the hands of the British authorities which ensured that a good deal of what was discussed and planned rapidly found its way back to the Castle, and given the fragmentation of the various militias. The outbreak of the First

World War increased this fragmentation. The majority of the Irish Volunteers supported the war effort and left or were expelled from the organisation, forming the National Volunteers; many of these would later volunteer for service on the Western Front, fighting alongside some of the same army regiments that had lately been stationed in Dublin. The remaining Irish Volunteers, holding to the maxim that England's difficulty would always be Ireland's opportunity, refused to support the war effort – a decision that was largely unpopular with the Irish public that was watching a good proportion of its young men going off to the trenches. Continuing in the more draconian atmosphere of war to drill and organise, the Volunteers – heavily influenced now by the leadership of the IRB and the ICA – even staged mock attacks on the Castle itself.

The atmosphere of these years, then, was theatrically charged. It is as if the Abbey unrest of 1907, when viewed coolly, was simply an unremarkable product of those years, when all manner of agendas were in play on the streets of Dublin, when theatre was a part of everyday politics, and when any reaction was conceivable. The socialism of Connolly, the earlier activism of Larkin, the nationalist politics of Pearse and many other threads – the actions on the streets, in processions and in marches and in symbolism and action of all kinds – these manifold threads were coming together to create an impulse for change and for movement. And this impulse could not for much longer be satisfied by the merely theatrical alone. Instead, it would have to morph into a drama in real life, a drama that would be played out in the very streets of Dublin itself.

Chapter 20

⧉

THE RISING

Easter 2006 and the great and the good gather on O'Connell Street for the ninetieth commemoration of the Easter Rising. The Irish Air Corps supplies a modest flypast overhead; and on O'Connell Street itself, the defence forces provide a military parade, featuring hardware and soldiers commensurate with the status of the small modern Irish state. The President, politicians and others gather on the dais outside the GPO to watch the army march past; and they themselves are subject to a certain amount of scrutiny. This is no mere ceremonial, after all: for many years displays of militarism, regardless of their scale, were not encouraged in Dublin, out of sensitivity to the fact of the Northern Ireland Troubles unfolding themselves just up the road.

Now, today, the Troubles appear to have come to some sort of end. Many modern commentators in Ireland were of the opinion that the military commemoration of Easter 1916 – any military commemoration, come to that – should be quietly dropped, since displays of hardware on the streets of the capital were in any case hardly fitting, not in this day and age. And to be sure, the spectacle does have a Cold War tinge to it – while it is not exactly Red Square, the sight of a tank rumbling through the city-centre streets offers something of its tone. Offsetting this, of course, is the fact that the soldiers on parade on O'Connell Street have a certain track record, as representatives of an Irish state with an honourable tradition of service with the United Nations.

In any case, debate over whether a military parade is appropriate in this day and age can be seen to be irrelevant, overtaken as it is by a powerful combination of the realpolitik of modern Irish politics and the contested nature of Easter 1916. The Rising signifies a range of meanings to a range of people, irrespective of their political affiliations; and therefore it is inevitable that it continues to be more than mere memory in the landscape of modern Irish politics. Its legacy is wholly ambiguous; conflict over and control of this legacy is therefore something precious to be grasped by the modern politician in the run-up to the centenary of the Rising in 2016.

O'Connell Street itself supplies much in the way of symbolism, for those who care to look. The Spire, a spike of glittering steel, rises on the site of the former Pillar. It is an oddly and vapidly disappointing symbol of the new Dublin: it seems to vanish at street level; its very height, so disproportionate to the surrounding streetscape, has a diminishing effect on the buildings around. The new paving, the expensive piazza that fronts the GPO, the modern lighting and new streamlined trees that replaced the gnarled old limes that once grew down the centre of the street – these are pleasing and have helped to lift O'Connell Street out of its twentieth-century dishevelment. So also do the tram lines that intersect with the street, running east towards the Abbey and Connolly Station, and west towards the Royal Hospital and out into the south-western suburbs. And the various signature buildings and memorials remain: the GPO, Clery's department store and Eason's bookstore, the Parnell Memorial and the Gate Theatre anchoring the north end of the street, Jim Larkin in full flow halfway down, O'Connell enthroned at the south. But the bitter north wind that funnels down and out through O'Connell

Street in winter weather cannot be tarted up or controlled; and neither can the jangle of fast-food outlets and sex shops that trade on the street, in spite of the best efforts of the authorities. So O'Connell Street, as the military parade winds ambiguously on, remains something of an ambiguity in itself, here in the centre of the city. All the modern streetlamps in the world will not change that fact.

It always was an odd area of the city. Marketed as self-contained Sackville Mall in the eighteenth century, as the most fashionable quarter in the city, and with the pleasure gardens of the Lying-In Hospital next door, it was agreeable enough for some time – before the engineers and planners connected it with the river and its history as a thoroughfare began. Its wide spaces and lack of intimacy have always marked it out as quite distinctive in Dublin terms; but it was never as fashionable – not really – as other city centre streets and neighbourhoods. All the same, it has remained the principal street of the city ever since the eighteenth century, and its decoration of statuary innumerable has gradually served to copper-fasten that status. And it was strategic too – commanding the bridge over the river, with clear views east and west along the Liffey, and south to College Green and to Trinity. It was as a result of this strategic value, and even more as a result of its iconic value, that the leaders of the Easter Rising chose to head-quarter themselves here, on the main street of the country.

— ◄◦► —

As a child in school, learning about the Easter Rising – although only briefly, and the subsequent War of Independence and Civil War were not covered at all – one of my tasks was to draw a map of Dublin city centre, contained within its circle of canals, fenced to the west by the Phoenix Park and to the east by the bend of the bay. The bridges over the Liffey and over the canals to be carefully placed – just so – and the grassy spaces of St Stephen's Green, Trinity and Merrion Square to be coloured a light pastel-green, the waters of the Liffey and the canals and their basins an improbable blue. All very neat. Then, the main focuses of the fighting during Easter 1916: the GPO at the centre of it all, the trench-lined park at the Green and the Royal College of Surgeons on its western side, City Hall on the shoulder of Dublin Castle with its long views east down Dame Street and north along Capel Street, Boland's Mill on the edge of the Grand Canal Basin, Jacob's Biscuit Factory in the Coombe, the domed Four Courts on the banks of the Liffey, the railway stations at Westland Row and Harcourt Street; and a set of others: a circle of buildings and positions that I coloured with bright green pencil and that could be seen to command the canal bridges and approaches to the city centre. Bisecting this rough circle of strong points, I filled other buildings in with (naturally) a black marker: the spacious quad-rangles of Trinity, the rambling buildings of the castle itself and the line of British army posts that were thrown up in haste to con-nect these two British bastions and to cut the circle in two. This was Dublin during Easter Week of 1916, I was told, and could I see – 'can you all see, boys? – can you see the strategy on both sides?' I nodded; we all nodded; what a neat map, and what a neat town, with its parks and gently curving canals. I was delighted with myself. Of course, this is the trouble with maps: they can only ever give one version of reality. There was nothing neat about the Easter Rising. It wasn't neat at the personal level, and it wasn't at the urban level either.

The lack of neatness in this story can be discerned before the Rising even begins. Connolly had been leading public calls in nationalist newspapers for an uprising against British rule and this ongoing public agitation had alarmed the IRB leadership inside the Irish Volunteers. This situation was eventually resolved with Connolly's co-option into the IRB itself; thereafter the Volunteers and the ICA, connected by the IRB, could be relied upon to operate in something approaching tandem and the preparations for the Rising itself could, in theory, proceed a little more smoothly.

The IRB leadership planned the operation in secret, and not even the ruling body of the Volunteers itself was permitted to know what was afoot until very late in the day. The date of the Rising had been planned initially for Easter Sunday, 23 April 1916 – but this was changed to Easter Monday in order to coincide with the races at Fairyhouse, just outside the city. The thinking went – reasonably enough – that most of the city's army officers would be at the races and would certainly not have the security situation in mind. In the days leading up to Easter, however, confusion reigned. The leader of the Volunteers, Eoin O'Neill, discovered what was afoot and the official order for the large-scale ostensible 'manoeuvres' in the city centre was issued, cancelled, reissued and then cancelled again, so that when Easter Monday finally dawned and the diminished group of rebels moved quietly across the city to secure their key points, the whole operation had already been shot through with a sense of instability and was seriously short of manpower. In all, only some 1,200 Volunteers and 200 members of the Citizen Army would answer the call, nowhere near enough to carry out in full the plan that had been drawn up. Women were present in nearly all of the main areas of conflict during that sunny Easter Week, principally as couriers and nurses, although the ICA included a cohort of women who had been drilled and trained alongside the men. Only Eamon de Valera, leading the contingent charged with occupying Boland's Mill, refused to countenance women fighting under his command. It is said that even he came to regret this decision, albeit for the most pragmatic of reasons: the absence of women in his base at the Mill, he said, had meant that his men had to waste time in cooking for themselves.

The declaration of the Proclamation of the Irish Republic was read by Pearse from the steps of the GPO on that sunny Easter

Monday, to a small and unimpressed crowd. The Citizen Army, as we have seen, began digging trenches in St Stephen's Green; de Valera's company duly took over Boland's Mill; other buildings were quietly captured too, with little in the way of opposition. It was judged that Dublin Castle itself would be too well defended to be successfully attacked by the diminished force of rebels, and so the plans to attack and occupy it were dropped. As it turned out, however, the complex was being held by only a small number of troops; it might easily have been taken, and the capture of what had been the seat of English and British power for a millennium would have provided the sort of symbolic ammunition that such uprisings dream of. As it was, the rebels had to content themselves with City Hall, sitting on its hill on the northern perimeter of the castle.

And, slow as the British had been on the uptake, their response when it eventually came was rapid and effective. Troops were hastily ferried over from Wales and by running their line of army posts between Trinity and the castle and on to Kingsbridge (now Heuston) station, they were able to sever the rebels' lines of communication very early in the week. By Wednesday, the gunboat *Helga* was in position on the river at the Custom House and the shelling of the city centre began in earnest. It transpired that *Helga*, for all of her musculature, could provide little in the way of support: the firing range of her guns was too great for the tight urban landscape in which the Rising was playing itself out and her shells were spraying uselessly across a wide area of Dublin. Instead, the main firing power came from the big guns in the main quadrangle of Trinity, which became the British military headquarters for the duration of the Rising, and from other strong points on the city quays. Soon, much of Sackville Street was in flames, and the GPO, a shattered and burning shell, was indefensible. Elsewhere, the other contingents were gradually holed up in their positions. On the Wednesday, as British reinforcements came into the city from the harbour at Kingstown, some 240 of them were killed or injured in an ambush at Mount Street Bridge, which spans the waters of the Grand Canal. But by Friday, the GPO had been evacuated and by Saturday nearly all of the rebels had surrendered.

Several features of the Rising stand out. The first is the sense that it was doomed from the very beginning, a fact that must have been well understood by the leaders themselves, albeit in very different ways. Pearse's doctrine of the blood sacrifice that was necessary to ensure national liberation, for example, implies not only an understanding of this stark fact, but a cool acceptance of it as an element of a greater national good. Connolly, meanwhile, must have carried with him the bitter knowledge that the strategy for holding Dublin city centre, flawed as it was, might have worked a little better if only sufficient numbers had cut through the fog of order and counter-order and turned out in support.

This in turn illustrates the range of opinions embodied by the rebels. Michael Collins – who was to become but the latest in a line of magnetic Irish personalities in those years, who was present in the GPO throughout Easter Week and who would later rise to prominence during the War of Independence – was painfully aware throughout of the basic flaws in the plan. Storming and holding strong buildings and positions throughout the city was all very well and looked good on a map, but such a strategy would serve them ill when they were pinned down in the face of superior British firepower. Pearse's acceptance of the concept of sacrifice had essentially little in common with Collins's fierce pragmatism and practical ability; it had even less in common with the class politics of Connolly, with whom he had allied himself, but whose views might well be summed up by a line from O'Casey's Rising play, *The Plough and the Stars*, 'There's only one war worth havin': th'war for the economic emancipation of th'proletariat.'[1] O'Casey's views, which were brought to dramatic life on the

Abbey stage ten years later, are significant in this context too – he had been involved with the ICA but disapproved of its association with the altogether more middle-class Volunteers, and he regarded the Rising as a mistake and a failure. These views, famously, would provoke yet further Abbey disturbances in 1926, but they also demonstrate well the texture and plurality of the debate at the time of the Rising itself. This was a disparate grouping of Irish citizens, united only by the cause of national liberation but by no means in concord as to what form this process of liberation, or the resulting nation, should assume.

On the outside, looking in, meanwhile, was Gregory's 'intellectual movement', and its responses to the events of Easter Week were charged with ambivalence and variety. Lady Gregory mourned the deaths, and wondered aloud in a letter to Yeats whether a course of improving lectures at the Abbey might have brought Pearse on side; and Yeats himself responded with 'Easter 1916', which speaks of bitter regret of his class-based disdain for the leaders of the Rising ('I have met them at close of day/Coming with vivid faces/From counter or desk among grey/Eighteenth-century houses') and which reflects his understanding of the new glitter-sharp reality which the rebellion has brought into being.

The second feature is the familiarity of the Rising's landscape. Unlike some other scenes of conflict, in which battle takes place on beaches and amid windy fields, the main theatres of conflict in Dublin were domestic, humdrum and profoundly everyday: post offices and university quadrangles, hotels, biscuit factories, mills and towpaths. And all, what is more, located within shouting distance of each other. Standing on College Green today, for example, with Grafton Street behind and the porticoed front of the GPO a few hundred metres away and tourists making their way west, maps in hand, towards Christ Church up on its hill, it takes an effort of the imagination to see a line of army posts stretching east amid the clutter and traffic of Dame Street, to hear shells emerging over the rooftops of Trinity, whistling overhead and crashing in flames on the other side of the Liffey. And yet this, amid the very domesticity of this familiar landscape, so human and so trafficked – this is what happened.

This sense of domesticity marks other aspects of the Rising too. Its history is marked by a proliferation of stories and urban myths – some doubtless true, some undoubtedly false. Every modern Dubliner's grandmother or great-grandmother, for example, would seem to have been sent on an errand across town at one time or another in the course of the week, carrying a mysterious bag that turned out to be filled with guns and ammunition; and many a young Dublin woman would appear to have spent that Easter week pushing a perambulator from one Dublin address to another – the treasured cargo of such perambulators being, not a baby, but yet more arms. Other cherished stories concern the orgy of looting that took place for the duration of the Rising. Easter 1916 stands as an exemplar in the art, with shops ransacked and rapidly emptied as though a plague of consumer-minded locusts had passed through on holiday. Clery's department store – almost opposite the burning GPO – was the best-known victim of this people power: it was ransacked and emptied of its goods, with Dubliners vanishing into the gathering chaos wearing looted clothes and coats, and carrying bags and sacks laden with everything they could lay their hands on. And Clery's was by no means the only victim of this particular art. Maybe this vein of anarchy runs just underneath the streets of Dublin: an Ulster Loyalist march in 2005 ended in disorder on the very same street, with paving stones being lobbed at police, heaved through invitingly stocked shop windows – and with looting being the result then too. Or maybe there is nothing especially amazing about such a scene, since looting is a game the whole family can play, given the opportunity. It remains, however, among the best-known aspects of the Rising.

But for all that, the effect of the Rising on Dublin city centre was considerable. In and around Sackville Street, large areas had been destroyed; and grainy contemporary photographs show Dubliners picking their way through the spring sunshine on the Sunday morning after the Rising ended and gawking into a shattered streetscape of burned and shelled buildings. The portico of the GPO remained, but the rest of the building and most of the neighbouring buildings too were burned shells; and the public response to the rebels was initially and predictably angry. As they were marshalled and marched as prisoners through the streets towards the barracks at Arbour Hill and at Kilmainham and later towards the docks on their way to internment camps in Britain, reports tell of Dubliners spitting and jeering in angry response to the scene of ruin that surrounded them. Almost 500 people, including over 200 civilians, had been killed in the fighting.

The public mood may have been angry, and the participants in the Rising may have been the initial target of this anger but this situation changed just as swiftly. The British response to the Rising was to separate out its leaders, bring them to the high-walled stonebreakers' yard at Kilmainham Gaol and there execute them by firing squad. By mid-May, nearly all of them – 15 in total – had been killed in this manner. Several escaped death: Markiewicz, for example, who was reputed to have told her jailers, 'I do wish your lot had the decency to shoot me', and who was spared death ostensibly by reason of her gender ('rubbish,' a tour guide told me at Markiewicz's childhood home at Lissadell in County Sligo, 'the British didn't shoot her because they wouldn't shoot one of their own'); and de Valera, who was spared because of doubts and anxiety surrounding his American citizenship. Certain facts stand out: Connolly, for example, whose ankle had been shattered by a sniper during the fighting and who had directed operations from then on from a stretcher, was brought from hospital to Kilmainham by ambulance, carried into the prison yard and set in a chair in order to be shot. Not good public relations, to put it mildly, and the backlash in public opinion was not long in coming. In this way, it can be seen that the Rising – for all that it failed in practical terms – did indeed achieve its objectives. The sands ran swiftly in its aftermath, and soon the British authorities became aware that the situation in Dublin, and in Ireland, had taken on a momentum of its own.

— ◄◦► —

Kilmainham Gaol itself appears as the navel of the world in any nationalist history of Dublin and of Ireland. Wolfe Tone never made it here, nor did O'Connell and nor did Collins – but, with these exceptions, virtually everyone who was anyone passed through the gates of the prison, some more than once. Some of these figures came out again too, while others were shot at dawn behind its high grey walls; many more, nameless in public memory, were hanged and swung above its front doors, in full view of crowds who came to watch and take notes. The old building is set well within the historic landscape of Kilmainham, for it forms a juxtaposition with the Royal Hospital, both being symbols of a colonial presence and authority. Today, though, that landscape is shifting, in Kilmainham as in the rest of Dublin: a hotel and a high-rise apartment development is going up directly opposite those same front doors, despoiling a historically significant environment, say some; people gotta live, say others – the usual debate. But the prison itself has lost none of its power to chill and to command attention. From the north – the main entrance – it looks imposing enough; but from the south and from a distance, as the land falls sharply and away, its fortress-like qualities, stone walls and particularly punitive air, become strikingly apparent.

Kilmainham Gaol begins featuring early in the pictorial record, appearing as a handsome and sturdy building set amid green fields a short distance from the new and handsome eighteenth-century Dublin. The Liffey flows in the foreground and the north front of the Royal Hospital rises in the centre of its demesne; the spires and towers of the city shimmer in the background. The prison was built and opened in 1796, set amid green fields as a replacement for an earlier, fetid and ruinous prison and reflecting the penal ideas of the time; but it was not long before the building became fetid in its turn, its soft limestone trapping moist air and rainwater and encouraging the spread of the disease through its low-roofed, narrow and claustrophobic corridors and cells. On the day I visit – an iron-grey January day, when temperatures have suddenly dropped alarmingly and the tour party I tag onto looks frozen to the bone – it is an easy matter to imagine the horror of the prison in its earliest days.

'I didn't think it would be like this,' one visitor murmurs forlornly, glancing up at the crumbling old roof, wrapping her pashmina around her head and presumably wishing she was safely back by the pool at Southfork. What did she think it would be like? Less utterly horrible, no doubt; so did I. The tour guide smiles cheerily, presumably pleased that we should be visiting on such a representative day. We head up crumbling stairs and down more crumbling stairs, as the claustrophobia presses around us. Those first prisoners slept on straw on the stone floor; no glass in the windows, of course; they could have extra food if they were able to pay for it and if not, they would subsist on the most meagre of diets.

The prison was hardly completed in 1796 when the first political prisoners arrived: Henry Joy McCracken, imprisoned here before being released on bail and going on to play a leading role in the 1798 Rising; Robert Emmet, held in 1803 prior to being dispatched to be executed – dropped, as Thomas Kinsella has it, into a crowd of redcoats – up at St Catherine's on Thomas Street.[2]

Emmet's servant, Anne Devlin, was held at Kilmainham too. In her case, she was kept for two years in complete darkness until she lost her sight and while being periodically threatened with death. We are shown to a large room complete with spy hole, where prisoners were taken to be checked for size by the hangman; and other areas too, where men and women could be held securely, though in appallingly crowded conditions, before being transported to the British penal colonies at Sydney and Van Diemen's Land. And this, in the first ten minutes of the tour. No wonder, really, that my fellow visitor should have tied her scarf around her ears.

We make our way, in a long chilly line onto another, slightly more lofty corridor. Here, the guide pauses and gestures to a double line of small cells. If ever there was a death row in an Irish prison, the guide says and smiles encouragingly, this was it. He reads out the list of names of the 1916 prisoners held here in the hours before their executions: the Pearse brothers, Tom Clarke, Thomas McDonough. Markiewicz too was held here, in one of these tiny cells. And Joseph Plunkett, who famously was permitted to marry his sweetheart, Grace Gifford, just before his execution. And one of de Valera's cells, pointed out in the corridor below.

A few minutes later, our party emerges from this warren of tiny and crumbling corridors into the striking main hall of the building. This is more as we imagine a prison to be, and my fellow tourists noticeably relax as they look up at the ranks of cells climbing into a vaulted ceiling, as the metal catwalks rise overhead. It's warmer too. This is Victorian Kilmainham, completed in 1862 with a view to possible redemption: the hall is bright and airy and the eye is caught and held by the long skylight in the ceiling. And this was the intention: to be incessantly reminded of the light of God, until one repented and mended one's ways. But one would be watched all the way – for, although not formed along the lines of Jeremy Bentham's famous panopticon, Kilmainham was built nevertheless so as to ensure high levels of observation and control. The prisoners were confined to tightly spiralled staircases as they came and went, thus limiting their room for manoeuvre; the edges of the hall were carpeted, so that inmates in their cells might be silently observed without ever being aware of this observation – and so on. This great echoing space is almost overwhelming in its sense of latent power and authority. And theatre too – for this is theatre embodied, with its galleried levels and tremendous acoustics and human drama and possibility of yet more drama to come. Appropriately, this nineteenth-century space at the centre of Kilmainham Gaol is now regularly the venue for opera and for plays.

Kilmainham is at the heart of nationalist histories – and fair enough too – but its significance is of a more fully rounded nature, for it fuses this national narrative with a social one. The smaller details of the prison are charged with poignancy and with shock: the children as young as six dispatched to Kilmainham, for example, for the crime of stealing flowers from the Phoenix Park, whipped by the prison authorities and sent back to their parents; the child inmates of the prison who as part of the exercise were required to walk in circles around the prison yard – boys in a clockwise direction, girls counter-clockwise – and forbidden to look up; those who did look up were brought into the prison building and whipped. In the years leading up to 1868, crowds of thousands gathered to witness the public hangings taking place over the front doors of the prison; after 1868, the hangings continued – but in private, behind the prison walls. As the location of a social history, or rather of the multitude of threads that constitute a social history – the straw beds, crumbling limestone cells, the hangman's spyhole, the solitary confinement in the dark, the hopeless waiting for transportation to Australia, the hangings in public and private, the children imprisoned in a shocking environment – Kilmainham takes some beating on this frozen day.

And yet, it is the nationalist narratives that dominate. The tour eventually brings us out into the icy air in the stonebreakers' yard, long and narrow, bounded by the highest walls we had yet seen in the prison and overlooked by no windows, where prisoners sentenced to hard labour worked on the stones for ten hours a day. This, of course, is significant enough to be going on with – but the guide points first to the small plaque on the wall, and then to the small black cross at one end of the yard, marking the spot on which 13 of the 14 Rising leaders were executed by a firing squad of a dozen men (six of them standing and six kneeling). At the other end of the yard stands another identical black cross: on this spot Connolly was sat in his chair to be similarly shot. Our little party of chilly tourists shifts on the balls of its collective feet and moves to keep warm in the lazy wind. It is difficult not to imagine the air of this yard as charged to saturation with emotion; the stonebreaking on its own would have been enough. The guide points to a gate in the stern stone walls, leading through to the front of the building.

'Grace Gifford waited there,' he says, 'until she heard the shots ring out. It was only then that she left Kilmainham.'

Later, as I have made my way through the exemplary museum section of the prison and am about to leave the building, I come across one last display – a measure of interactivity to round off the experience. A computer display takes the casual visitor through the rights and wrongs of the death penalty, lists those countries where it is current and those where it is not and invites the visitor to vote. The current tally – the number of previous visitors who have voted in favour, the number against – is displayed on the large screen. A young man, short of hair and with ear diamond-studded, pauses briefly in front of the display and then punches the red button, votes in favour of the death penalty, walks on. He isn't alone either; in spite of the Kilmainham Experience, the public vote is running more than three to one in favour of capital punishment.

Kilmainham Gaol had officially closed in 1910 and had been reopened in 1916 specifically to receive the leaders of the Rising.

As the tide of Irish history ran on swiftly, however, it was to see yet more action, more prisoners and more deaths before its last and final closure in 1924. In the intervening years, its British wardens would hand the prison to the new Irish order, the final inmates would be processed, and the prison's final executions would be those of Irish citizens shot by Irish citizens as the Civil War gathered pace in 1922. The prison can be seen, then, to be a barometer of those final, anarchic years of British rule in Dublin, and the first traumatic months of the Irish Free State.

A powerful building – but Kilmainham Gaol almost lost its power, having spent a good part of the twentieth century neglected and abandoned behind its locked front doors. It presented a symbolic and practical problem for the new Irish state – what to do with such a building, with emotion embedded in its very stones? Preserve it, as a silent witness? Or demolish it and wipe away its memory? Or – the third option – do nothing and leave the problem for someone else to deal with? The third option wins every time; and it was left to an army of volunteers to begin a slow conservation of the building, repairing it little by little until the state eventually took the enterprise into its embrace in the 1980s. The initial hesitancy can in this case be readily understood, however, such is the symbolic resonance of this building – not merely as a scene of unspeakable and silent horrors as year followed year, and not merely as a crucible of Irish nationalist experience, but most of all in the ambiguity and hatreds of its final, closing months as a prison, when men were put up against a stone wall and shot by their compatriots.

— ◄o► —

In the museum at Kilmainham Gaol is a facsimile of the first edition of the *Irish Times* to be published in the aftermath of the Rising. The banner headline reads, 'Sinn Féin Rebellion in Ireland'.

It was a dramatic headline – all the more dramatic for being wholly inaccurate, in that the relatively new Sinn Féin party had had no part in the planning of, or playing out of, the Rising. Indeed, Sinn Féin ought by rights to have seemed suddenly out of step with popular sentiment, now radicalised by the executions at Kilmainham. After all, the party had in the years leading up to the First World War notionally championed the now suddenly quaint policy of establishing a dual monarchy of Great Britain and Ireland, along the lines of the fractious relationship between Austria and Hungary; and moreover had been on the financial rocks in the run-up to the Rising. For all that, however, the party was blamed for the Rising – by the British administration, by the *Irish Times*, and by a good many other people besides – and the party's title began to be used as an umbrella term for any movement of individuals opposing the administration in Ireland. The result of this was that Sinn Féin now abruptly morphed into a republican party. It was taken over by those who had been radicalised by or imprisoned as a result of the Rising and, having weathered the internal storms caused by such a rapid expansion and change in direction, the movement began to gain political and electoral momentum, culminating in a decisive victory over the constitutional nationalists in the November 1918 United Kingdom general election, when it took 73 out of the 106 Irish parliamentary seats.

Sinn Féin adopted an abstentionist policy, refusing to take its seats at Westminster and instead summoning the first Irish Dáil, which met at the Mansion House on Dawson Street on 21 January 1919. Most of these elected representatives were in jail, with a mere 26 members present to take their seats. This Dáil meeting was proclaimed as the first meeting of a new parliament of a new republic. The Irish Volunteers became the IRA – the Irish Republican Army – and swore allegiance to this new republic. This date can be, in hindsight, viewed as the beginning of a war of Irish independence. The Dáil ratified the Proclamation of Independence that had been read from the steps of the GPO in 1916, issued a new declaration of independence and demanded the evacuation of the British military garrison from Irish soil. But contemporary opinion in the new Dáil and among the public at large was by no means united in favour of a process of military engagement with the British authorities. For all that, however, it is the case that this date marks the beginning of a full-scale slide of Ireland into civil unrest and widespread rebellion against British rule.

These years were marked by widespread political and economic anarchy in Ireland. Dublin partook of its full share in the resulting violence, which left its mark on the city's people and its environment alike. The main Republican policy in this period was to create in Ireland a state within a state, by means of withdrawing cooperation from the British administration. It was a strategy that proved remarkably successful; by the summer of 1920, for example, both the court service and tax collection had ceased in most parts of Ireland. In Dublin, Michael Collins organised a 'Squad', the aim of which was to assassinate members of the so-called 'G-Division', the dedicated intelligence-gathering operation of the British authorities. By 1920, the ITGWU workers ceased to cooperate in the handling of military materials on the Dublin docks. These actions, and many more like them, resulted in a gradual and inevitable disintegration of British authority across most of Ireland.

The British response to this escalating situation was heavy-handed and clumsy and had the effect of firming up Irish public opinion against the authorities. In particular, the arrival in 1920 of two new military forces can be seen in retrospect to have hastened the British collapse in Ireland. The 'Black and Tans' and the Auxiliaries were militia forces recruited by a British administration reluctant at this point to send regular army units into what was becoming a guerrilla-dominated situation. These two militia groups rapidly gained a fearsome reputation for aggression and ill-discipline: no man, as Austin Clarke notes in his poem 'Black and Tans', could drink quietly in a Dublin pub for fear of the door being broken in by 'these roarers' looking for trouble. [3]

A pattern rapidly emerged: IRA activity in one locality was followed by rapid reprisals, in which (for example) houses and sometimes whole localities might be raided and torched. These episodes were well publicised in the British media by, among others, Lady Gregory, who wrote a series of pieces describing the impact of Black and Tan activity on Irish society. And this violent period in Irish affairs was dramatised in other ways too: in prose, with Frank O'Connor's first short story collection *Guests of the Nation* appearing in 1931 and highlighting the effect of such conflict on the human spirit; and on the Abbey stage too, when O'Casey's *The Shadow of a Gunman* opened in April 1923.

In Dublin, the most infamous of these violent occasions took place on 21 November 1920. This day had begun with the assassinations, in various locations across Dublin city centre, of 13 British intelligence agents by members of Collins's 'Squad'. The operation had been meticulously planned and was ruthless in its execution, with some of the men pulled from their beds and shot in front of their wives. It is also the case, however, that Collins had originally planned for some 35 agents to be killed but some of these operations had been botched; and that the various sweeps resulted in the deaths of several innocents. In spite of such awkward facts, however, the operation essentially achieved the objectives set by Collins, which were of breaking and confusing the British intelligence-gathering machine in Ireland.

The plan had been timed to coincide with a Gaelic football match scheduled to take place between Dublin and Tipperary at Croke Park, in the north inner city, that afternoon. The city would be packed, Collins reasoned, and so the getaway of his operatives would be so much easier. The match took place as planned, although it was late in starting and much of the crowd stayed away as news of the morning's killings spread. Some ten minutes into the match, however, British security forces surrounded the stadium, with regular troops coming down from the west, and a troop of police and Auxiliaries up from the east. The latter group rapidly forced their way into the park, and began firing. It was a confused scene and confused too were the narratives that emerged later. The British commander on the day admitted that his men had become over-excited; British newspaper reporters noted that the armed IRA men that the police claimed to have seen were actually ticket vendors. But it is certainly the case that the police fired from the pitch into the crowd as it surged away from them; that more members of the police and Auxiliaries waiting outside the ground fired into the crowd as it emerged; and that regular army units waiting outside the ground, startled by the sight of a panicked crowd and the sound of gunfire, opened fire over the heads of the crowd. In all, 14 people were killed in Croke Park that day – mainly as a result of gunfire, although two were crushed to death in the stampede to escape the ground – and another 60 injured.

The authorities' later claims that shots fired by IRA infiltrators within the ground had panicked the crowd and caused a stampede were ridiculed from all sides, including elements in the British media. The stadium at Croke Park was already, at this point, a potent symbol of national aspirations, and not only because of the specifically Irish football and hurling matches that took place there; a section of the stadium itself, for example, was constructed with rubble taken from the ruins of Sackville Street in the aftermath of the Easter Rising. One result of the killings was to further emphasise the stadium's symbolic significance and to burn the events of the day into the city's collective memory, so much so that almost a century later in 2007, the decision to permit 'foreign' games – specifically soccer and rugby – to be played at Croke Park for the first time was still capable of provoking high emotions. In particular, the first rugby fixture between Ireland and England was keenly observed, with many commentators seeing the match – complete with a rendition of 'God Save the Queen' by the English contingent in the stadium – as loaded with significance. In the event, the game passed off without incident.

The aftermath of the Croke Park killings inflamed public opinion even further and hastened the ending of British authority in Ireland; it also raised to even greater heights the violence in the city and across the country. A potent symbol of this ever-increasing unrest came several months later, on 25 May 1921, when the IRA, at de Valera's instigation, attacked and burned the Custom House, at that time the centre of local government in Ireland. The building was reduced to a shell and its vast store of documentation lost in the flames. But five IRA members were killed in the operation, which not only exposed a rift in policy between Collins and de Valera but also demonstrated vividly that the IRA could not engage effectively in conventional operations with the British military. There was a sense of mutual exhaustion and a realisation that both sides had too much to lose if the confrontation carried on for much longer, and a truce was declared on 11 July 1921. The following day, de Valera led a deputation to London to meet the British Prime Minister, David Lloyd George, thus beginning a process that would culminate in the Treaty of December 1921, which outlined the terms under which an Irish state would come into being.

Until this point, of course, the plurality of opinions on the Irish nationalist side could be set aside in the cause of an independent Ireland. A time was always going to come, however, when this common cause would shatter. The Treaty, as negotiated by Michael Collins on the Irish side, provided for a self-governing Irish Free State, but also set the partition of the country in stone, by stating that the Unionist-dominated six counties of Northern

Ireland could opt out of the Free State if they so chose – they did. It also set the status of the Free State not as an independent republic, but as a Dominion of the Empire along the same lines as New Zealand, Canada, Newfoundland, Australia and South Africa, with – vitally – the British monarch remaining as head of state and requiring an oath of allegiance from all parliamentarians of the new Irish state. Moreover, the Royal Navy retained in its possession several naval bases on the south and north coasts of Ireland. These stipulations would prove to be acceptable to the pragmatic majority of delegates to the Dáil. It was the best that could be achieved, went the argument, under the circumstances and would do for the time being. But they proved to be unpalatable to a substantial minority of delegates. The vote ratifying the Treaty took place on 7 January 1922 and was passed by 64 votes to 57, and de Valera led the anti-Treaty wing of Sinn Féin out of the Dáil in protest.

The Civil War did not begin right there and then, instead, there followed a period of uneasy peace characterised by rising tension. Through January, Collins was ensconced in the Gresham Hotel on Sackville Street negotiating the final terms for a surrender of Dublin Castle – which took place by mid-January – and the removal of the British military from Ireland. Neither side wanted a civil war – but a civil war was nevertheless what they got. Violence erupted once more in Dublin at the end of June 1922 when Free State troops first shelled and then stormed the Four Courts, which had been occupied by anti-Treaty forces. Two days later it was surrendered. Like the GPO and the Custom House before it, the great building was ablaze and the Irish national archives lost in the fire. The fighting then moved to Sackville Street, and it and its inhabitants too suffered yet more damage, reflected later by O'Casey in *Juno and the Paycock*. Over 60 people died in this last bout of bloodletting on Dublin's streets. In its aftermath, the pro-Treaty side had firm control of Dublin and within a few months of the rest of the Free State too, but the city was to witness some final deaths before the Civil War ended – executions this time, sanctioned under Emergency Powers legislation passed in the autumn of 1922. The anti-Treaty activist and author Erskine Childers was executed by firing squad at Beggar's Bush Barracks on 22 November 1922, and 80-odd additional executions were sanctioned, some at Kilmainham, before the Civil War came to its painful conclusion in the spring of 1923 and Dublin was able to take on its role once more as a capital city.

Chapter 21

⧉

CONTENTS AND DISCONTENTS

A clear day at the very end of winter, and the granite and green circular dome of the Four Courts glints under afternoon sunshine. There has been no snowfall in Dublin at all this year, only a mere day or so of February sleet in the city itself and a little icing-sugar dusting on the tops of the mountains on the southern skyline; and this afternoon the air is mild with a touch of spring. A scene of industry plays out around the Four Courts as legal people dart to and fro, carrying files and papers. On the steps of the building, overlooking the Liffey, other people are lingering with rather less of an air of busy industry – they are witnesses, maybe, in some hellish case of Jarndyce and Jarndyce. And yet more wait and loiter inside the doors, under the great, humming rotunda. So I fancy, at any rate. I don't know, because I am sitting on the tram and heading west past the courts and taking my ease; no legal quagmires and hellishly bulging files for me.

'The Four Courts,' says a recorded, posh female voice, and then, 'Na Ceithre Cúirteanna' in what even I recognise to be poorly accented Irish. A few punters get off and a whole lot more get on and off we go again. This is the Red Line, heading west and south into the suburbs and always, so far as I can tell, packed. I am enjoying the experience all the same; I hardly ever tram it and thus can experience the ride as though I am a tourist on my holidays. These trams are a relatively new sight on the streets of the city, and, smooth and silver-sleek and quietly efficient as they are, they still manage to appear improbable, as though they ought really to be slipping silently through the streets of Zürich.

Behind the Four Courts – to my right as I sit on the gleaming tram, gliding west – lies one of the urban seams that is so characteristic of Dublin, both in the past and today. The ramble of courts and Land Registry and a hurrying and expensive legal world give way, beyond the tram lines, to public housing from the 1930s and 1940s and to old pubs like Hughes that sits opposite the courts and that still features trad music two and three nights a week. A little to the west lies Smithfield, its long cobbled square that was once home to the city's horse market now lit by modern and striking gas burners and its old working-class houses now cheek by jowl with dense new apartment buildings, Thai restaurants and hotels. Nearby too is Oxmantown, where the native Irish settled after their repeated expulsions from medieval walled Dublin, and, as Stoneybatter, remains a neighbourhood of tightly packed terraces and narrow streets. In the past, this seam, stitched between the world of the Four Courts and the neighbourhoods that adjoined it, was a good deal more apparent. These days, however, the old houses are being gentrified and the barristers that work in and around the Four Courts today might actually live in the neighbourhood.

There is much in the way of symbols and irony dancing about this urban scene. The changing fabric of the city, for one thing, is well encapsulated by the process of gentrification, for good or ill, that is now under way in such districts as Stoneybatter. This is an atmospheric part of town, its terraces and small streets still lending themselves to a distinct sense of community and of place, even as its property prices bob higher and higher and out of reach. And these expensive legal folk symbolise neatly, meanwhile, the ties that continue to exist between a now decolonised Dublin – once an entrepôt for British trade and a seat of British authority, now the capital city of an independent republic – and that other country across the Irish Sea. They represent well the continuity that was a feature of life in the city even after the bitter conflicts of the War of Independence and Civil War – even as the gentrification and those mobile property prices demonstrate the extent to which Dublin has changed, radically and breathtakingly, in the last decade.

In the dying days of the colonial administration in Dublin, as we have seen, the nationalist side worked to make the city and country ungovernable. It achieved this end by taking the tools of government – the collection of taxes and administration of justice – and successfully subverting them. The so-called Dáil courts, answering to the authority of the parallel Dáil government, were one of the more potent and subversive tools at the disposal of the nationalists. Being in essence part of a second judicial system that ran parallel to the existing British one, these courts paralysed at a stroke the existing system of governance – not merely by means of rejecting the colonial authority but also filling the resulting vacuum by supplying a new focus of allegiance. And naturally they were so clean a departure from the previous judicial system, so radical in their conception and execution (they were based in part on the notion of restorative justice, which has become legally fashionable today) and so striking a success in their management of the new law – that they were rapidly disposed of as soon as the new Free State came into being.

In a sense, the reasoning can be readily understood. The new Irish state that was asserting itself in the period following the War of Independence and Civil War was – naturally – concerned with establishing itself and its institutions as rapidly as might be. For this reason, it was evident that what had proved useful in the tumultuous pre-independence years might be a potential menace once that independence had been achieved. The Dáil courts, as part of a system dedicated to an alternative dispensation, symbolised this potential menace better than most – and so it was hardly surprising that they should be swept away in the twinkling of an eye and a new and official judicial structure be created to take their place. It is significant, however, that this new structure was strikingly similar to the old one, right down to the costume, the language, the very rules and mechanisms. So much for change: it is only in the last few years, indeed, that barristers in the Irish courts have been ordered, once and for all, to address Irish judges as 'Judge' – instead of 'yer Honour', 'yer Worship' and all the other titles beloved of courtrooms. And as it was for the legal system, so it was for the civil service, which continued to be organised and run as it had been by the British administration.

The fate of the Dáil courts exemplifies the mindset of the new Irish state and in so doing illuminates the sudden and sharp change in the character of post-independence Dublin. The writer and trades unionist Peadar O'Donnell, who hailed from Donegal, who had sympathised with the Republican side in the Civil War and who had been holed up in the Four Courts on the eve of its shelling and destruction by government forces, characterised the behaviour of the new Irish state as 'a hatching hen fussiness'.[1] The administration was, like that of the hatching hen, concerned to an overwhelming extent with incessantly arranging and controlling its environment – a good deal too concerned, in fact, to have much time for the greater world that surrounded it. As a result, this politically independent Dublin was famously marked by a degree of insularity and self-absorption that can seem startling today.

The culture of censorship that was such a consistent aspect of life in the new state is a good illustration of this self-absorption. As early as 1923, the Dáil had passed the first Censorship of Films Act, and this would be followed by successively amended Acts designed to keep track of the evolving cinematic technology and to close any legislative loopholes. A Committee on Evil Literature was appointed in 1926, and from its meeting room on Kildare Street, its members (including one Catholic and one Church of Ireland clergyman) advised the government on means by which public morality might best be protected, including the banning of pictures of dancers, of information on birth control and of any publication that demonstrated an undue fascination with crime. In 1929, the first Censorship of Publications Act was passed – it was concerned to catch in its net any book or publication 'that was in its general tendency indecent or obscene'. And so on.

One is inclined to titter at such strictures today. As is the way with all acts of censorship, they tend rather to draw more attention to the lewd and obscene than would otherwise be the case, and they draw attention also to the state of mind of those drawing up the rules in the first place. But in the context of the time, the censorship laws – which would be a feature of life in Ireland for decades – filled the useful function of unifying a legislature that otherwise remained desperately divided by the memory of the Civil War. They posited the notion of creating and protecting a pure and unsullied new nation, and protecting it from British contamination in particular. As a result, the entire political spectrum of opinion in Dublin could be relied upon to support such legislation, which acted as a sticking plaster on the wounds of the Irish body politic. The Republican organ *An Phoblacht*, for example, had earlier praised the efforts of the Committee on Evil Literature in seeking to 'check the flow of filth from Britain into this country' – and a few years later, it would take to task the artists and writers of Dublin for their innate filth of mind:

Some will wonder that they have to take the Holyhead boat to look for fame. Their bright, beauteous souls love to hover around the prostitutes of Dublin, the thieves and murderers of Dublin.

These writers cannot have healthy brains, cannot have brains at
all but a slack mass of matter like frog-spawn where grim, filthy
ideas crawl and breed like so many vermin.[2]

Certainly it was the case that the Censorship Acts, in all their
manifold variety, would impact grievously on Dublin's cultural
life in the years following independence. Although they could not
be relied upon to work in practical terms – the new Irish border
was at all times porous, boats came and went from the harbours
of Dublin and Dún Laoghaire as they ever did and filth would
always spew its way onto the streets of the city, the sandbags of
censorship notwithstanding – the symbolic importance of the Acts
cannot be underestimated. Moreover, as book after book was
added to the list of the banned, it was no wonder that many Irish
writers and intellectuals would, as the years passed, give up the
ghost and join the swelling ranks of those emigrating from Ireland
for good. Some, but not all: the *Bell* periodical in Dublin, which
ran from 1940 to 1954, was created by a group of writers and
intellectuals including O'Donnell and Seán Ó'Faoláin who
remained in Ireland in spite of the prevailing culture. Its foundation, indeed, can be seen to be partly in response to the censorship
that stalked the land; and it and other phenomena give the lie to
the notion of stagnancy gripping the country in these years.

Such censorship laws were just one manifestation of the striking cultural conservatism of official Ireland in the years and
decades following independence. And there are other indicators
too, notably the steady eclipse of a female presence in public life.
Indeed, the roles played by the suffrage movement in Ireland and
by women in Dublin in the political events of 1916 to 1923 are
striking when viewed with the benefit of hindsight, because both
are thrown into sharp relief by the nature of public life thereafter.
In this new national dispensation, room for female manoeuvre
became limited. Constance Markiewicz might have been the first

female minister to sit in Cabinet in Dublin, for example, but it says rather more about the political climate of the country that there would not be another such for 60 years. Rather, the woman's place was to be in the home from this moment on – a point that would be spelt out in the new Irish Constitution of 1937 that placed women firmly in the domestic sphere.

The new climate in Dublin can be glimpsed in other ways too: in the final elimination of Monto and its red lights in the 1920s by the combined forces of the police and the Legion of Mary, and most notably by the staging in the city in 1932 of the Eucharistic Congress, an extravaganza of Catholic piety that was designed to celebrate the millennium and a half that had passed since the coming of Christianity to Ireland. The Congress took the form of a variety of vast gatherings in venues across the city, including masses celebrated at St Mary's Pro-Cathedral[3] at the opening of the five-day event, and in the Phoenix Park at its close. Hundreds of thousands of pilgrims, indeed, gathered in the Phoenix Park; not quite on the scale of the papal visit four decades later, but still gargantuan enough in its own right. The city went wild for Catholicism in all its manifestations, and the close identification of the new state with the Church was made manifest when de Valera and the ministers of his brand-new government assembled at Dún Laoghaire harbour to welcome the ship bearing the papal representative to the Congress. At the close of the event, and in another demonstration of these close Church–state relations, the Blessed Sacrament was carried in procession from the Park down to O'Connell Street, flanked both by units of the army and by representatives of Church orders in strict hierarchical order. 'Women' brought up the rear.

— ◄◦► —

'Museum,' the posh female voice now says reprovingly and shakes me out of my virtuous reverie. 'Ard-Mhúseum.' The tram is packed now and nobody else seems to be getting off, and so I deploy my elbows in my best passive–aggressive style to get through the scrum, off the tram, out into the bright air. The tram glides away, Zürich-style, and I climb up the steps to the National Museum.

The view from this modest height seems designed to encapsulate Dublin for the benefit of passing tourists. The Museum complex faces south, down to the narrow chartered waters of the Liffey and across to the Guinness complex. And complex is the very word, for gleaming silver tanks – do they hold millions of gallons of Guinness, I wonder idly? – jostle cheek by jowl with chimneys and factories and administrative buildings, all set along the old steep hill of Dublin that falls down to the level of the river. To the west rises the confident Victorian façade of Heuston – formerly Kingsbridge – Station, with the spire of the Royal Hospital on the hill behind; to the south the mountains line up, not plumb-blue on this sharply bright day but rather green and brown and silent against the skyline.

As for the Museum itself, this vast building sits ranged on its own hill, a series of austere and uncompromising elevations gazing across the city. Taken over by the new state in 1922 but built by the British and named by them the Royal Barracks, the complex was built on this prominence and in this tough style with an intention in mind: to be seen and to communicate an unspoken authority and control. Walk underneath its arch and into the main quadrangle and this sense of austerity becomes even more pronounced, in spite of the alterations and additions that have been undertaken to change the complex from barracks to museum. The façades are bare, undecorated; the modern glazed interventions added by the architects to connect the buildings are understated too; and the parade ground itself is empty and furnished with no modern fripperies like fountains or furniture to relieve its sparseness. The sense of sternness is admirable, but also mildly shocking – I wonder what passing tourists make of it.

The Royal Barracks is now Collins Barracks. It is just one of a number of buildings that today house Ireland's much expanded National Museum, but by far the largest and (that word again) the most authoritative too. For me, though, its principal significance lies in its altered status. While the original museum buildings on Kildare Street and Merrion Street were purpose built as museums and treasuries, Collins Barracks has only recently been made over, and its original purpose and function and motives – these remain tangible. For this reason, the visitor experience can feel sharper and more disconcerting – or at any rate it seemed for me on that mild day in early spring. I took in the Easter Rising exhibition and the Irish at War exhibition, and a monumental stacked display of Irish glass and Japanese lacquer boxes and Burmese statuary. I rounded a corner and came face to face with a de Havilland Vampire suspended from the ceiling, almost cartoon-comic in its minuteness and its bulbous pilot's cabin. This tiny plane was acquired in the 1950s by the Irish Air Corps; acquired second-hand from the British, one can deduce, for such was the general practice of the day. It is a useful reminder that a politic life continued apace, even as the pious set about organising Eucharistic Congresses and the censors set about putting into practice the recommendations of the Committee on Evil Literature. Even so, a million contacts were carried on regardless between the new state and the old coloniser, and pragmatism always won the day.

The devotion with which the new state tended the morals of its population appears even more odd when one sets it against the social problems faced by post-Independence Dublin. The historical experience of this city, of course, has always been distinct from that of the country that surrounds it – first as isolated colonial bridgehead, and then as principal urban centre in a predominantly agrarian society. With independence, these paths were still divergent, and this is nowhere more apparent than in the living conditions of the city's poor. Although the effect of late nineteenth-century land reform in the countryside had been to raise the housing conditions of rural labourers – by most estimations they were in a better condition at the turn of the century than most of their European counterparts – poor Dubliners remained in as bad a way as ever. The same miserable litany repeats itself: ghastly living conditions, inadequate water and sewage supplies with all its consequences, and families living huddled in one decaying room in one decaying inner-city Georgian town house. The antagonism between the Castle and the nationalist-dominated Corporation that was such a feature of the nineteenth century continued into the twentieth, and the inevitable result was stalemate. In the last desperate days of British administration, the situation worsened even more: as a consequence of the prevailing political anarchy, the struggling colonial authorities withheld funds designed for new housing in an attempt to bring the population into line. So it was that the new Irish government inherited a social situation in Dublin that was as bad as it could possibly be.

And yet there had been floated monumental visions of the city's future. A scheme that was first mooted in 1914 and that appeared in various forms in the following years called for an ambitious remodelling of the city along contemporary – and specifically Parisian – lines. This plan would have seen the running of a grand processional route from the Phoenix Park along to Sackville – soon to be O'Connell – Street; this new road would intersect at the Four Courts with a new city square that would in turn be home to a new National Gallery. A new Catholic Cathedral would sit at the top of Capel Street on the north side of the Liffey, looking down the length of the street and across to the green dome of City Hall, south of the river. A new National Theatre would gaze down the length of O'Connell Street and across to College Green, where the Bank of Ireland would be reclaimed as a home once more to a national parliament. Parts of Dublin Bay would also be reclaimed, and new infrastructure – including rail lines and brand-new railway stations – would bring the city most definitively into the modern age.

Naturally, the destruction wrought on Dublin by the Rising and its aftermath was seen by many planners and architects as a golden and wholly unlooked for opportunity for the city to rebuild itself along these or other ambitious lines. As we know, however, the authorities were content to rebuild rather more modestly – certainly nothing like along the lavish lines that had been outlined. O'Connell Street was rebuilt and the GPO, Custom House and Four Courts eventually restored, but no triumphant processional route would be carved through the north city. Dublin would not mirror Paris. Rather, it would remain Dublin and the energies of the new state would be channelled, instead and at last, into dealing with the housing needs of the city's population. It is a measure of how times had changed from the nineteenth-century attitude of laissez-faire that the state now accepted the pressing case for intervening in the housing market. It was a case of the greater good being served by building for the new Ireland, by clearing the slums and eliminating the diseases that festered there.

In those early days, ideological motives also loomed large. The authorities had never been enthused by the idea of building blocks of flats and requiring people to live there; such notions were felt to be not in keeping with an Irish way of doing things. By the 1920s opinions had hardened further: mindful, perhaps, of the coterminous experience of post-war 'Red Vienna', in which vast urban apartment blocks had become a stunning norm, the authorities and the Church now conceived of flats as positively Communist. Shared hallways and staircases, it was considered, formed the road to hell – they led certainly to vice and possibly to revolution as well and ought, wherever possible, to be avoided. To be sure, flats were built – notably as the 1930s went on and some of them excellent examples of public housing – but a stigma was consistently attached to them and they continued to be seen as the last redoubt of the poorest and most unfortunate in society. This particular mindset persisted in Dublin well into the twentieth century and left a legacy that has contributed in the present day to the endless and environmentally unsustainable expansion of the modern city's ribbons of suburbs into the countryside.

The first housing built in Dublin after independence, in the north-eastern suburb of Marino, consisted of so-called 'cottages': small terraces of two-storey dwellings, the form and execution of which was influenced by similar developments then taking place in the burgeoning London suburbs. On street maps of the modern twenty-first-century city, the lines of the Marino development still stand out quaintly, branching out as they do like so many dinky, circular toy trees. The scheme had been long in the gestation, first appearing on plans well before the First World War and put on hold in the troubled years that followed. The houses that at last rose from the green fields were prettily detailed: they featured baths among other luxuries, as well as delicate many-paned windows and small gardens front and rear; and allotments were inserted as part of the scheme's general emphasis upon clean, healthful living. Green space in the form of 'circuses' was provided, together with neat signposts and freshly planted trees, and the general dimensions of the whole development were human and comforting. The Marino scheme was recognised, then as now, as among the most successful of the early developments undertaken by the Corporation – even if the original narrow roads are not much favoured by SUV drivers in these later and slightly less pastoral times.

But other, rather larger, schemes were less successful. In the 1930s, the city authorities unrolled a vast new housing development in what is now Crumlin, on the gently rising land south and west of the city centre. Like Marino, the development consisted of a good many cul-de-sacs interspersed with green circuses – but the sheer scale of these vast, bare greens, so unlike the intimate open spaces of Marino, was daunting. The scale of the entire development was pretty daunting too, come to that, and the new inhabitants who were shifted from their central-city tenements into these new houses suffered the effects of such an extreme dislocation. Crumlin was not sufficiently provided with the paraphernalia of everyday life – shops, schools and playing fields took their time in arriving – and many of the new inhabitants, accustomed as they were to the communality and intricate social networks of life in the city centre, were isolated in their new homes. Dublin was no different in this regard, of course, than many other European cities at this time – but such various failures of urban planning help to illustrate the fact that in many cases the remote state mindset of the nineteenth century had simply been swapped for a paternalistic one that failed to equate bricks and mortar with actual human lives and needs. Add to this the fact that the very poorest members of society could not afford the rents on these new houses and so remained where they were and in the same desperate conditions, and one would be excused for thinking that history in Dublin had a very nasty habit of repeating itself – irrespective of who was in charge.

The development of the city was proceeding apace, then – even if the various aspects of this development were not all equally successful. In terms of building and of urban character, the changes and expansion of post-independence gives the lie to the easy assessment of Dublin as a Georgian city. It is, of course, nothing of the sort. Look again at that street map with the intimate ring of the canals, the large green circuses of Crumlin still intact south and west of the city centre, and the narrow branching lines of Marino in the north and east. Even by the 1930s, as Dublin's twentieth-century expansion was still in its earliest stages, the space taken up by the city's Georgian squares and terraces seems small in comparison with these unrolling suburbs where a new city was being created and new lives being lived.

Chapter 22

∞

WAR AND PEACE

In Elizabeth Bowen's story 'Sunday Afternoon', a visitor returns to Dublin on a short visit. He is a member of the old Anglo-Irish class and is now living in a London that is experiencing the Blitz. He has been invited to visit a circle of old friends who are still living in the suburbs of south Dublin – in this case, an agreeable villa in an outer and well-heeled suburb set on a shoulder of the hills. It is May but by no means warm: a cold wind plays around the group as they take tea on the lawn, although at first they strive to deny this fact. They sit gamely in the chilly garden, and they silently wish they could move into the house and close to the fire that is dancing, most necessarily, in the hearth.

In the course of the story, the visitor observes once more the gap that has opened up between his own life, in the blitzed London he has temporarily left, and the lives of his former friends who now seem becalmed in their hillside suburb. The former friends observe the phenomenon too and they shiver – but repressively, this is not a topic they wish to explore in any great depth, any more than they want to admit to the coldness of the day and the dampness of the lawn – at the thought of his war-shadowed life, his destroyed home. He, in his turn, silently wishes himself far away from these Dublin lives that are safe – they are certainly safe – but becalmed and drained of passion. The story ends with the visitor returning down the long drive of the suburban villa to catch the bus back into Dublin once more, en route to what has become home.

The story plays and tugs at certain thoughts and sensations. In one way, it feels as though it is a stripped and transplanted version of Bowen's earlier novel *The Last September*, which describes the last days of an aristocratic Big House during the War of Independence. In this novel, the IRA are burning neighbouring houses in that corner of County Cork and a military presence is all pervasive – but the members of the family must still play tennis as they have ever done and eat chocolate cake on the lawn as though their lives depend upon it. In 'Sunday Afternoon', although the characters are now suburban, and the scene is anything but militarised, the conversations remain the same, and tea is still taken on the lawn as though everything is at stake. A chilly wind may be whipping down from the mountains above but nobody must mention it. A war may be taking place nearby but it is someone else's war and can therefore by discounted. These people and this caste are marooned or maybe anaesthetised, living their lives in a place that is quite outside of history. Cool observation of this stratum of society was a favourite topic of Bowen, who, after all, was by birth – in Dublin, in 1899 – a member of this Anglo-Irish caste, and who spent a lifetime observing and recording its cultural and political predicament.

The parallels between *The Last September* and 'Sunday Afternoon' – the people, the claustrophobia and silences and codes – these are evident and readily traced. To my mind, though, the story encapsulates and frames a Dublin that is at once living and not living in a world at war. And Henry Russel, the protagonist of the story, might well be taken to be Bowen herself, who personifies much of the ambiguity felt within Ireland during the war years, who spent these years shuttling back and forth between Dublin and London, and who was one of a number of Irish figures

– including Louis MacNeice and Kate O'Brien – who contributed reports to the British government on the state of Irish society. Bowen's *Notes on Éire* may be summed up thus: leave the country alone; do not think of invasion. Which was, more or less, the conclusion to which the British government would eventually come in any case.

The Second World War in Ireland was referred to, euphemistically, as the 'Emergency'. At the outbreak of war, the state took to itself a series of emergency powers, but the country remained neutral for the duration of the conflict. It was a situation that was not much to the liking of many – of Winston Churchill, say, who publicly condemned Irish 'disloyalty' and who engaged in a well-publicised spat on the subject with Eamon de Valera, Taoiseach throughout the war years. Many supported the attitude of Churchill and others, but many also understood the immense cultural complexity and necessary cultural ambiguities of the situation.

Irish wartime neutrality has always been a vexed issue. In the years after 1945, the Lutyens-designed War Memorial Gardens on the weir of the Liffey at Islandbridge, which had been created in 1938 to commemorate those Irish citizens who had died in the First World War, was allowed to slide into neglect and was restored only in the 1990s – a physical expression in Dublin of the discomfort and discord that accompanied any thought of the Irish role in these international wars.[1] And, as the years have passed, documents released and memories set down on paper or film with relief or with bitterness, the issue has become more and not less complex. Some commentators have pointed out that a fresh war for Ireland in 1939 – and a war that would essentially be in support of the old enemy – was politically and culturally impossible, for it would have opened anew the rents and wounds of the Civil War. New papers have illustrated British plans to use poison gas along the eastern coasts of Ireland in the event of a German invasion of the country. Others have shown that Irish neutrality was in any case a flickering, shadowy affair. Lost or downed Allied service personnel, for example, were by no means interned – as were downed Germans – but were instead hastily bundled up and pushed across the border into Northern Ireland as quickly as possible; the Irish government permitted overfly rights to Allied planes taking off or landing in the North; and Irish Intelligence shared its findings with the Allies. On the other hand, not too many Jewish refugees were permitted into the country, and de Valera famously called at the German legation in Dublin to offer his sympathies in the aftermath of the death of Hitler.

The psychology of this doubtful neutrality is fascinating. My mother remembers, as a small girl in north Donegal, hearing the rumbling blast of torpedoes finding their dreadful goal out in the Atlantic and the bodies of sailors, Allied and German, washed up on the local beaches in the following days. And Irish lives were lost – not only on service overseas, say, or in a Blitz-ravaged London, but in Ireland itself. On the west Donegal coast, an isolated monument commemorates the 19 young men and boys killed when a sea mine floated to shore and exploded as they played football on the strand. The monument was raised only in 2003, a full 60 years after the event and people still flinch from discussing it. When I asked a Donegal acquaintance about what happened, he told me coolly, 'Sure, they shouldn't have been playing there in the first place, should they?'

I mention this context, this rapid pen-and-ink sketch of a wartime situation, in order to illustrate the pressing nature of the Emergency in Dublin – fencing the city and country in on all sides and generating ambivalence at all times, a psychological drama that continued for a full six years. An acquaintance of mine, as a child growing up in wartime Dublin, was in the habit of always keeping a freshly washed, starched and ironed nightdress neatly on a hanger on the back of the bedroom door. That way, if a bomb fell at night, if they needed to get out of the house in a hurry, she could always count on having a fresh nightdress to wear in front of the neighbours.

And of course, this lady, this girl, was quite right to do so – for bombs did fall on a Dublin essentially defenceless against any attack from above. In January 1941, German planes attacked the southern suburbs, but on the night of 31 May 1941, a more severe attack took place across the north of the city. It was assumed that the German pilots thought they were over a British city, but it is difficult to see how they could have made such a mistake; while United Kingdom cities were blacked out during the war, the lights of Dublin were subject to a mere dimming order that was in any case infrequently obeyed. There has been speculation that the raid, in fact, might have been ordered as retaliation for the assistance sent from Dublin, in the form of fire tenders, when Belfast had been subjected to devastating German raids in the previous month. However it was, bombs fell on the North Strand area of the city and along the North Circular Road, and in the process killed over 30 Dubliners.

Rationing was introduced throughout the country from 1942. Dublin had the worst of it – in the countryside there were always provisions to be had, especially for those fortunate enough to be farming – for most foodstuffs had to be imported into the city and were more expensive to boot. Tea and cigarettes became precious commodities and tempers probably stretched as these most precious of resources ran down; coal became rare and then disappeared altogether and the population was forced to rely exclusively on turf; and high stacks of coal and then of turf became, as we have seen, part and parcel of the topography of the Phoenix Park throughout the Emergency and in the years that followed too. The smell of a turf fire is evocative indeed, but it does not do to imagine the pollution that must have resulted from the population of an entire city burning turf for cooking and heating. Maybe Bowen imagined her fire in 'Sunday Afternoon' as built of turf; in such a way her characters might be reminded, with each unwelcome whiff of turf smoke in their delicate nostrils, that Dublin too was part of this wartime world.

Fresh film matter was a precious resource in those years. Hollywood was at war and a good many of the new releases either didn't make it as far as Dublin, or were censored if they did, and the city was forced to fall back on its own resources. Indeed, the war years touched off an emphatic cultural response. A home-grown film industry was sparked; the *Bell* was as much a reaction to this manifest national need for self-sufficiency that accompanied the outbreak of war as it was to the climate of censorship; and both phenomena and others like them, came to serve a vital function in the Dublin of those times. Not all travel had to be abandoned: daytrippers from Belfast became a common sight, arriving at Amiens Street (now Connolly) Station on the train in order to escape the atmosphere of war and occasional German bombs falling in the militarised North. 'They are tolerated,' notes Bowen in her *Notes on Éire*, 'as having money to spend ... they frequent the cheaper hotels, crowd the shopping streets and the cafés and restaurants. Dublin is undoubtedly flattered to find herself in the role of a pleasure city.'[2]

The end of the war in Europe brought with it wider horizons once more: travel across the continent was possible again and the proximity of a larger and more colourful world contrasted sharply with Dublin's more muted colours and its economic and cultural circumscriptions. The country's persistent economic woes and demographic decline showed no signs of being addressed and the policies of self-sufficiency were demonstrably failing. A lack of employment opportunities in the rapidly depopulating countryside was leading, not only to the flood of overseas emigration that was such a feature of twentieth-century Irish life, but to a resulting swelling in the population of Dublin, as country people arrived in the city in search of better prospects. Some of these, doubtless, came with the intention of taking the boat to Britain – and many did, with the boat trains at Westland Row Station seeing much in the way of desperate departures; others, however, were unwilling to go any further and to leave Ireland for good. Dublin has always, as we have seen, been a receiving house for the rest of the population of Ireland – this has traditionally been one of its functions in Irish life – but this movement of people was now more substantial than it had ever been. The result of this was that, by 1951, one-fifth of the population of the state lived in the greater Dublin area, and this proportion would swell yet more dramatically as the century went on.

The Catholic Church began its ambitious programme of suburban church-building in order to tend to the souls of these newcomers, and most of the vast, barn-like places of worship scattered across the city today date from this period. The phenomenon of urban drift was to the obvious detriment of smaller towns and cities across Ireland, but it was a situation that was socially tolerable. The small size of the country meant that these new Dubliners could flee the city for frequent weekends at home, and any witness standing in the main concourse of Busáras – the city's modernist bus station – on a Friday evening in the 1950s would have seen great flocks of folk undertaking this very journey with fleets of buses departing the city for all corners of the island. Such a national redistribution of population strained the ability of the city to cope – but naturally it assisted in the generation of new cultural energy too, insofar as a great many people cannot be brought together in a slowly shrinking world without many sparks, of whatever complexion, being touched off.

Censorship of course remained ubiquitous in those years, but it is a sign both of changing times and of a moral backlash against them that these sparks of new energy can be detected readily enough in the post-war city. An atmosphere both of possibility and of repression is best summed up by the fate of the Pike Theatre, which had been founded in 1953 in a tiny auditorium off Baggot Street – one of a number of small, ad hoc theatre companies established in those years and operating on a shoestring. The Pike founders, Carolyn Swift and Alan Simpson, had opened their theatre with the intention of presenting 'plays of all countries on all subjects, written from whatever viewpoint, provided they appear to us to be of interest and to be dramatically satisfying'. With this in mind, the work of Jean-Paul Sartre and of Eugène Ionesco were presented to Dublin audiences for the first time, together with the Irish premieres of Brendan Behan's *The Quare Fellow* and of Beckett's *Waiting for Godot*, which opened at the Pike in October 1955 and which has always been the institution's most significant claim to fame.

In 1957, however, the Pike chose to stage Tennessee Williams's *The Rose Tattoo*, as part of the inaugural Dublin Theatre Festival. The theatre was packed, the public jostled for precious tickets and all seemed set fair. Alas! What nobody took into account was the fact that Williams's script featured a prophylactic dropped on stage – dynamite in a country in which such items were illegal. In the Pike production, the guilty condom was actually mimed and therefore strictly speaking non-existent, but to no avail. Simpson was arrested on the charge of lewdness, of 'presenting for gain an indecent and profane performance', and the case went to court. It took a year before the state's case was dismissed in the Supreme Court, but arguably it had made its point: the Pike had won the battle but lost the war, for it was crippled by its legal expenses and forced to close its doors. And in 1957, as though to underscore the point yet more heavily, the entire Theatre Festival was cancelled after the Church objected to several proposed productions.

There are plenty more where that one came from too, all serving to point out the prevailing censorious mood in the Dublin of those years. Take the reception, now infamous, of Edna O'Brien's first novel, which appeared in 1960:

> My first book, *The Country Girls*, was a simple little tale of two girls who were trying to burst out of their gym frocks and their convent, and their own lives in their own houses, to make it to the big city. It angered a lot of people, including my own family. It was banned; it was called a smear on Irish womanhood. A priest in our parish asked from the altar if anyone who had bought copies would bring them to the chapel grounds. That evening there was a little burning. My mother said women fainted, and I said maybe it was the smoke. When I wrote my second book (*The Lonely Girls*), the opinion was the first was a prayer book by comparison. My mother had gone through the book and inked out any offending words.[3]

The experiences of the Pike and of O'Brien point to the close relationship between Church and state in the Dublin of those years and show the extent to which the moral position of the one was generally reflected in the actions, legislative and practical, of the other. And yet, of course, there was a good deal more ambiguity to the relationship than met the eye. De Valera, who was Taoiseach for the greater part of these years, was not in the habit of taking orders, even from a man of the cloth and John Henry McQuaid, who was Archbishop of Dublin from 1940 to 1971, was no less pragmatic than he was profoundly doctrinaire.

A glance at the history of these times demonstrates this ambiguity, as well as the limits of this culture of authority and censorship. Take, on the one hand, the state funeral in 1949 of President Douglas Hyde, which – in view of Hyde's Anglican faith – was held in St Patrick's. Rather than enter a Protestant church in order to attend the funeral service, the largely Catholic Cabinet instead loitered outside in the porch. But on the other hand, take the fact that the new and enormous Catholic cathedral for Dublin, due to be erected in Merrion Square, was never actually built. Or take the famous public bar on Catholics attending Trinity College without special dispensation. In public, McQuaid took the very clear position that Catholic attendance at the College was manifestly undesirable, and yet in practice Catholic students happily studied at Trinity even before the official lifting of the ban in 1970. Similarly, O'Brien's books – and a great many others like them – were readily available in Dublin, censorship or no censorship, even if some of them went on to become kindling; and the Pike court case amply demonstrates the limits of even the most elaborate system of censorship and authority.

The subtle tension and changes of these ostensibly bleak post-war years in Dublin can also, with hindsight, be read against a background of greater change to come. The 1960s in Dublin would be the decade of genuine transformation, and one in which progressive ideas would begin to circulate more widely in the aftermath of the Second Vatican Council. The city's universities began a phase of rapid expansion: University College moving from the city centre and settling into its new greenfield campus in the southern suburbs, while Trinity's expansion is best expressed in Paul Koralek's superlative Berkeley Library building, completed in 1967. In these years too, the national economy would begin a process of lifting itself out of the doldrums – albeit fitfully and with much in the way of reverses – and to set aside a doctrine of self-sufficiency in favour of what we might today tentatively call globalisation. Specifically, it was the decade in which successive Irish governments set their sights on eventual membership of the European Economic Community (EEC), a goal that would be achieved in 1973. And arguably, this decade was instrumental in establishing the circumstances that brought contemporary Dublin into being. Shifts and breaks, then, generated by education and by the modern world, and fitful at first – but signifying that certain movements were under way and would bring momentous social changes in their wake.

— ◄o► —

The last three decades of the twentieth century in Dublin encapsulate both the best of urban life and the worst: the bursting optimism, the sense of recurring economic despair and the eventual and startling economic upturn as the city's world expanded once more. EEC membership led inevitably to a new envisioning of identity for the city and the country: Dublin was now officially a city of Europe, its people were European citizens for the first time after decades of apparent isolation, and the world, commensurately, began to change to reflect this reality. The old trading patterns with Britain, which national independence had scarcely altered – the great majority of the goods entering the Port of Dublin still came from British harbours and the country still exported its goods to Britain as it had ever done – now began slowly to shift. Emigration continued, but the city's educated youth might now choose more readily to go, not to London on the boat train, but to Paris or Brussels or Munich. And to return home, knitting Dublin with each visit a little more tightly into the European orbit.

It was by no means all plain sailing. The state attempted to follow EEC membership with a great economic leap forward, to be achieved by means of heavy foreign borrowing. It was not a gamble that paid off: the oils shocks of the 1970s and resulting global economic downturn impacted grievously on the small national economy. And if the 1970s had offered hope, the 1980s brought renewed and chronic economic weakness. These years also brought salutary lessons to those who still believed that minor national economies could make their own way in the world. And yet, in spite of a sometimes gloomy economic situation, the tectonic plates were slowly moving, and these shifts began to affect the way people lived. More and more Dubliners had money to spend and the city began to change, as shops and restaurants and travel agents sprang up to meet these new consumer needs.

The flip side of these changes, of course, was also readily apparent to anyone with eyes and ears. It could be seen in the rapidly expanding but poorly planned and serviced suburbs that fostered chronic social isolation. It could be seen too in the steadily increasing levels of crime and drug abuse – Dublin developed a heroin problem that was giddying in its scale. Social stratification was bleakly evident, incubated and magnified by the country's starkly unequal health and education systems. Some people had a good deal of money in their pockets, in other words – but many more certainly did not.

The changes are nowhere better expressed, perhaps, than in the position of the Catholic Church, which, in recent years, has altered dramatically in the life of the city. It is a situation that has come about – in part, at least – as a result of the cultural shifts that have taken place in the latter half of the twentieth century that have left the Church under pressure in Dublin as elsewhere in the world. In other words, the result of the impact of the modern world, of consumerism and materialism, of shopping malls and Sunday trading laws, on spiritual life. It is also, however, the result of knowledge of the Church's own actions and policies being disseminated and becoming better known in what is now a rather less hierarchical and a rather more critical society. In Dublin, as in the rest of Ireland and across the world, a probing media, a more responsive legislature and changing cultural attitudes have resulted in a flood of information about Church activities becoming public knowledge. Once occupying the position of moral guardian and arbiter of what was and was not acceptable in the life of the people – in education, culture, health and much more besides – the Church has fallen from grace most dramatically as various actions perpetrated in its name and by its agents have become public.

The abuse of children – physical, sexual, psychological – by priests and religious within the community is perhaps the best known of these scandals; and investigations into such incidents are ongoing in the Dublin diocese. To this can be added literal institutional abuse: the abuse of children in the so-called 'industrial schools', which first appeared on the Irish social landscape in the middle of the nineteenth century. In the aftermath of independence, the industrial school system had been maintained and expanded by the new state; such schools were state-funded to provide an 'industrial' education for the children on their books, but were administered by various religious orders. They were scattered across Ireland – in Dublin, the best known of them were the schools at Artane and at Goldenbridge – and the children on their rolls were there principally because their families were poor, and for no other reason. It is not the case, for example, that the schools were orphanages, although they frequently have been referred to as such. Neither were they reform houses – only a small proportion of their inmates had any sort of criminal conviction. Instead, the industrial schools reflected a partnership that existed between Church and state in Ireland, premised on the need to educate the poorest children in society in the cheapest way possible and in a way that bolstered most effectively the temporal power of the Church. Add to this a knowledge of the fact that religious orders not infrequently ran a complex of operations – including industrial schools and Magdalen laundries – simultaneously and on adjoining sites, and it is difficult not to see these operations as truly 'industrial', in a literal and profoundly shocking sense of the word.

The abuse that has been documented, in the form of legal hearings in modern Ireland, took a giddying variety of forms, ranging from a simple failure to provide the education that were the schools' raison d'être through physical and psychological mistreatment of all kinds, all the way to thoroughgoing sexual abuse. Of course, this abuse was not always and everywhere present; men and women of conscience worked in these institutions. It is also the case, however, that the abuse was systemic.

Evidence has been and continues to be collated, both in book form and in the form of state-sponsored inquiries, but it is worth quoting from one testimony, in order to catch a glimpse of the material presently under investigation. This is a section of one testimony of a boy at Artane, run by the Christian Brothers until its closure in 1969:

From the very beginning in Artane you had fear instilled into you. I remember someone saying: 'You see that door over there? There's whips and hanging ropes and things in there, and that's what you'll get if you run away or get into trouble.'

The main thing about Artane, and everyone will tell you this, was the size of it. It was huge. Hundreds of boys, all of us in short trousers, runny noses, shivering in the yard.

There was one Brother in school who'd put you up against the wall if you got something wrong, or didn't know an answer. Then he'd take out his hurley and sliothar, and he'd hit the ball at you with his full force. Often, he'd miss, or you might duck. But he'd keep at it until he got you, and it really hurt when he did.

At night it was bad. I often heard a Brother come into the dormitory in the middle of the night, and take some boy off up and out the door. You'd hear the screaming then and shouting and beating. There didn't seem to be any reason why they'd pick any particular boy. Just for kicks, I suppose.

There was another Brother that used to have a certain number of boys that he used to carry on with – sexual abuse, I suppose you'd call it now.[4]

The flood of information and evidence that has come to us in recent years has been so great that it becomes all too easy to become inured to it, to become numb to its substance and to forget the horrible impact that such abuse had on so many lives, in Dublin and in Ireland as a whole. One response of the various Church orders that have been implicated in this process was to issue a series of apologies, both conditional and unconditional. Another has been to move rapidly to protect their financial assets: in particular, an indemnity deal negotiated with the state in 2002 capped the financial contribution that the religious orders would make to a victims' compensation scheme at €128 million. The state – that is to say, the taxpayer – will pay the balance, which is estimated today to stand at well over one billion euro.

Today, those great barn-like churches of the 1950s and 1960s that are scattered across the suburbs of Dublin are seldom filled; neither are the ornate Victorian churches of the city centre; and the number of Catholic Dubliners who now go to mass each Sunday morning continues to dwindle year by year. To some commentators, this diminishing of the authority of the Church is a shift to be bitterly regretted, symbolising as it does the loosening of the ties that bind the society of the city and of Ireland as a whole. To others, it is a necessary change to what had become a dysfunctional situation. To still others, it would seem that the Church has taken certain decisions far-reaching in their future impact – specifically that the religious orders that ran Artane, Goldenbridge and other industrial schools have opted to sacrifice their spiritual authority in order to maintain their temporal assets largely intact.

In other ways too, the role and self-image of the city has shifted decisively in these last decades. Thirty years ago saw the beginning of the Troubles in Northern Ireland – which was, after all, only a few miles up the road from O'Connell Street. Not very far away, as became clear in January 1972, when the British Embassy on Merrion Square was set alight and destroyed in the aftermath of the Bloody Sunday killings in Derry. Or, as became clear in May 1974, when bombs exploded on Parnell and Talbot Streets, north of the Liffey, and on South Leinster Street, south of the river. Twenty-seven people died in these three explosions, responsibility for which was claimed by Loyalist paramilitaries in Northern Ireland. There have been persistent claims in the intervening years that the operation was planned by members of the British intelligence services in collusion with these Loyalist groups; and it has also been noted that the authorities in the Republic did not investigate the bombings with the appropriate rigour and energy. The most recent inquiry into the bombings was hampered in its work by a catalogue of missing and destroyed evidence. It left many of the salient points unanswered, and it seems increasingly likely that they will remain unanswered in the years to come.

Many commentators have noted such ambivalence and noted too the sense that Dublin's ostensible destiny, as publicly underlined by successive governments (that of the capital city of an undivided Ireland), sits uneasily alongside the actual goal as pursued by those same successive governments – that of the modern capital city of an economically and culturally successful, if partitioned, state. In the aftermath of the Good Friday Agreement of 1998, the electorate in the Republic voted by 94 per cent to 6 per cent to relinquish the territorial claim to Northern Ireland and to amend the Irish Constitution accordingly. This, at any rate, has removed some of that chafing ambivalence, but it is clear nevertheless that this particular phase in Irish history has yet to be fully played out.

In the meantime, it has become abundantly clear that a different political and economic reality has been created in Dublin in any case, regardless of what the politicians choose to say or not say. Take the commodification of culture that has been such a feature of life in the city since the 1990s, and that is best epitomised in the Riverdance phenomenon that first took to the stage in the unlikely setting of the Eurovision Song Contest held in Dublin in the spring of 1994. Riverdance took the traditional art of Irish dancing and worked to sex it up for an international market, and the attempt succeeded beyond the wildest dreams of commerce; the results of this success, in fact, has been touring the world ever since. Like it or loathe it – few people feel merely indifferent to it – Riverdance symbolises the success with which an image of Dublin and of Ireland has been turned into cultural capital and exported, with surpassing and steady success, around the world. It is all far removed from previous orthodoxies that emphasised the notion of preservation of the national culture. Today, the stress is laid rather on its utilisation and the result has been an Ireland and a Dublin that markets itself relentlessly to the world.

It is a process that has brought the world to Dublin in search of U2, that perfect pint of Guinness in an authentically Irish pub, that perfect sunset shot of the Ha'penny Bridge framed in the viewfinder of a digital camera and those other potent local trademarks that have been capitalised on around the globe. And, as one moves through the streets of the contemporary city, the results of such cultural and marketing exercises are everywhere to be seen, for today tourism fills the streets of the city throughout the year. Even on gloomy winter mornings – the buildings grey and the sky grey and a chill mizzle falling – the tourist coaches appear on Nassau Street, line up along the railings of Trinity College and decant their inmates who set out across the cobbled quadrangles in search of the essence of Ireland. On such dim days, this authenticity will take the form of a brief glimpse of the *Book of Kells* resting in its unpleasantly claustrophobic room in the Old Library, of the purchase of a tweed jacket or a package of linen napkins, a CD of traditional music or a pair of Waterford crystal goblets in a tourist shop across the road, all rounded off with a dish of Dublin coddle and a pint in the local Irish bar. Chop-chop though, the coach leaves at 2.00 p.m. sharp for Newgrange. And, in the midst of this cultural refashioning, it can be difficult to catch at the living and breathing and working Dublin that rests alongside its brazen and highly coloured cultural twin.

EPILOGUE

All things counter, original, spare, strange ...

'Pied Beauty' GERARD MANLEY HOPKINS

On a chill, blasting morning late in March, with an icy wind blowing snow through the air – and perhaps we are not done with winter after all – I hurry along Baggot Street and into our friendly neighbourhood cheesemongery. It is a new joint, more or less, and its existence is indicative of much that is distinctive about Dublin today, some 12 or 15 years into this present surge of complacent half-prosperity. Dedicated cheese shops were thin on the ground back in 1990, for there was simply not the money sloshing around to make too many of them viable.

Nor was there the interest in food that there is today. Dublin has never had much of a reputation for food indulgence and quite right too: the most cursory of glances through this city's history is enough to demonstrate that there never was much of a chance for the populace to sample voluptuous living. Good brown bread, tender spring lamb, a pint of Guinness and a plate of once scorned oysters – that was about the height of it; and besides, the oysters could give you typhoid. But today, amid the dross of mediocre restaurants in Temple Bar offering bad bruschetta and platefuls of clotted, knotted spaghetti carbonara, there are others offering food locally sourced and grown and produced. A certain old and famous bookshop on the Liffey quays that closed quietly a few years ago, for example, has lately reopened as a restaurant offering local beef and fresh-caught fish (once so scorned) and fine Irish charcuterie – all set against a sensational backdrop of a Ha'penny Bridge glimpsed floodlit through high sash windows.

And our cheesemongers. The world's best cheeses, for sale in our local shop. Maybe the existence of such establishments signifies not only a triumph of slick bourgeois consumption but a fleeting rejection of anonymous globalisation too. Certainly I feel good about myself – in a Fairtrade kind of way – as I turn into the old grey Georgian building and bounce virtuously downstairs into the icy cheesemonger chill. I plan to buy some cheese produced by a local goat; and who could not feel good about that?

The cheese person behind the counter is deep in conversation with another customer. They are discussing appropriate cheeses for an upcoming and clearly expensive dinner party; I will have to wait my turn. I amuse myself, faint with greed though I am, by trying the samples set out on the cold marble counter: the vast array of Irish cheese from Munster and Leinster, the Ardrahans and Crozier Blues and Gubbeens, all jostling with French and Swiss and Italian cheeses and hams. And it is well that I have something to distract me; the other customer, large from a surfeit of cheese, confident of voice and manner, and clad in what looks like a chinchilla fur coat (lots and lots of little chinchilla skins, all stitched together in a charming fashion) is not in a hurry. So much is clear. A few minutes' steady grazing takes place before I turn away from the produce before me (there being only so much cheese a body can take, be he glutton or no) and into their conversation that has taken a sudden and startling lurch into a netherworld of drink and drugs.

'We have to be careful in Ireland,' the woman in the fur coat says, staring intensely at the cheese person. 'Do you know what I mean?'

'I do, I do.'

'Because what I think is this: that we carry a gene for it in this country.'

'We do. We do carry a gene for it. That's what I think too. I remember an uncle of mine ...'

The chinchilla woman sweeps away the uncle. 'When I think about my aunt – and even today I get upset when I see friends of mine drinking too much.'

'Well, and quite right too. I think everyone in Ireland is affected by alcoholism in some way.'

They swivel towards me. 'We're not keeping you,' they tell me, 'are we?' and gaze down at me – for I am sitting now on the cold tiled ground, busily scribbling in my notebook. I know there is no other way I'll remember this conversation; I need to write it down now, instantly.

'I'm in no hurry,' I tell them, 'I forgot to put something on my list, so take your time.'

The chinchilla woman nods and says, 'Right so,' and she snuggles back into her nest of fur and the two of them plunge back into their conversation: alcoholic aunt following alcoholic uncle and friend and cousin in a giddy line, and it is all I can do to keep up. When at last she leaves the shop, she looks purged, as if she has taken a laxative and can now properly concentrate on the North Face of the dinner party that is looming before her. She leaves a brief silence in her wake, before I complete my shameless notes, scramble to my feet, rub my chilled bottom and begin pointing at cheeses.

Such a scene, such a conversation: though hardly representative of one's daily interactions on the streets and in the shops of the city, they nonetheless crystallise certain aspects of life in Dublin.

For one thing, they point to that old intimacy of the city, as manifest a characteristic of Dublin today as it was a thousand years ago, or five hundred, or a hundred. They point also to the fluency of the language in the city, noted by generations of travellers and equally vibrant today. Maybe they also mark a change in Dublin life too, in facing up to the emotional and social problems that have traditionally scarred life here and that have only recently been addressed. Incidents of schizophrenia are eerily high in Ireland (not that this is a fact we'll see bandied about in the guidebooks), and incidents of alcoholism among young people and of suicide specifically in young men have assumed epidemic proportions. And these last can be witnessed in full flow on any night of the week on the streets of Dublin. Such social ills and epidemics are in part the responses, maybe, to a city and a society that has become wealthy in a short space of years, and to the consumerism that has come as a result. Consumerism, as we have seen, is on parade night and day in Dublin: in the shop windows; in the expensive bags clutched by those sated shoppers on Grafton Street; in the ranks of brand-new cars gridlocked on those overburdened streets; at a Dublin Airport that is bursting at the seams.

Dublin's economic success throughout the 1990s and beyond has been largely underwritten by international capital, the inevitable result of an economic model that maintains corporation tax at the lowest possible level in order to welcome foreign investment. The computer chip and pharmaceutical plants that gleam white and anonymous in the suburbs have kept a new generation of Dubliners from emigrating in search of work and brought in a generation of new immigrants to fill the host of vacancies that now, suddenly, exist. These plants and other, tangible symbols of economic buoyancy have brought prosperity, but also concomitant risk – for today, the city's economy is wholly exposed to the global market, and a recession abroad will bring shocks for Dublin too. They have also brought difficulty in their wake: as house prices have spiralled ever upwards and the cost of living soared, so levels of personal indebtedness have leaped accordingly. Today, the Irish are the most indebted people in Europe and Dubliners are the most indebted in Ireland. It is difficult to see how such a situation can sustain itself indefinitely, even if the crash that commentators have been foreseeing for years shows little sign of arriving.

In these years, the twentieth-century city that was seedy and faded, 'Part elegant and partly slum', sometimes seems to have vanished beyond recall; and this exposure to the world, moreover, is sometimes seen as having diluted Dublin's particular qualities:

> Beyond/the backlit tree-tops of Fitzwilliam Square
> a high window is showing one studious light,
> someone sitting late at a desk like me.
> There are some die-hards still on the upper floors,
> a Byzantine privacy in mews and lane,
> but mostly now the famous Georgian doors
> will house a junk-film outfit or an advertising agency.
> The fountain's flute is silent though time spares
> the old beeches with their echoes of Coole demesne;
> foreign investment conspires against old decency,
> computer talks to computer, machine to answering machine.[1]

Dublin is Everycity, or so it goes; its citizens are Everyman and Everywoman, as they rush along to work in their Swiss and American banks in the mornings, balancing iPods and litre-beakers of coffee; as they get snagged in traffic congestion, grey-faced in the evenings. Globalisation has caught us, and made us queue up for our sandwiches at lunchtime, and wrung the colour out of us; and now we are all the same.

But the specific character of the city, to my mind, will always bob, cork-like, to the surface. The specific character of any city, come to that, for I make no special claims for Dublin in this regard. Rather, the weight and experience of history brings a specific texture, flavour and tang to each locality – an energy that can never be matched or mirrored in any other one. The effect of lives lived and embedded and wired into Dublin, and at last laid down here – this puts paid to the notion of a flattened, anodyne place. Everyman surely has no role in this city of Dublin. He never did have.

Similarly, these years have frequently been heralded as ushering in some notional post-national era in the city and in the country – a glib formula that fails to take into account the consistent presence of a national debate in Irish life, and in the life of the city. Dublin is a capital, with all the national paraphernalia – cultural, commercial and political – that goes along with this role. It is perhaps more apt, rather, to suggest that the very terrain and meaning of nationalism has been stretched and contested in recent years. This contest can be seen to be at work in Irish discourse: in the way in which history is read in modern Ireland and taught in its schools, for example, with the meaning of episodes like the Rising and the Famine the subject of sometimes bitter dispute.

At the same time, Dublin's experience in a history of Ireland is, as we have seen, a distinctive and different one: now an economic bridgehead, now a bitterly contested meeting place, an urban centre marked as much by dire poverty as by gracious living and spectacular architecture, a port city, a cultural capital, a military encampment, a dour administrative hub in a struggling new nation state, a modern European capital, a zone inhabited by international capital and banks and corporations, a city chronically overstretched and with an infrastructure that clearly cannot cope. In all these roles, Dublin's world transcends the merely national; instead it is, as Louis MacNeice in 'Snow' would have it, 'incorrigibly plural'. With this knowledge, then, comes the understanding that history – whether it is a national history, a natural history, a local or a civic history – is by no means united or monolithic. Instead, it is manifold in nature, composed as it is of a million voices and a million different stories.

——— ◄○► ———

I write this sitting on the roof of my apartment building. Mild spring sunshine but fitful at best; I keep my fleece about me and out of a sharp wind that is still blowing from the north-east. On one side, I can see the green copper dome, the clock tower, the gleaming stone of the Pepper Cannister Church peeping through the rooftops; on the other, the waters of the Grand Canal are sparkling and the beeches in the park are putting out their first delicate, veined, translucent leaves. Last night, I was at the Good Friday concert at St Patrick's and I listened as Fauré's *Requiem* filled the soaring, vaulted spaces of the old cathedral. A planning application has been lately bolted to the walls of the development site next door; and already emails are flying from neighbour to neighbour, letters are drafted and redrafted, spears and swords sharpened and oiled and chariot wheels cranked up for the fresh battle ahead. I drafted a letter today, too, to Dublin Tourism this time, enquiring about the possibility of having two memorial plaques created for this sturdy building remembering Frank O'Connor and Liam O'Flaherty who lived and wrote here in years gone by; and I might even get around to mailing it. The daffodils are over for another year but the tulips are blooming, parrot-yellow and red, in their pots beside me; and I read in the paper about a plan to build barrages out in Dublin Bay to protect the city from future flooding caused by global warming.

This, all of it – this is Dublin, a thousand and more years later, as the chain of plum-blue hills still runs serenely on the southern skyline.

NOTES

Chapter 2: The Heathen Men

1   G. N. Garmonsway (trans. and ed.) *The Anglo-Saxon Chronicle* (London: J. M. Dent, 1953), 55–6.

Chapter 5: A Map of the World

1   Elizabeth Bowen, *Seven Winters* (London: Vintage, 1999), 492.

Part Two

1   Jonathan Swift, letter to Charles Ford, 20 August 1718, cited in Irvin Ehrenpreis (ed.), *Swift: The Man, the Works and the Age*, Vol. 3 (Cambridge: MA: Harvard University Press, 1983), 242.

Chapter 7: Lenders and Borrowers

1   Cited in Muriel McCarthy, *Marsh's Library: All Graduates and Gentlemen* (Dublin: Four Courts Press, 2003), 39–40.

Chapter 8: Life and Liberty

1   Whitelaw, Revd J., 'An Essay on the population of Dublin, being the result of a survey taken in 1798 with great care and precision, to which is added the general return of the district committee in 1804, with a comparative statement of the two surveys, also several observations on the present state of the poorer parts of the city of Dublin, 1805', cited in Joseph Brady and Anngret Simms (eds), *Dublin Through Space and Time c. 900–1900* (Dublin: Four Courts Press, 2001), 155–6.

2 Gilbert, J. T., 'Calendar of ancient record of Dublin in the possession of the municipal corporation', Vol. 5 app. XIV, pp. 606–7, cited in Brady and Simms, 79–80.

Chapter 9: Laws and Order

1 'Letter to Sir Hercules Langrishe, Bart. M. P., on the subject of the Roman Catholics of Ireland, and the propriety of Admitting them to the Elective Franchise, Consistent with the principles of the Constitution, as Established at the Revolution', in *The Works of Edmund Burke* (Boston: Little, Brown, 1839), 530.

2 National Library of Ireland, Pos. 3142.

Chapter 10: The Truth According to Laetitia

1 From *Dublin 1742*, by John Banville, performed at The Ark, Dublin, summer 2002.

2 Virginia Woolf, *The Common Reader*, Chapter Eleven, 'The Lives of the Obscure' (London: Hogarth, 1925). See also University of Adelaide eBooks: http://etext.library.adelaide.edu.au/w/woolf/virginia/w91c/chapter11.html.

3 A. C. Elias Jr, *The Memoirs of Laetitia Pilkington* (Athens, GA and London: University of Georgia Press, 1997), 1.

4 ibid., 13.

5 ibid., 88.

6 ibid., 161.

7 ibid., 23.

8 ibid., 33.

9 ibid., 29.

10 ibid., 281.

11 Harold Williams and David Woolley (eds), *The Correspondence of Jonathan Swift* (Oxford: Clarendon, 1965), III, 285.

Part Three

1 Caitríona O'Reilly, 'Sunday', in *The Nowhere Birds* (Tarset: Bloodaxe, 2001), 33.

Chapter 13: The Green

1 Ruth Delaney, *Ireland's Inland Waterways* (Belfast: Appletree, 1986), 106.

2 1823 Royal Canal Company Minutes, Vol. 5, 24 March 1823, cited in Ruth Delany, *Ireland's Royal Canal 1789–1992* (Dublin: Lilliput, 1992), 83.

3 Elizabeth Bowen, *Seven Winters* (London: Vintage, 1999), 478.

4 George Moore, *A Drama in Muslin* (London: Vizetelly, 1886), 220.

5 Elizabeth Bowen, *The Shelbourne* (London: Vintage, 2001), 125.

Chapter 15: Riverrun

1 It is important to emphasise how utterly different the shoreline was in the early city. South of the Liffey's treacherous mouth, the shoreline of the sea itself ran where now the districts of Irishtown, Ringsend and Sandymount now stand, inland from the sea. North of the river mouth, meanwhile, today's East Wall and North Wall remained underwater until late in the eighteenth century; and further north, Bull Island that stretches alongside the coast parallel to Clontarf – so fixed a part of the landscape today, home to two famous links courses and to kite-fliers and birdwatchers and to boy racers screaming along Dollymount Strand on summer evenings – Bull Island too is a thoroughly modern phenomenon.

2 In fact, the release of this flotilla of yellow plastic ducks was part of an experiment to gauge tidal flow on the Liffey. Each duck was marked with contact details and members of the public were invited to log the time and location of each avian discovery. I should like to thank David Norris for this information.

3 See Thomas Kinsella, 'Baggot Street Deserta', in *A Dublin Documentary* (Dublin: O'Brien, 2006), 71.

Part Four

1 Louis MacNeice, 'The Closing Album I: Dublin', in *Selected Poems,* Michael Longley (ed.) (London: Faber, 1988), 74.

Chapter 16: Consumption

1 See Thomas Kinsella, 'Baggot Street Deserta', in A *Dublin Documentary* (Dublin: O'Brien, 2006), 71.

Chapter 17: A Sky for the Favoured

1 George Moore, *A Drama in Muslin* (London: Vizetelly, 1886), cited in W. J. McCormack, *Sheridan le Fanu and Victorian England* (Oxford: Clarendon, 1980), 197.

2 Elizabeth Bowen, *Seven Winters* (London: Vintage, 1999), 493.

3 ibid.

4 Letter to Bishop Doyle, 1831, in *Correspondence of Daniel O'Connell*, Vol. IV (Dublin: Irish Academic Press, 1972), 492.

5 Bowen, *Seven Winters,* 482–3.

6 *Irish Times*, 4 March 1892, cited in Mary Daly, *Dublin. The Deposed Capital: A Social and Economic History, 1860–1914* (Cork: Cork University Press, 1984), 208.

Chapter 18: 'Part Elegant and Partly Slum'

1   Sheila Wingfield, 'A Melancholy Love', *Collected Poems, 1938–83* (London: Enitharmon, 1983), 146.
2   Hansard, 17 February 1845, reprinted in P.S. O'Hegarty, *A History of Ireland under the Union* (London: Methuen, 1952), 296.
3   George Moore, *A Drama in Muslin* (London: Vizetelly, 1886), 158–9.
4   A situation graphically illustrated in the following description of conditions in the city's tenements, recorded late in the nineteenth century:
> There is no direct means of removing the refuse from the several floors, the common stair soon therefore becomes fouled: while the height of the houses – seldom less than three, and generally four storeys high – in no slight degree operates against cleanliness. Many of these houses possess unoccupied cellars, the atmosphere of which cannot fail to injuriously affect the health of the occupants of the upper rooms.

C. Eason, 'The Tenement houses of Dublin: Their condition and regulation (1899)', in *Journal of the Statistical and Social Inquiry Society of Ireland*, 10 [79], quoted in Joseph Brady and Anngret Simms (eds), *Dublin Through Space and Time c. 900–1900* (Dublin: Four Courts Press, 2001), 188.
5   *Irish Times*, 7 June 1897, cited in Mary Daly, *Dublin. The Deposed Capital: A Social and Economic History, 1860–1914* (Cork: Cork University Press, 1984), 300.
6   Cited by Malcolm Shifrin in 'Victorian Turkish Baths', see www.victorianturkishbath.org.
7   *Bristol Times*, 15 December 1860, see www.victorianturkishbath.org
8   *Irish Times*, 7 October 1902, cited in Daly, 304.

Part Five

1   Austin Clarke, 'Inscription for a Headstone' in *Selected Poems*, Hugh Maxton (ed.) (Dublin: Lilliput, 1991).

Chapter 19: The Shift

1   Elizabeth Bowen, *Seven Winters* (London: Vintage, 1999), 491.
2   *Exhibition Expositor and Advertiser*, May 1853.
3   *Shan Van Vocht*, January 1897.

Chapter 20: The Rising

1   Sean O'Casey, *The Plough and the Stars*, Act 2 (London: Faber, 1998), 191.
2   See Thomas Kinsella, 'from a non-contemporary nationalist artist's impression', in *A Dublin Documentary* (Dublin: O'Brien, 2006), 92.
3   See Austin Clarke, 'Six Sentences: Black and Tans', in Hugh Maxton (ed.), *Selected Poems* (Dublin: Lilliput, 1991), 29.

Chapter 21: Contents and Discontents

1   *An Phoblacht*, 26 May 1933, cited in Peter Hegarty, *Peadar O'Donnell* (Cork: Mercier, 1999), 203.
2   *An Phoblacht*, 11 June 1926, in Hegarty, 185.
3   'Pro-' is an abbreviation of *pro tempore*, meaning 'temporary' or 'provisional', and because Dublin has no 'actual' Catholic cathedral, the Catholic Church has continued to view Christ Church, Anglican since the Reformation, as the 'official' cathedral of Dublin. This will remain the situation until such time as St Mary's is formally raised to full cathedral status.

Chapter 22: War and Peace

1   In an edition of the *Bell* in 1947, Peadar O'Donnell summed up the lack of official clarity that accompanied the position of the island of Ireland in what had been a global conflict:

> It would startle even the best informed among ourselves to have accurate figures of the recruitment of Irish men and women into the British armed forces and war industry ... soldiers home on leave were welcomed by their neighbours. An air raid in Britain brought anxiety to every parish in Southern Ireland. One met the joke often ... that what the Irish were doing dare not be told because the facts would embarrass both the Belfast Government [of Northern Ireland] who wished the world to believe their people were in the war, and Mr de Valera who wanted the Southern Irish to believe they were out of it.

2   Elizabeth Bowen, *Notes on Éire* (Aubane: Aubane Historical Society, 1999), 28.
3   Edna O'Brien, cited on Salon.com, 2 December 1995.
4   Cited in Mary Raftery and Eoin O'Sullivan, *Suffer the Little Children: The Inside Story of Ireland's Industrial Schools* (Dublin: New Island, 1999), 117–20.

Epilogue

1   Derek Mahon, 'The Yellow Book: Axel's Castle' in *Collected Poems* (Oldcastle: Gallery, 1999), 227.

FURTHER READING

The following titles may be useful in exploring further the story of Dublin:

A broad national context is provided by Terence Brown's *Ireland: A Social and Cultural History, 1922–2002* (London: HarperCollins, 2004); by Seamus Deane's *Strange Country: Modernity and Nationhood in Irish Writing Since 1790* (Oxford: Clarendon, 1997); and by Declan Kiberd's *Inventing Ireland: The Literature of the Modern Nation* (London: Cape, 1995).

The Making of Dublin City series, edited by Joseph Brady and Anngret Simms and published by Four Courts Press, provides an immensely satisfying geographical and social study of the city in the last thousand years. Titles in the series include: Brady and Simms (eds), *Dublin Through Space and Time c. 900–1900* (2001); Ruth McManus, *Dublin 1910–1940: Shaping the City and Suburbs* (2002); and Gary A. Boyd, *Dublin 1745–1922: Hospitals, Spectacle and Vice* (2006). Christine Casey's *The Buildings of Ireland: Dublin* (New Haven and London: Yale University Press, 2005) is a superlative architectural guide to the central city.

Dublin by Peter Somerville-Large (Frogmore: Granada, 1979); and *Dublin 1660–1860* by Maurice Craig (Dublin: Allen

Figgis, 1980) present portraits of the city down the centuries; Séamas Ó'Maitiú's *Dublin's Suburban Towns 1834–1930* (Dublin: Four Courts Press, 2003) illustrates the suburban growth of the city; Flora Mitchell's evocative *Vanishing Dublin* (Dublin: Allen Figgis, 1966) recalls in watercolours the Dublin of the 1960s; and Frank McDonald's *The Destruction of Dublin* (Dublin: Gill and Macmillan, 1985) and *The Construction of Dublin* (Kinsale: Gandon, 2000) demonstrate the remarkable changes in the city's built environment in the late twentieth century.

The medieval city is thoroughly explored in *Medieval Dublin: Proceedings of the Friends of Medieval Dublin Symposium* (Dublin: Four Courts Press, 1999–2005), edited by Seán Duffy; and Maria Kelly's *The Great Dying: the Black Death in Dublin* (Stroud: Tempus, 2003), and *A History of the Black Death in Ireland* (Stroud: Tempus, 2001) explore the impact of the plague on the medieval city.

Dublin and its natural environment through the years are explored in the following titles: J.K. De Courcy, *The Liffey in Dublin* (Dublin: Gill and Macmillan, 1996); Ruth Buchanan, *Ireland's Royal Canal* (Dublin: Lilliput, 1992) and *Ireland's Inland Waterways* (Belfast: Appletree, 1986); and Brendan Nolan, *Phoenix Park: A History and Guidebook* (Dublin: Liffey Press, 2006). Brendan Lynch's *Parson's Bookshop: At the Heart of Bohemian Dublin 1949–1989* (Dublin: Liffey Press, 2006) is the story of that famous bookshop perched above the waters of the Grand Canal.

The eighteenth-century city can be further studied in Patrick Fagan's *Catholics in a Protestant Country: The Papist Constituency in Eighteenth-Century Dublin* (Dublin: Four Courts Press, 1998); in *The Journals of Laetitia Pilkington*, edited by A.C. Elias (Athens, GA and London: University of Georgia Press, 1997); in *The Correspondence of Jonathan Swift*, edited by

Harold Williams and David Woolley (Oxford: Clarendon, 1965–72); in Ian Campbell Ross's *Swift's Ireland* (Dublin: Eason, 1983); and in *Locating Swift: Essays from Dublin on the 250th Anniversary of the Death of Jonathan Swift*, edited by Aileen Douglas, Patrick Kelly and Ian Campbell Ross (Dublin: Four Courts Press, 1998); while the history of Marsh's Library is explored by Muriel McCarthy in *Marsh's Library: All Graduates and Gentlemen* (Dublin: Four Courts Press, 2003).

The social history of nineteenth-century Dublin is explored in Mary Daly's *Dublin. The Deposed Capital: A Social and Economic History, 1860–1914* (Cork: Cork University Press, 1984).

The theatricality of Dublin life is illuminated by Fintan O'Toole in *A Traitor's Kiss: the Life of Richard Brinsley Sheridan* (London: Granta, 1997); by Colm Tóibín in *Lady Gregory's Toothbrush* (Dublin: Lilliput, 2002); and by Chris Morash in *A History of Irish Theatre, 1901–2000* (Cambridge: Cambridge University Press, 2002).

Peter Hegarty's *Peadar O'Donnell* (Cork: Mercier, 1999) brings to life the altered atmosphere of post-Independence Ireland; and Elizabeth Bowen's take on various aspects of Irish life is amply explored in *Bowen's Court & Seven Winters* (London: Vintage, 1999) and in *Notes on Éire* (Aubane: Aubane Historical Society, 1999). The story of the 'Emergency' is contextualised in Robert Fisk's *In Time of War: Ireland, Ulster and the Price of Neutrality, 1939–45* (London: Andre Deutsch, 1983); and the war years in Ireland and Dublin are evoked in Clair Wills's *That Neutral Island: A Cultural History of Ireland during the Second World War* (London: Faber, 2007).

The history of the Pike Theatre is retold in Gerald Whelan and Carolyn Swift's *Spiked: Church–State Intrigue and The Rose Tattoo* (Dublin: New Island, 2002); and Mary Raftery and Eoin O'Sullivan's *Suffer the Little Children: The Inside Story of*

Ireland's Industrial Schools (Dublin: New Island, 1999) tells the frequently harrowing story of the abuse of children in Dublin's industrial schools.

PICTURE CREDITS

⚭

P. 1 *(top)* John Speed's Map of Dublin in *Theatre of the Empire of Great Britain* (1611), (NLI 16 G 17 (1)), with the permission of The Board of The National Library of Ireland *(bottom)* John Rocque's *Exact Survey of the City and Suburbs of Dublin* (1756), (NLI 16 G 2 (1)) with the permission of The Board of The National Library of Ireland; p. 2 *(top)* William Ashford: *A View of Dublin from Chapelizod*, courtesy of The National Gallery of Ireland, photo © The National Gallery of Ireland *(bottom)* Flora Mitchell: *Tailors' Hall, Back Lane*, courtesy of The National Gallery of Ireland, photo © The National Gallery of Ireland; p. 3 *(top)* Flora Mitchell: *No. 5 Henrietta Street (Illustrations for 'Vanishing Dublin')*, courtesy of The National Gallery of Ireland, photo © The National Gallery of Ireland *(bottom left)* Laetitia Pilkington (née Van Lewen) by Richard Purcell © National Portrait Gallery, London *(bottom right)* Study portrait of Jonathan Swift/Private Collection, © Philip Mould Ltd, London /The Bridgeman Art Library; p. 4 *(top left)* Sir Arthur Guinness, courtesy of Guinness Archive, Diageo Ireland *(top right)* Photo © Fennell Photography, 2002 *(bottom)* Harry Clarke: *'He Takes the Gift with Reverence and extends'*, courtesy of The National Gallery of Ireland, photo © The National Gallery of Ireland; p. 5 *(top)* Edwin Hayes: *An Emigrant Ship, Dublin Bay, Sunset*, courtesy of The National Gallery of Ireland, photo © The National Gallery of Ireland *(bottom)* William Orpen: *Merchants' Arch, Dublin*, courtesy of The National Gallery of Ireland, photo © The National Gallery of Ireland; p. 6 *(top)* Charles Russell: *The O'Connell Centenary Celebrations*, courtesy of The National Gallery of Ireland, photo © The National Gallery of Ireland *(bottom)* Erskin Nicol: *Donnybrook Fair*, © Tate, London 2007; p. 7 *(top)* Patrick Collins: *Liffey Quaysides*, courtesy of the National Gallery of Ireland, © The Artist's Estate, Photo © The National Gallery of Ireland *(bottom)* Photograph by ILN, Camera Press, London; p. 8 *(top)* Harry Kernoff: *The Forty Foot, Sandycove*, © The Artist's Estate, reproduced courtesy of the AIB Group *(bottom)* James Malton: *St Stephen's Green, Dublin*, (NLI PD 3181 TX 143), courtesy of the National Library of Ireland

337

INDEX

Index

Unionists 258, 286–7
United Irishmen 82
United Nations (UN) 87, 267
United Nations Biosphere 176
United States 74–5, 118, 220
University College 312
  rowing club 179
Urquhart, David 230

Van Diemen's Land 278
van Lewen, John 104, 112
venereal disease 223, 235
Viceregal Lodge (later Áras an
  Uachtaráin) 162–4
Viceroys 161–4
Victoria, Queen 163, 220
  Golden Jubilee 253
Victorian architecture 225, 227, 228–30,
  233, 278
Victorian values 230–1, 233, 234–5,
  244–5, 248
Vikings 5, 7–21, 27–8, 34, 36, 130, 178,
  184, 195, 211, 223
  archaeology 12, 13, 14, 41–2
  Dublinia exhibition 39
Volta Cinema 216
Voltaire 257
voting 208–9

Wakefield 45
Wales 29–30, 37
War Memorial Gardens 13–14, 85, 179,
  305
Wars of the Roses 54
Wasaki Global Corporation 183
Waterford harbour 31
waterways 142–7
  see also specific rivers and canals
weaving 76, 134, 135

  see also Woollen Act 1699; woollen
    industry
Weir's jewellers, Dublin 191, 192
Wellesley, Arthur, Duke of Wellington
  197
Wellington Bridge, Dublin 197
Wellington Quay, Dublin 8
Wellington Testimonial, Phoenix Park
  166, 179
West Germany 148
Western Front 265
Westland Row Station 309
Westminster Parliament 134, 208, 261,
  282
  Renunciation Act 1783 135
  under Cromwell 58, 59
Whitelaw, James 77
Wicklow Mountains xiv, xv, 32, 47, 49,
  53, 173
Wide Streets Commission 118, 130, 189,
  222
Wilde, Oscar 128, 251
wildlife 184
Williams, Tennessee 310
Wingfield, Sheila x
Woffington, Peg 98
women
  role in the Easter Rising 270
  role in public life 294–5
Wood Quay, Dublin 8, 172
  controversy, 1970s 41–2, 43
Woolf, Virginia 102–3
Woollen Act 1699 71, 76, 108, 133–4
woollen industry 71
  see also weaving
workhouses 219, 230, 236
Wynne, John 68

Yeats, W.B. 250–5, 258–9, 263, 273